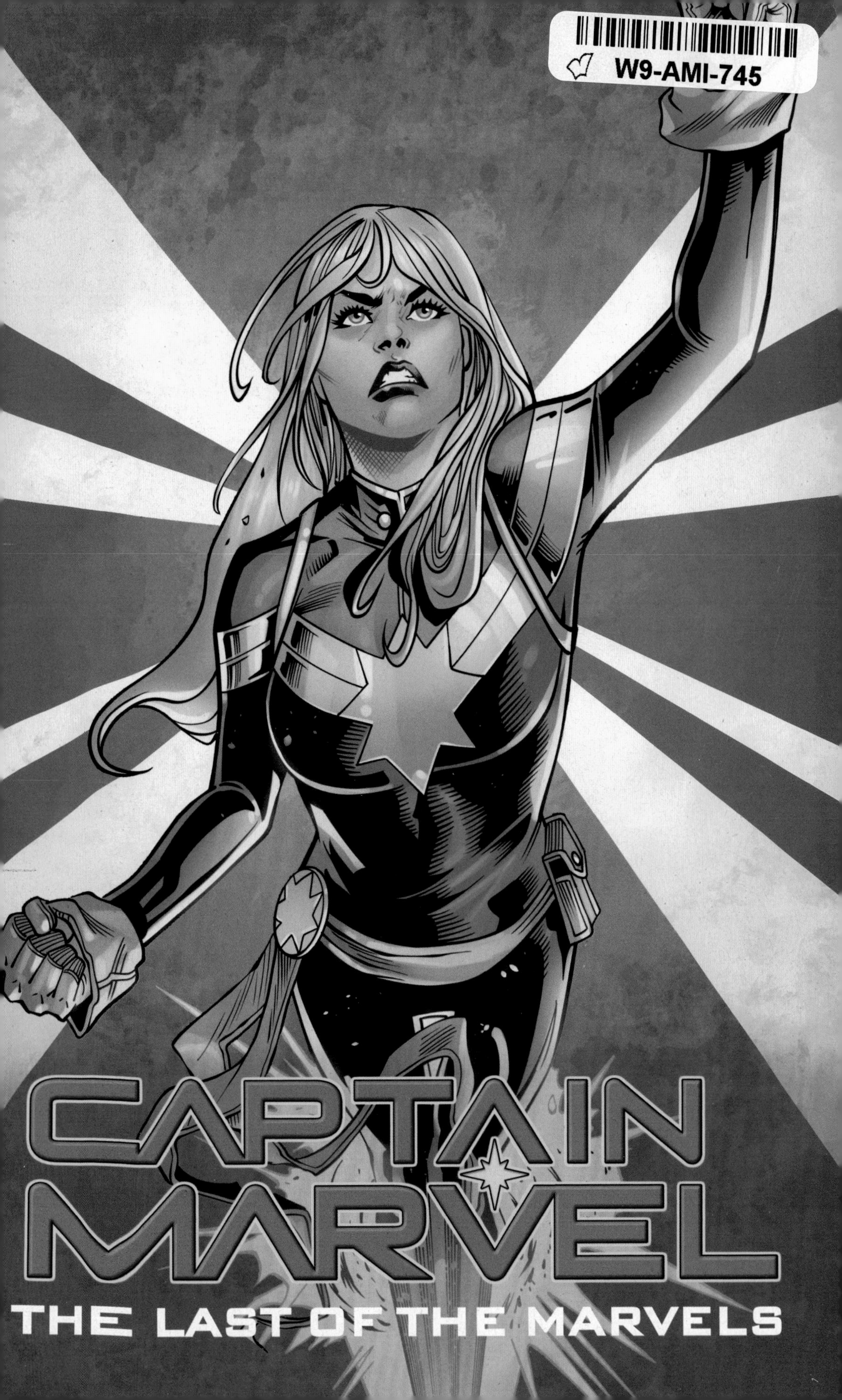
CAPTAIN
MARVEL
THE LAST OF THE MARVELS

Born to a Kree mother and human father, former U.S. Air Force pilot Carol Danvers became a super hero when a Kree device activated her latent powers. Now she's an Avenger and Earth's Mightiest Hero.

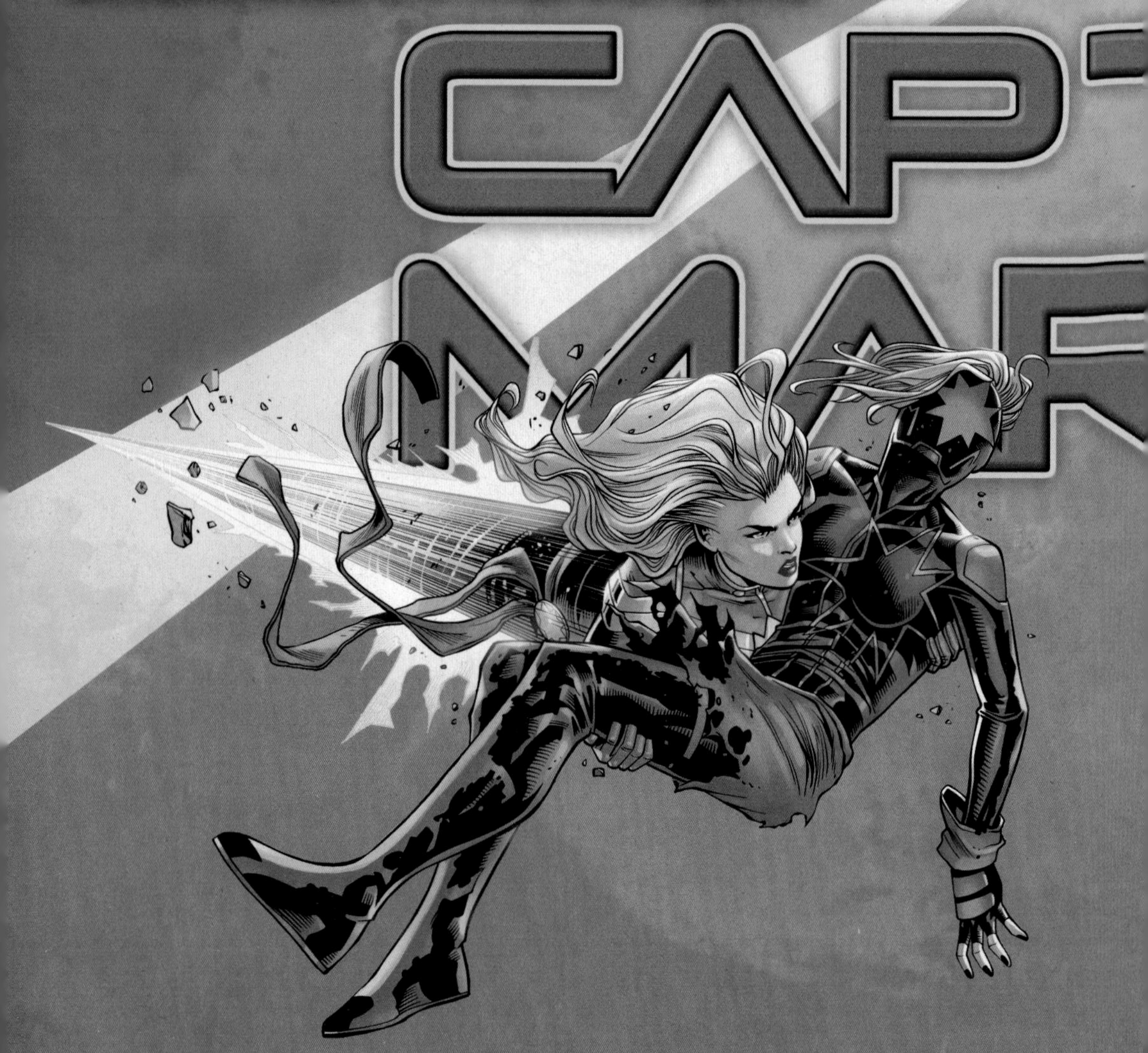

Carol's been through the wringer lately. Her Kree heritage was outed to the public, and then aliens invaded Earth — not a good look. But perhaps it was meant to be, because it led her to the discovery of her half sister, the Kree Accuser Lauri-Ell.

And speaking of meant to be, Carol broke up with James Rhodes after a traumatic glimpse of his potential future family, but when he came to her rescue in a fight with the super villain Ove, the star-crossed lovers made up.

Now, with their relationship rekindled, Carol and Rhodey are in dire need of some TLC. and are finally taking a long-awaited vacation together. With any luck, they'll get an escape from all the hero business for a bit.

CAPTAIN MARVEL VOL. 7: THE LAST OF THE MARVELS. Contains material originally published in magazine form as CAPTAIN MARVEL (2019) #31-36. First printing 2022. ISBN 978-1-302-92884-1. Published by MARVEL WORLDWIDE, INC., a subsidiary of MARVEL ENTERTAINMENT, LLC. OFFICE OF PUBLICATION: 1290 Avenue of the Americas, New York, NY 10104. © 2022 MARVEL No similarity between any of the names, characters, persons, and/or institutions in this book with those of any living or dead person or institution is intended, and any such similarity which may exist is purely coincidental. **Printed in Canada.** KEVIN FEIGE, Chief Creative Officer; DAN BUCKLEY, President, Marvel Entertainment; JOE QUESADA, EVP & Creative Director; DAVID BOGART, Associate Publisher & SVP of Talent Affairs; TOM BREVOORT, VP, Executive Editor; NICK LOWE, Executive Editor, VP of Content, Digital Publishing; DAVID GABRIEL, VP of Print & Digital Publishing; JEFF YOUNGQUIST, VP of Production & Special Projects; ALEX MORALES, Director of Publishing Operations; DAN EDINGTON, Managing Editor; RICKEY PURDIN, Director of Talent Relations; JENNIFER GRÜNWALD, Senior Editor, Special Projects; SUSAN CRESPI, Production Manager; STAN LEE, Chairman Emeritus. For information regarding advertising in Marvel Comics or on Marvel.com, please contact Vit DeBellis, Custom Solutions & Integrated Advertising Manager, at vdebellis@marvel.com. For Marvel subscription inquiries, please call 888-511-5480. **Manufactured between 1/28/2022 and 3/1/2022 by SOLISCO PRINTERS, SCOTT, QC, CANADA.**

10 9 8 7 6 5 4 3 2 1

...AIN ...VEL

THE LAST OF THE MARVELS

KELLY THOMPSON
Writer

#31

TAKESHI MIYAZAWA
Artist

IAN HERRING
Color Artist

MARCO CHECCHETTO & MATTHEW WILSON
Cover Art

#32-35

SERGIO DÁVILA
Penciler

SEAN PARSONS
Inker

JESUS ABURTOV
Color Arist

IBAN COELLO & ALEJANDRO SÁNCHEZ [#32]; **IBAN COELLO & JESUS ABURTOV** [#33-34] and **R.B. SILVA & DAVID CURIEL** [#35]
Cover Art

#36

SERGIO DÁVILA
Penciler

SEAN PARSONS with **ROBERTO POGGI**
Inkers

ERICK ARCINIEGA
Color Arist

R.B. SILVA & JESUS ABURTOV
Cover Art

VC's CLAYTON COWLES
Letterer

SARAH BRUNSTAD
Editor

KAT GREGOROWICZ & ANITA OKOYE
Assistant Editors

TOM BREVOORT
Executive Editor

Collection Editor: JENNIFER GRÜNWALD
Assistant Editor: DANIEL KIRCHHOFFER
Assistant Managing Editor: MAIA LOY
Associate Manager, Talent Relations: LISA MONTALBANO

VP Production & Special Projects: JEFF YOUNGQUIST
Book Designers: SARAH SPADACCINI with CLAYTON COWLES & NICK RUSSELL
SVP Print, Sales & Marketing: DAVID GABRIEL
Editor in Chief: C.B. CEBULSKI

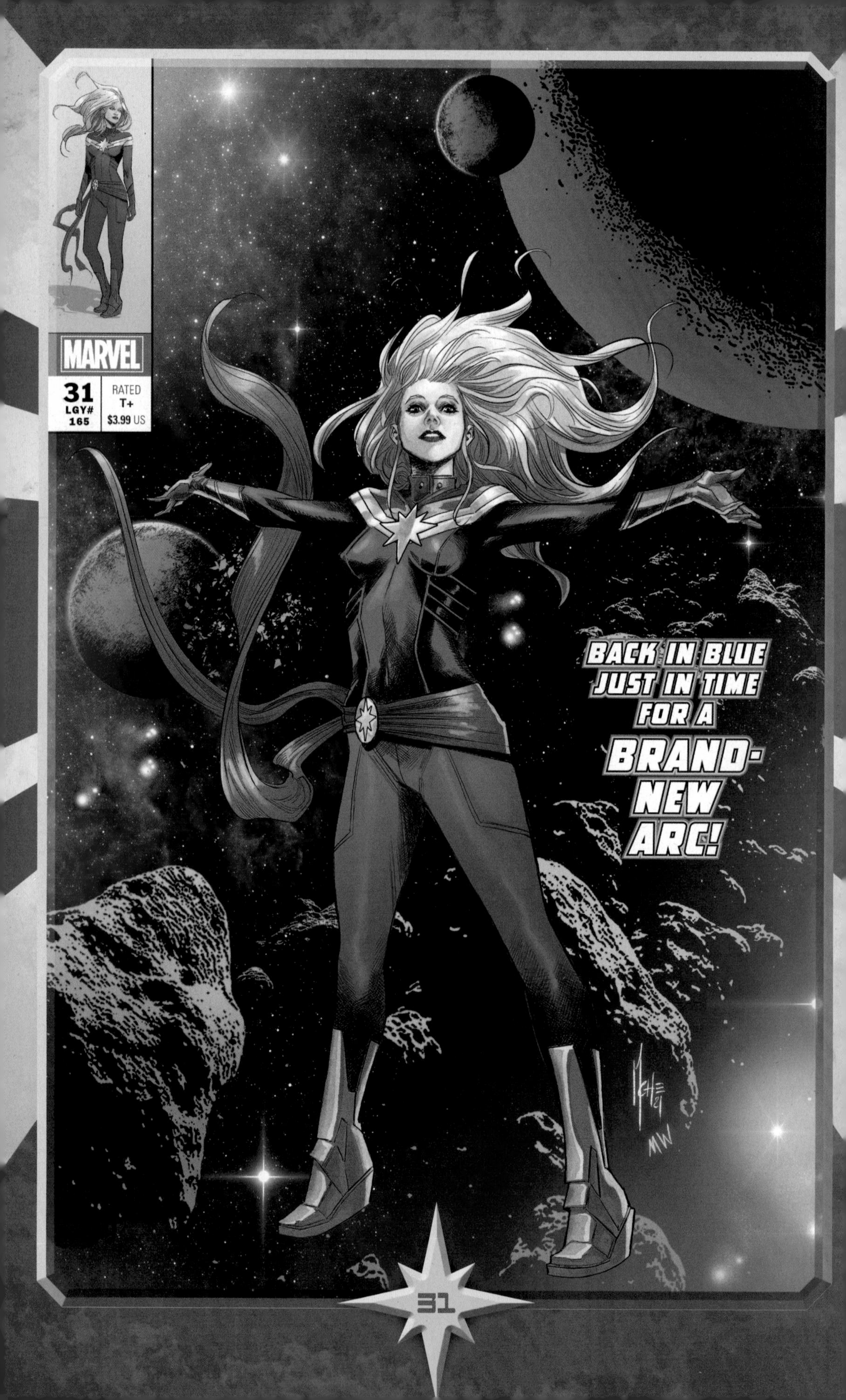
MARVEL
31
LGY#
165
RATED
T+
$3.99 US
BACK IN BLUE
JUST IN TIME
FOR A
BRAND-
NEW
ARC!
31

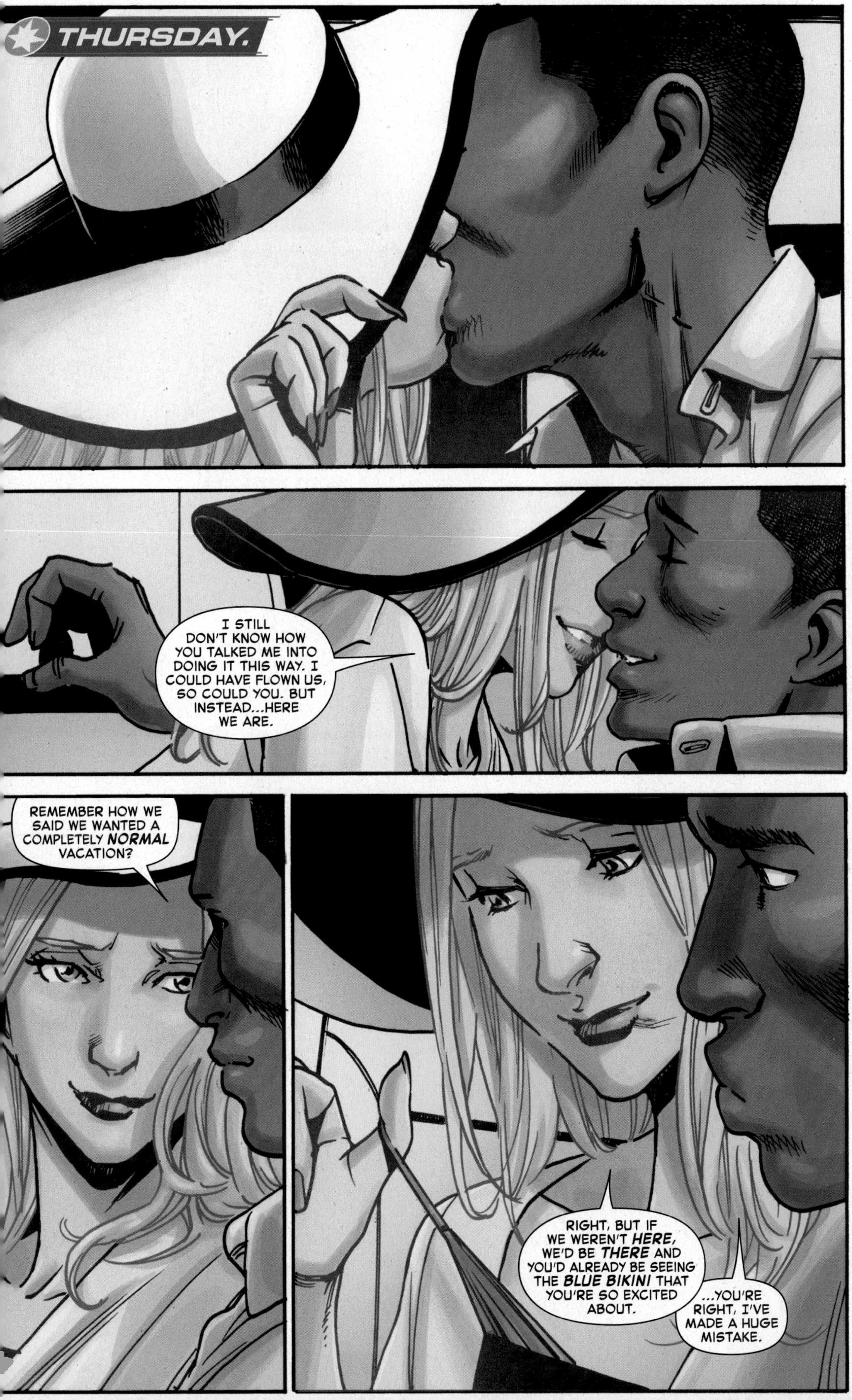
THURSDAY.
I STILL DON'T KNOW HOW YOU TALKED ME INTO DOING IT THIS WAY. I COULD HAVE FLOWN US, SO COULD YOU. BUT INSTEAD...HERE WE ARE.
REMEMBER HOW WE SAID WE WANTED A COMPLETELY NORMAL VACATION?
RIGHT, BUT IF WE WEREN'T HERE, WE'D BE THERE AND YOU'D ALREADY BE SEEING THE BLUE BIKINI THAT YOU'RE SO EXCITED ABOUT.
...YOU'RE RIGHT, I'VE MADE A HUGE MISTAKE.

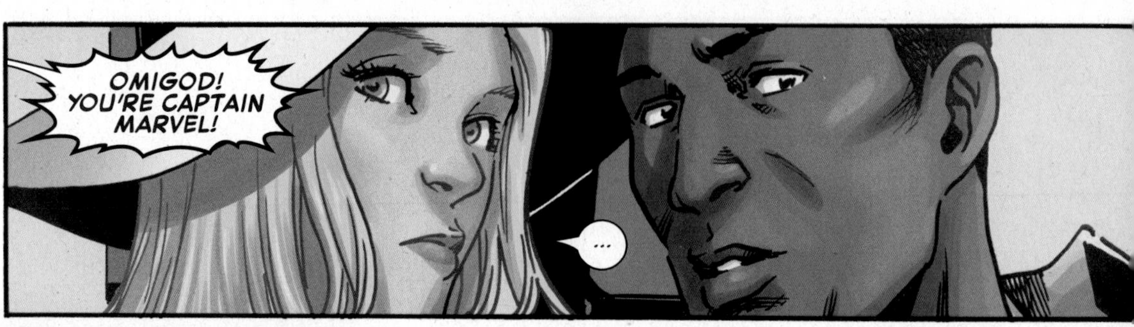
OMIGOD! YOU'RE CAPTAIN MARVEL!
...

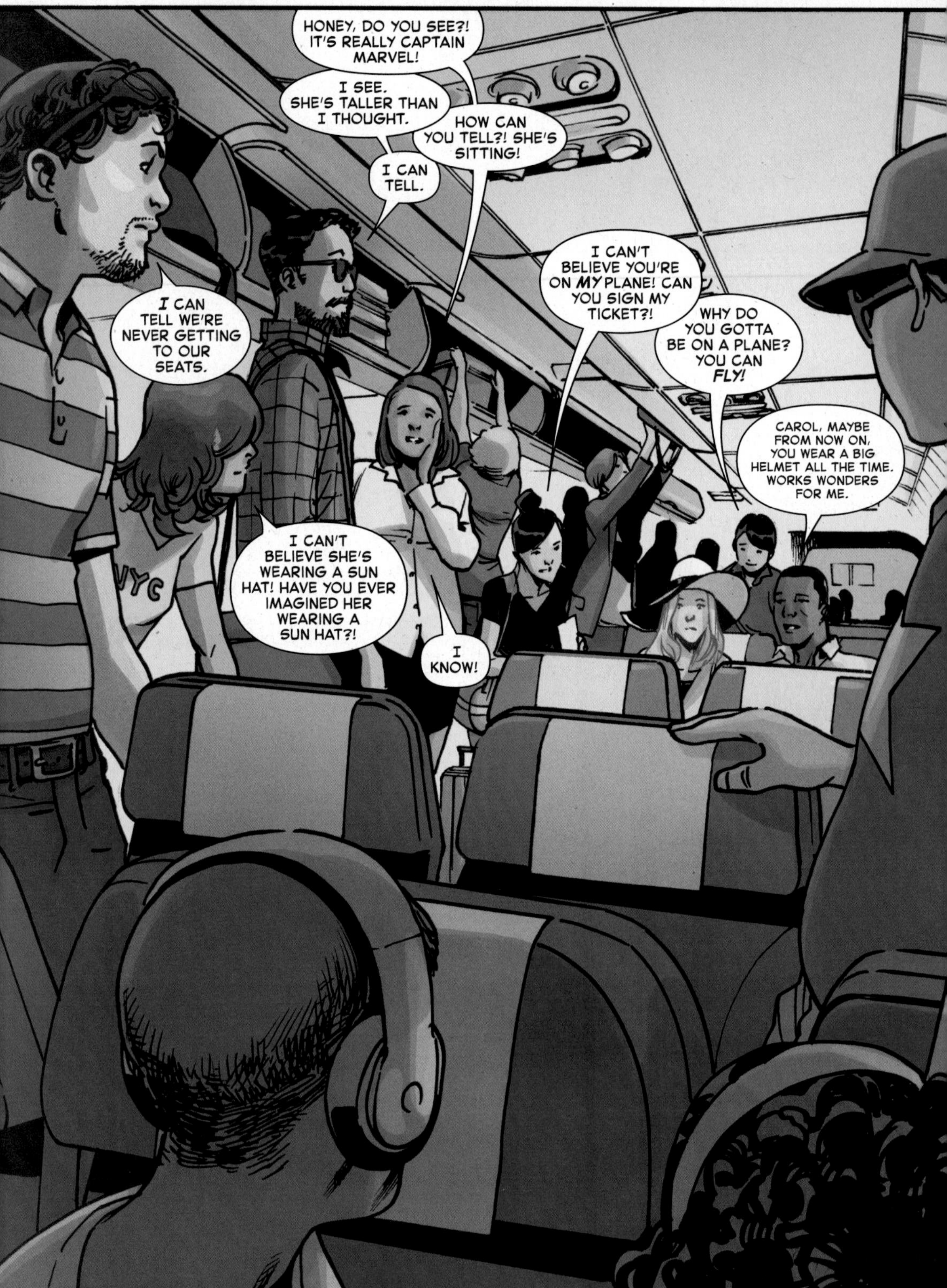
HONEY, DO YOU SEE?! IT'S REALLY CAPTAIN MARVEL!
I SEE. SHE'S TALLER THAN I THOUGHT.
HOW CAN YOU TELL?! SHE'S SITTING!
I CAN TELL.
I CAN TELL WE'RE NEVER GETTING TO OUR SEATS.
I CAN'T BELIEVE YOU'RE ON MY PLANE! CAN YOU SIGN MY TICKET?!
WHY DO YOU GOTTA BE ON A PLANE? YOU CAN FLY!
CAROL, MAYBE FROM NOW ON, YOU WEAR A BIG HELMET ALL THE TIME. WORKS WONDERS FOR ME.
I CAN'T BELIEVE SHE'S WEARING A SUN HAT! HAVE YOU EVER IMAGINED HER WEARING A SUN HAT?!
I KNOW!
NYC

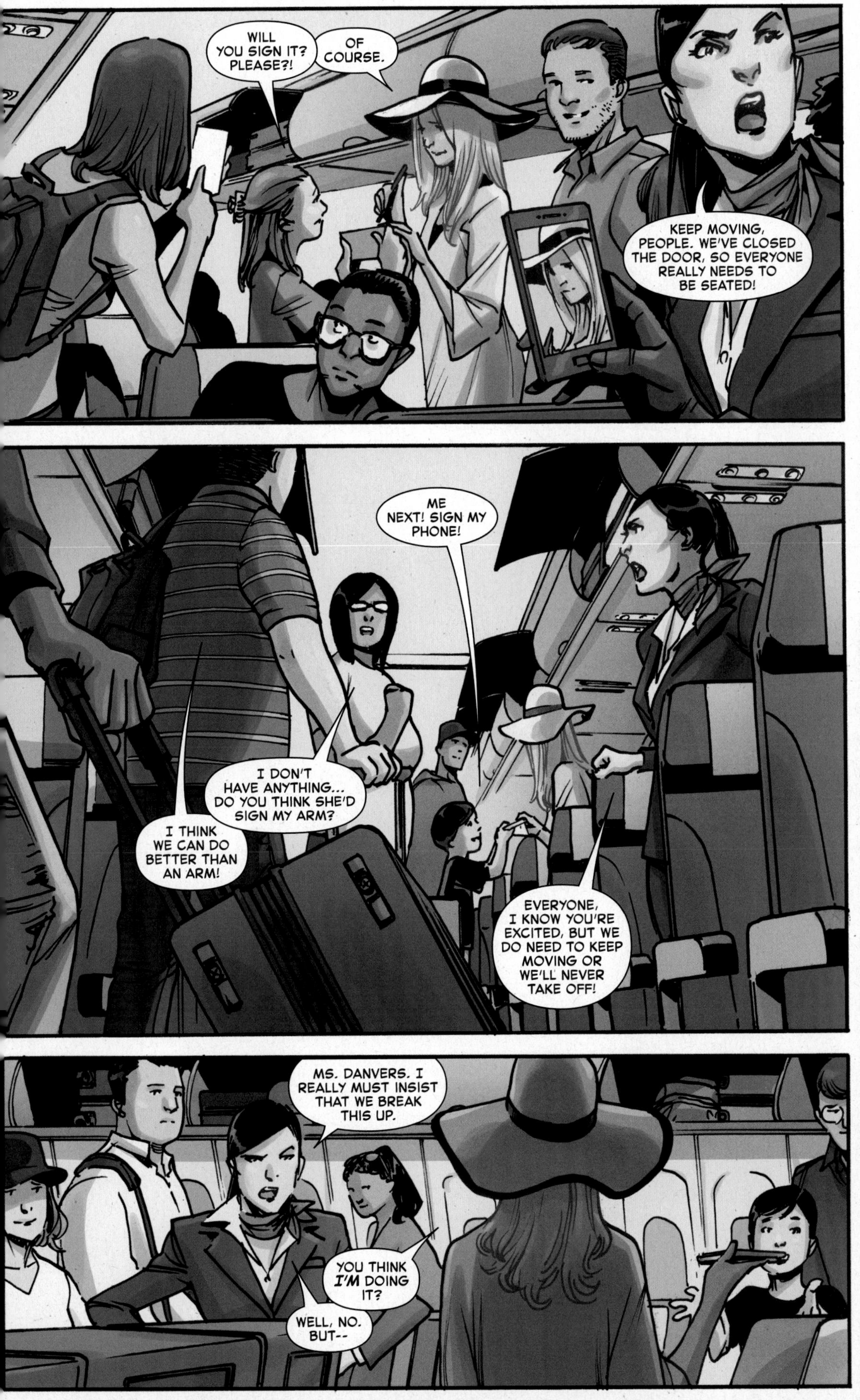
WILL YOU SIGN IT? PLEASE?!
OF COURSE.
KEEP MOVING, PEOPLE. WE'VE CLOSED THE DOOR, SO EVERYONE REALLY NEEDS TO BE SEATED!
ME NEXT! SIGN MY PHONE!
I DON'T HAVE ANYTHING... DO YOU THINK SHE'D SIGN MY ARM?
I THINK WE CAN DO BETTER THAN AN ARM!
EVERYONE, I KNOW YOU'RE EXCITED, BUT WE DO NEED TO KEEP MOVING OR WE'LL NEVER TAKE OFF!
MS. DANVERS. I REALLY MUST INSIST THAT WE BREAK THIS UP.
YOU THINK *I'M* DOING IT?
WELL, NO. BUT--

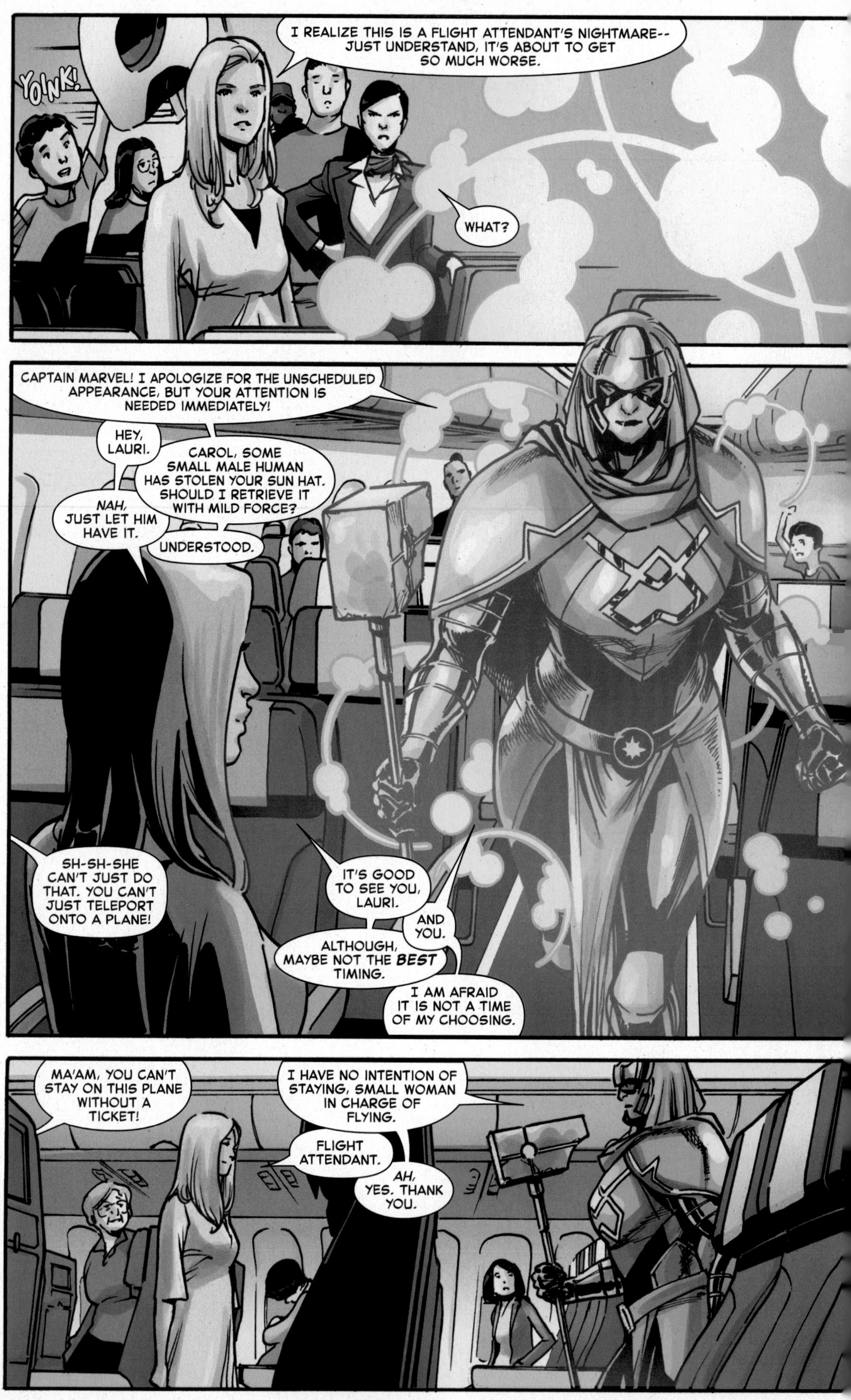
YOINK!
I REALIZE THIS IS A FLIGHT ATTENDANT'S NIGHTMARE-- JUST UNDERSTAND, IT'S ABOUT TO GET SO MUCH WORSE.
WHAT?
CAPTAIN MARVEL! I APOLOGIZE FOR THE UNSCHEDULED APPEARANCE, BUT YOUR ATTENTION IS NEEDED IMMEDIATELY!
HEY, LAURI.
CAROL, SOME SMALL MALE HUMAN HAS STOLEN YOUR SUN HAT. SHOULD I RETRIEVE IT WITH MILD FORCE?
NAH, JUST LET HIM HAVE IT.
UNDERSTOOD.
SH-SH-SHE CAN'T JUST DO THAT. YOU CAN'T JUST TELEPORT ONTO A PLANE!
IT'S GOOD TO SEE YOU, LAURI.
AND YOU.
ALTHOUGH, MAYBE NOT THE BEST TIMING.
I AM AFRAID IT IS NOT A TIME OF MY CHOOSING.
MA'AM, YOU CAN'T STAY ON THIS PLANE WITHOUT A TICKET!
I HAVE NO INTENTION OF STAYING, SMALL WOMAN IN CHARGE OF FLYING.
FLIGHT ATTENDANT.
AH, YES. THANK YOU.

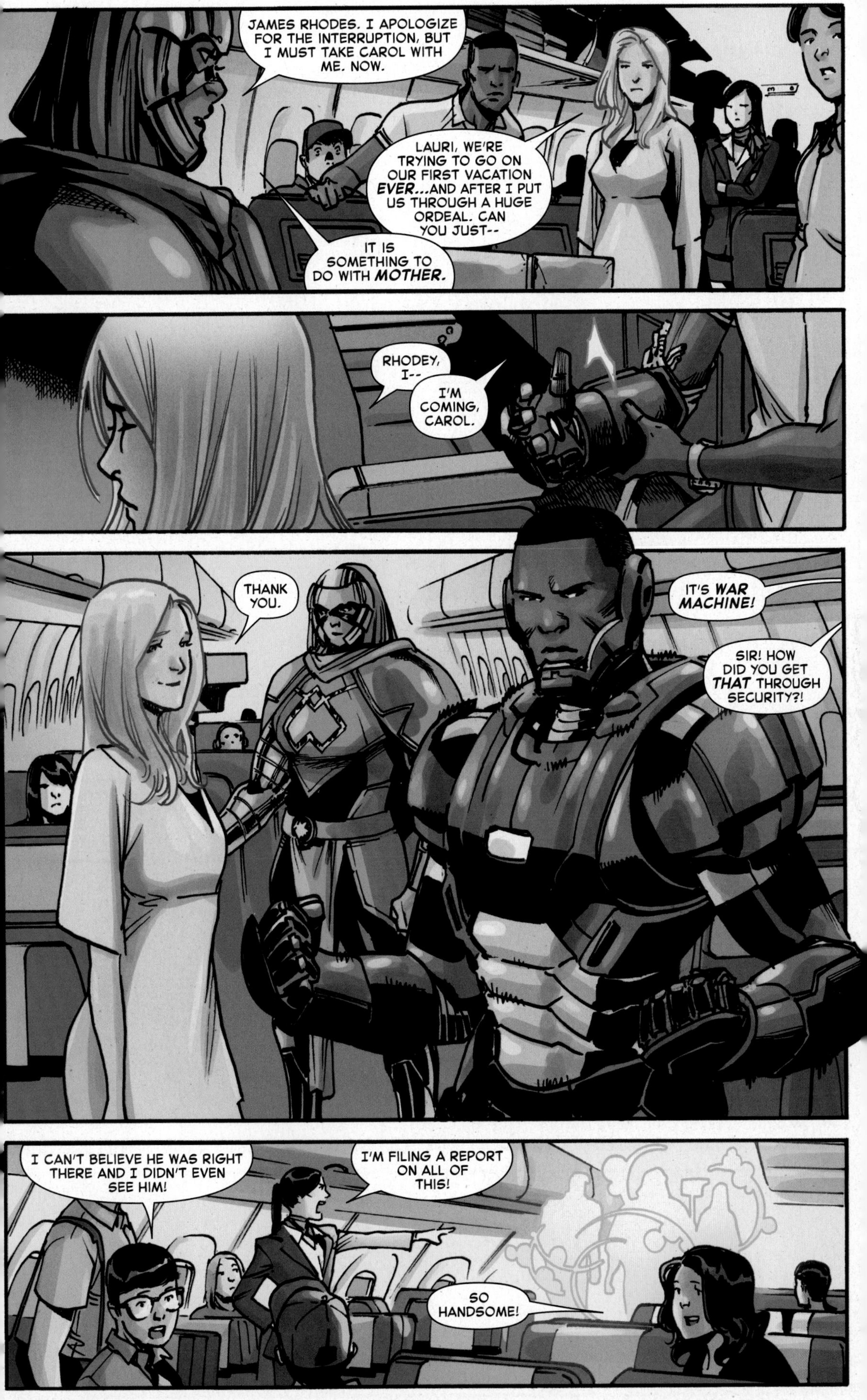
JAMES RHODES. I APOLOGIZE FOR THE INTERRUPTION, BUT I MUST TAKE CAROL WITH ME. NOW.
LAURI, WE'RE TRYING TO GO ON OUR FIRST VACATION EVER...AND AFTER I PUT US THROUGH A HUGE ORDEAL. CAN YOU JUST--
IT IS SOMETHING TO DO WITH MOTHER.
RHODEY, I--
I'M COMING, CAROL.
THANK YOU.
IT'S WAR MACHINE!
SIR! HOW DID YOU GET THAT THROUGH SECURITY?!
I CAN'T BELIEVE HE WAS RIGHT THERE AND I DIDN'T EVEN SEE HIM!
I'M FILING A REPORT ON ALL OF THIS!
SO HANDSOME!

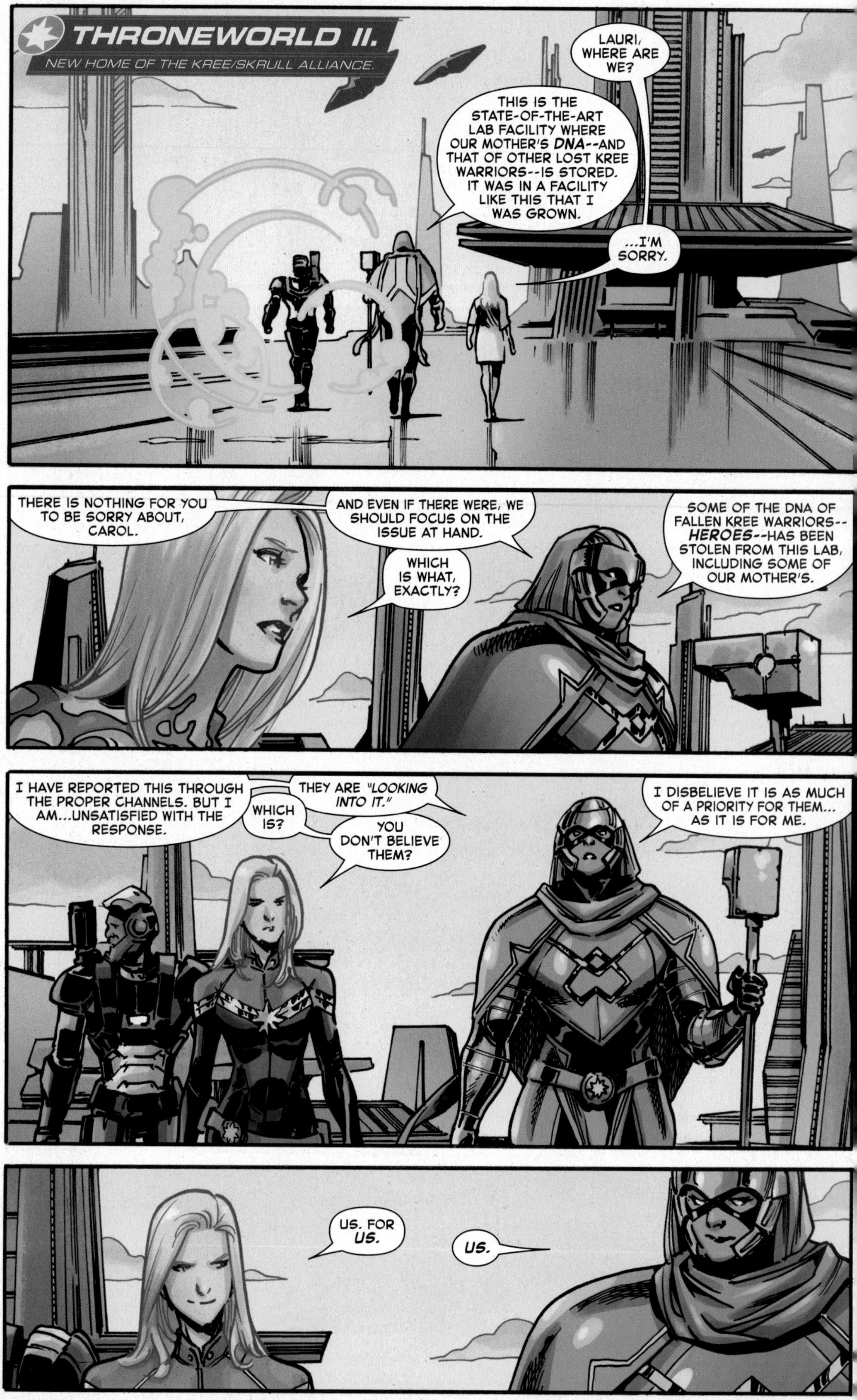
THRONEWORLD II.
NEW HOME OF THE KREE/SKRULL ALLIANCE.
LAURI, WHERE ARE WE?
THIS IS THE STATE-OF-THE-ART LAB FACILITY WHERE OUR MOTHER'S DNA--AND THAT OF OTHER LOST KREE WARRIORS--IS STORED. IT WAS IN A FACILITY LIKE THIS THAT I WAS GROWN.
...I'M SORRY.
THERE IS NOTHING FOR YOU TO BE SORRY ABOUT, CAROL.
AND EVEN IF THERE WERE, WE SHOULD FOCUS ON THE ISSUE AT HAND.
WHICH IS WHAT, EXACTLY?
SOME OF THE DNA OF FALLEN KREE WARRIORS--HEROES--HAS BEEN STOLEN FROM THIS LAB, INCLUDING SOME OF OUR MOTHER'S.
I HAVE REPORTED THIS THROUGH THE PROPER CHANNELS. BUT I AM...UNSATISFIED WITH THE RESPONSE.
THEY ARE "LOOKING INTO IT."
WHICH IS?
YOU DON'T BELIEVE THEM?
I DISBELIEVE IT IS AS MUCH OF A PRIORITY FOR THEM... AS IT IS FOR ME.
US. FOR US.
US.

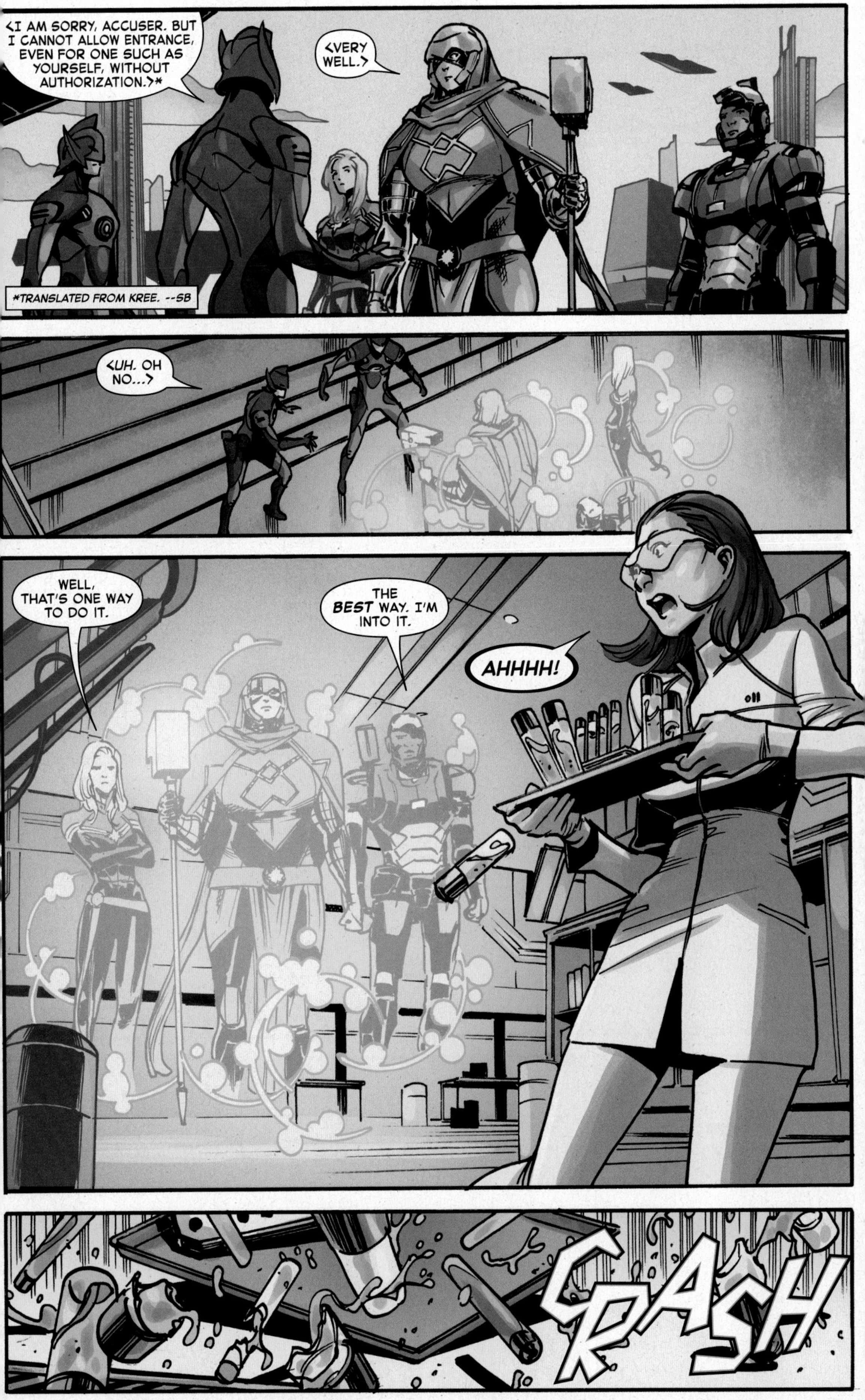
<I AM SORRY, ACCUSER. BUT I CANNOT ALLOW ENTRANCE, EVEN FOR ONE SUCH AS YOURSELF, WITHOUT AUTHORIZATION.>*
<VERY WELL.>
*TRANSLATED FROM KREE. --SB
<UH. OH NO...>
WELL, THAT'S ONE WAY TO DO IT.
THE BEST WAY. I'M INTO IT.
AHHHH!
CRASH

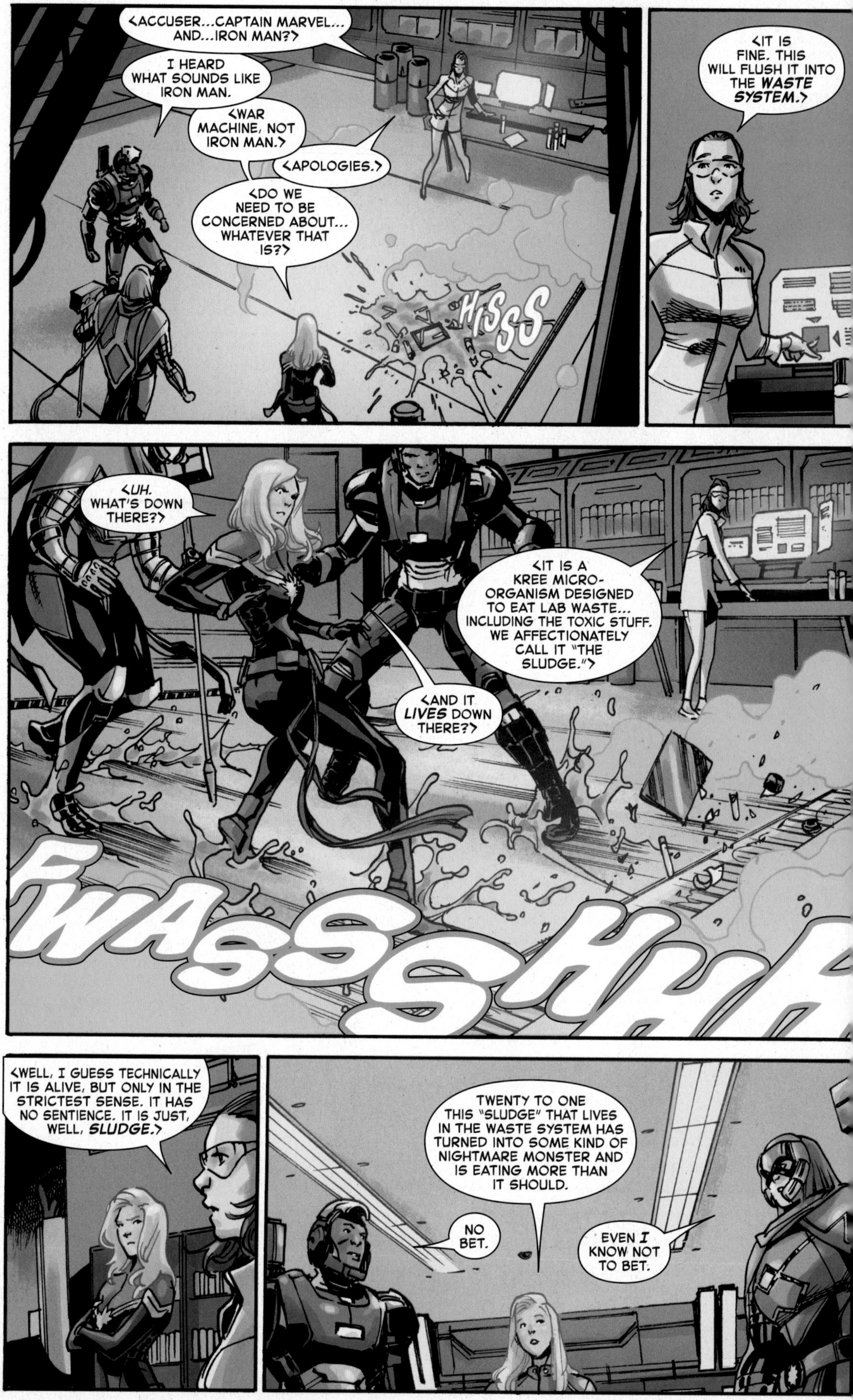
<ACCUSER...CAPTAIN MARVEL... AND...IRON MAN?>
I HEARD WHAT SOUNDS LIKE IRON MAN.
<WAR MACHINE, NOT IRON MAN.>
<APOLOGIES.>
<DO WE NEED TO BE CONCERNED ABOUT... WHATEVER THAT IS?>
HISSS
<IT IS FINE. THIS WILL FLUSH IT INTO THE WASTE SYSTEM.>
<UH. WHAT'S DOWN THERE?>
<IT IS A KREE MICRO-ORGANISM DESIGNED TO EAT LAB WASTE... INCLUDING THE TOXIC STUFF. WE AFFECTIONATELY CALL IT "THE SLUDGE.">
<AND IT LIVES DOWN THERE?>
FWASSSHH
<WELL, I GUESS TECHNICALLY IT IS ALIVE, BUT ONLY IN THE STRICTEST SENSE. IT HAS NO SENTIENCE. IT IS JUST, WELL, SLUDGE.>
TWENTY TO ONE THIS "SLUDGE" THAT LIVES IN THE WASTE SYSTEM HAS TURNED INTO SOME KIND OF NIGHTMARE MONSTER AND IS EATING MORE THAN IT SHOULD.
NO BET.
EVEN I KNOW NOT TO BET.

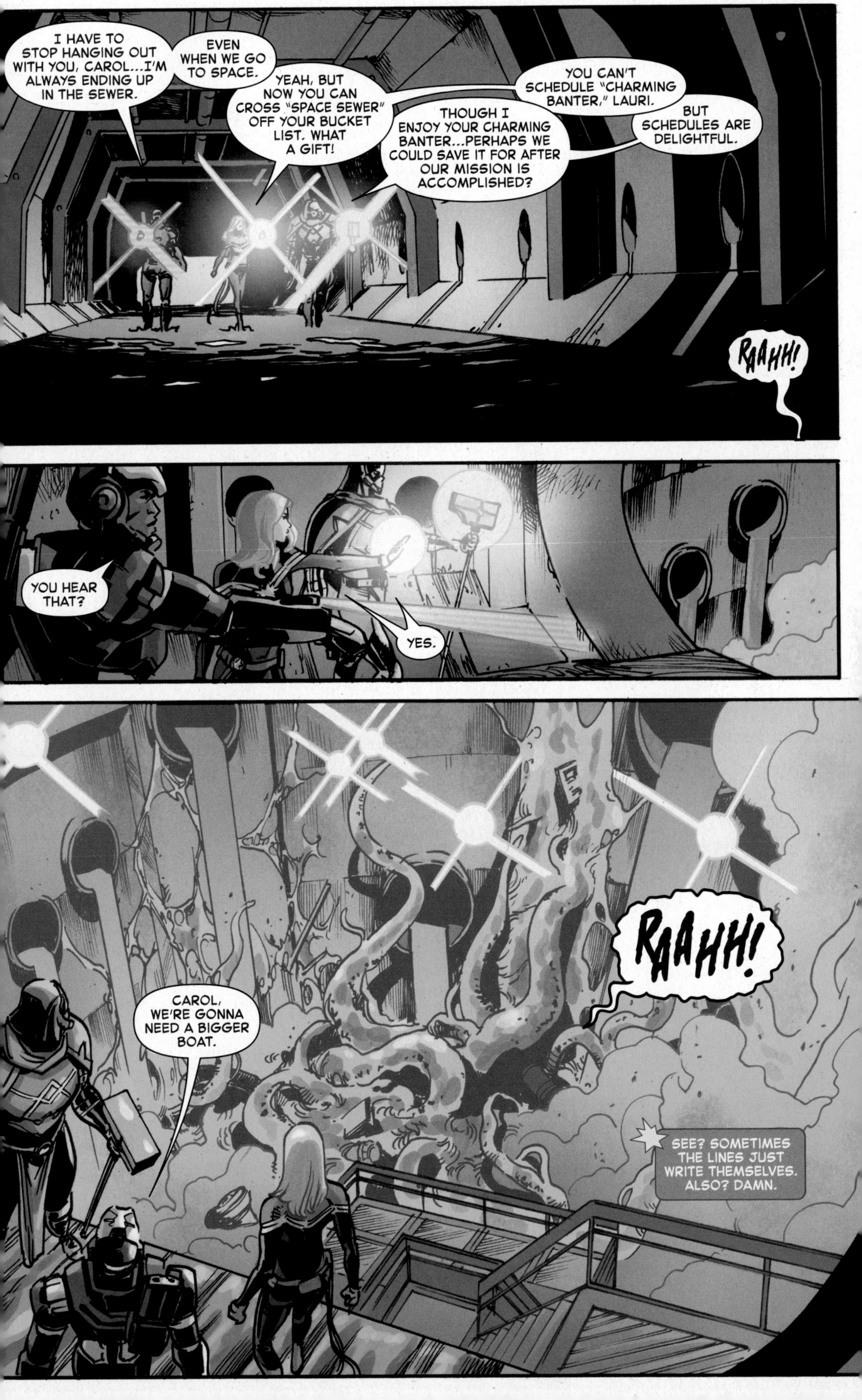
I HAVE TO STOP HANGING OUT WITH YOU, CAROL...I'M ALWAYS ENDING UP IN THE SEWER.
EVEN WHEN WE GO TO SPACE.
YEAH, BUT NOW YOU CAN CROSS "SPACE SEWER" OFF YOUR BUCKET LIST. WHAT A GIFT!
THOUGH I ENJOY YOUR CHARMING BANTER...PERHAPS WE COULD SAVE IT FOR AFTER OUR MISSION IS ACCOMPLISHED?
YOU CAN'T SCHEDULE "CHARMING BANTER," LAURI.
BUT SCHEDULES ARE DELIGHTFUL.
RAAHH!
YOU HEAR THAT?
YES.
RAAHH!
CAROL, WE'RE GONNA NEED A BIGGER BOAT.
SEE? SOMETIMES THE LINES JUST WRITE THEMSELVES. ALSO? DAMN.

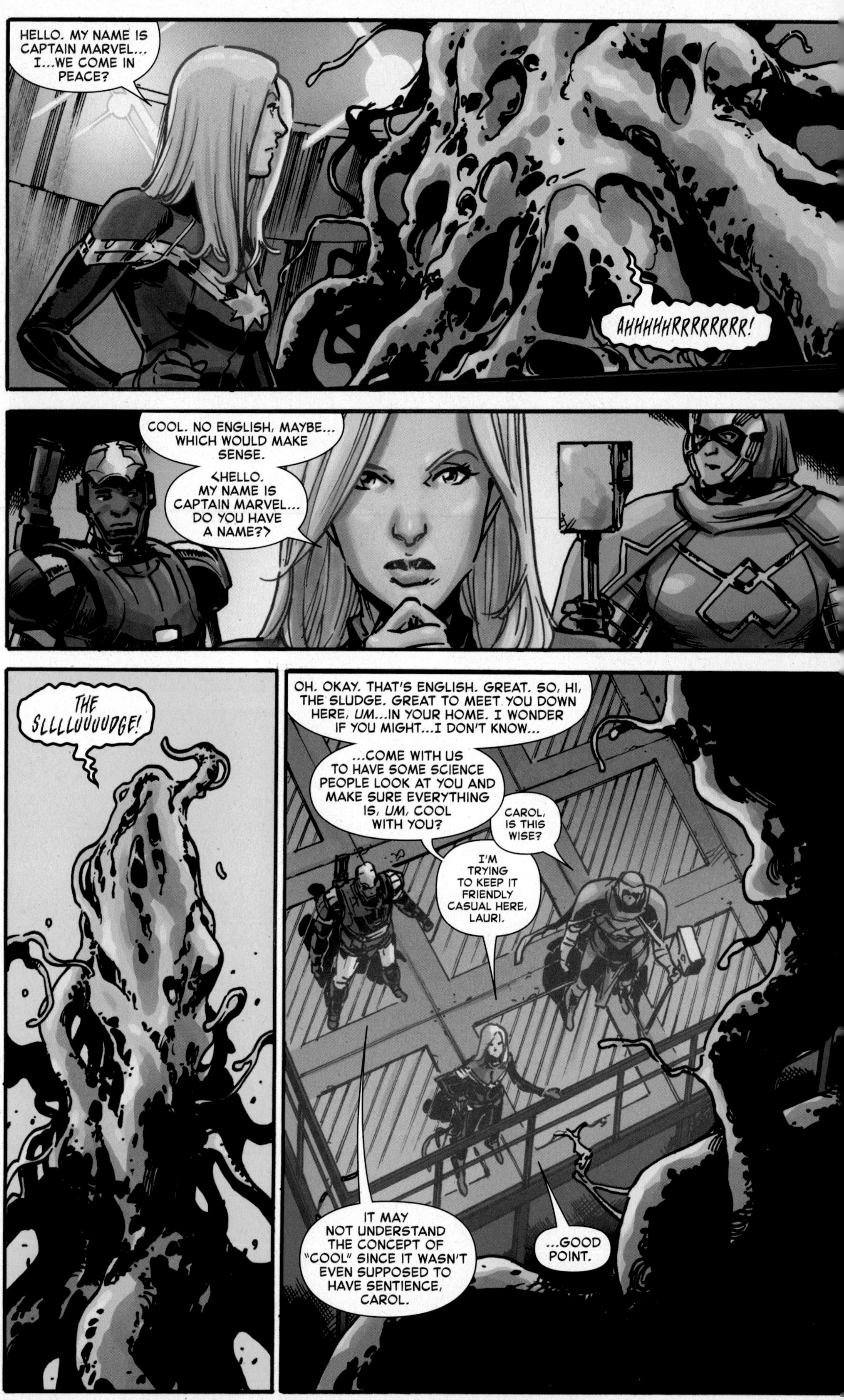
HELLO. MY NAME IS CAPTAIN MARVEL... I...WE COME IN PEACE?
AHHHHHRRRRRRR!
COOL. NO ENGLISH, MAYBE... WHICH WOULD MAKE SENSE.
<HELLO. MY NAME IS CAPTAIN MARVEL... DO YOU HAVE A NAME?>
THE SLLLLUUUUDGE!
OH. OKAY. THAT'S ENGLISH. GREAT. SO, HI, THE SLUDGE. GREAT TO MEET YOU DOWN HERE, UM...IN YOUR HOME. I WONDER IF YOU MIGHT...I DON'T KNOW...
...COME WITH US TO HAVE SOME SCIENCE PEOPLE LOOK AT YOU AND MAKE SURE EVERYTHING IS, UM, COOL WITH YOU?
CAROL, IS THIS WISE?
I'M TRYING TO KEEP IT FRIENDLY CASUAL HERE, LAURI.
IT MAY NOT UNDERSTAND THE CONCEPT OF "COOL" SINCE IT WASN'T EVEN SUPPOSED TO HAVE SENTIENCE, CAROL.
...GOOD POINT.

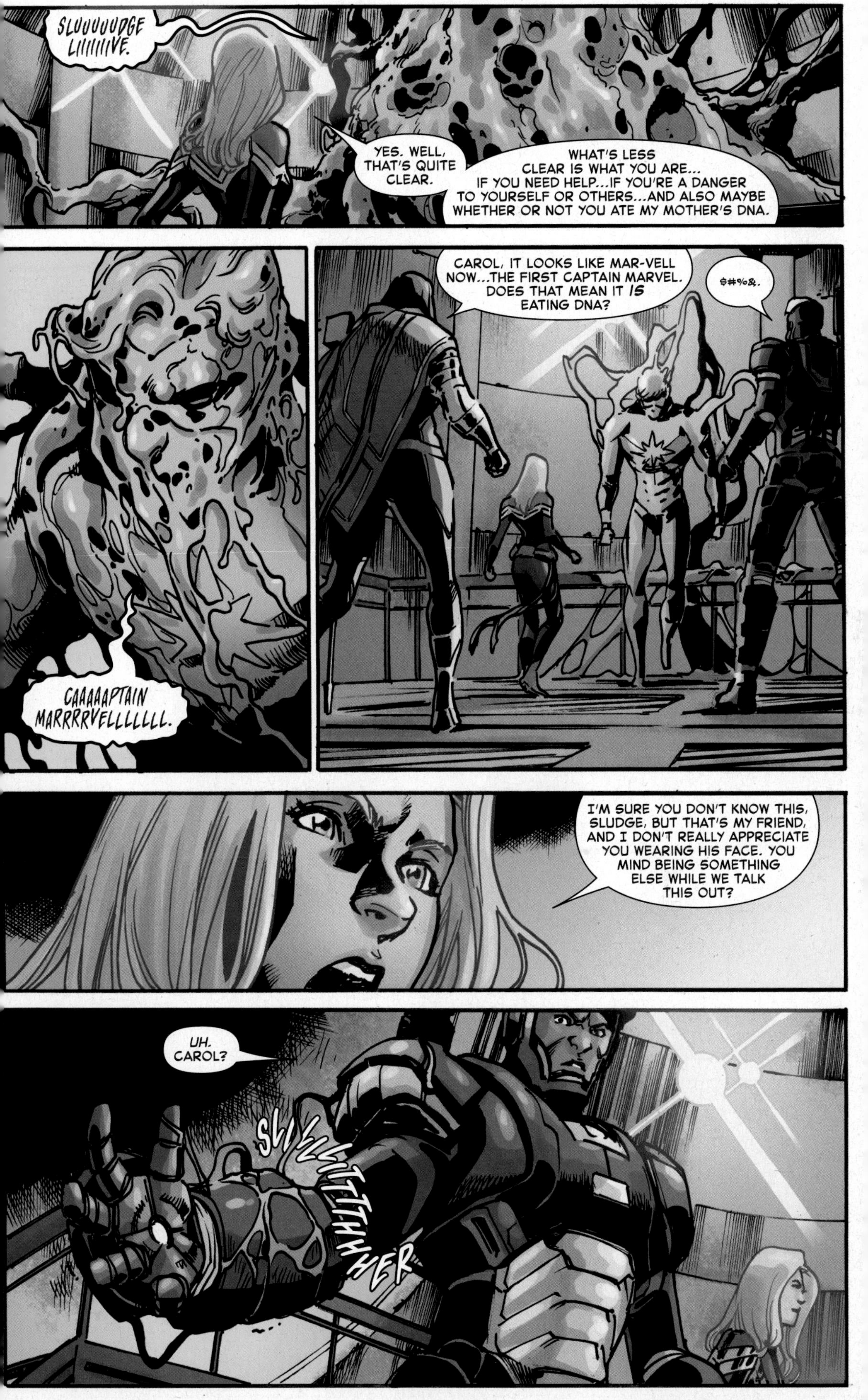
SLUUUUUDGE LIIIIIIVE.
YES. WELL, THAT'S QUITE CLEAR.
WHAT'S LESS CLEAR IS WHAT YOU ARE... IF YOU NEED HELP...IF YOU'RE A DANGER TO YOURSELF OR OTHERS...AND ALSO MAYBE WHETHER OR NOT YOU ATE MY MOTHER'S DNA.
CAAAAAPTAIN MARRRRVELLLLLLL.
CAROL, IT LOOKS LIKE MAR-VELL NOW...THE FIRST CAPTAIN MARVEL. DOES THAT MEAN IT *IS* EATING DNA?
$#%&.
I'M SURE YOU DON'T KNOW THIS, SLUDGE, BUT THAT'S MY FRIEND, AND I DON'T REALLY APPRECIATE YOU WEARING HIS FACE. YOU MIND BEING SOMETHING ELSE WHILE WE TALK THIS OUT?
UH. CAROL?
SLIIITHHHER

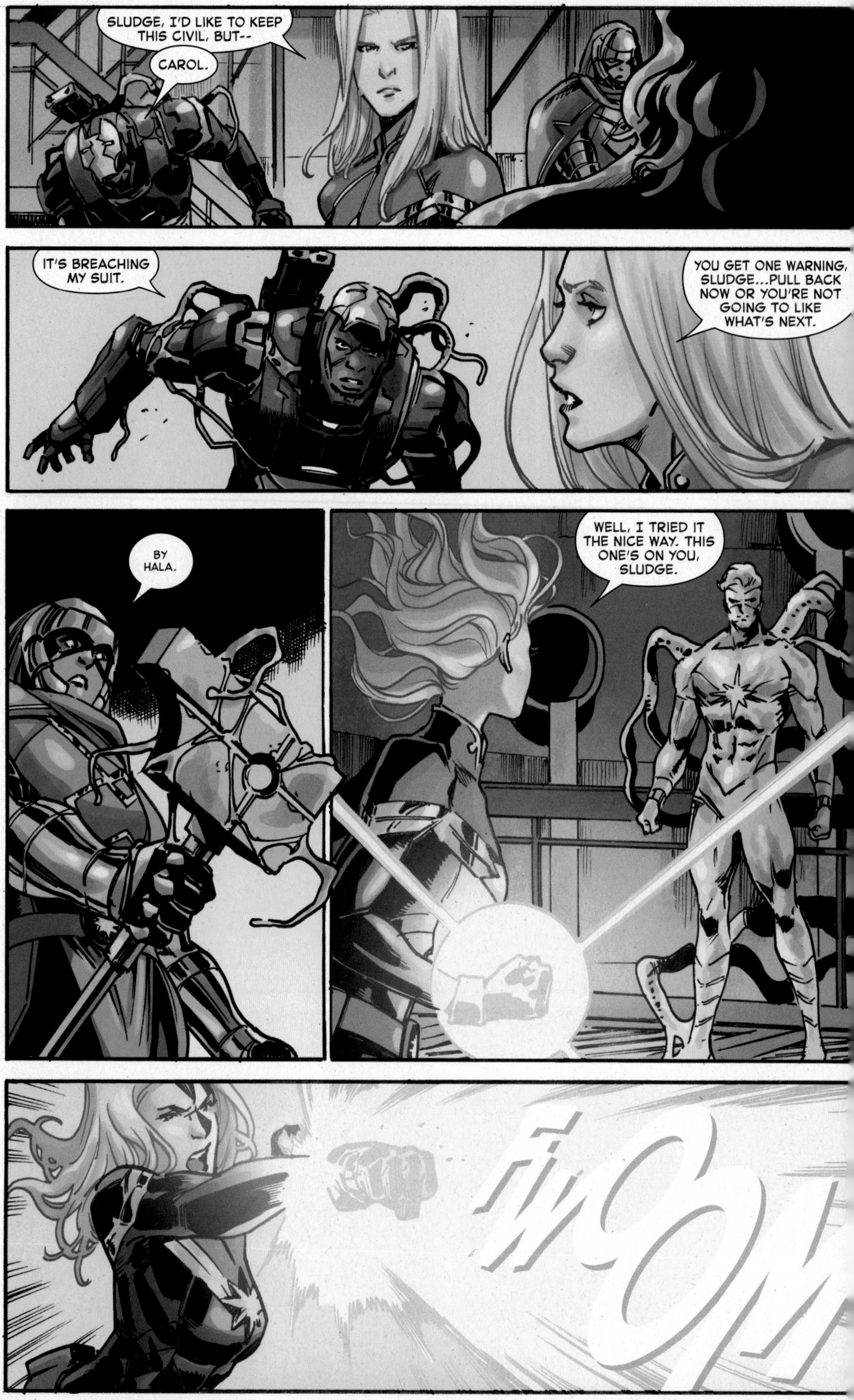
SLUDGE, I'D LIKE TO KEEP THIS CIVIL, BUT--
CAROL.
IT'S BREACHING MY SUIT.
YOU GET ONE WARNING, SLUDGE...PULL BACK NOW OR YOU'RE NOT GOING TO LIKE WHAT'S NEXT.
BY HALA.
WELL, I TRIED IT THE NICE WAY. THIS ONE'S ON YOU, SLUDGE.
FWOOM

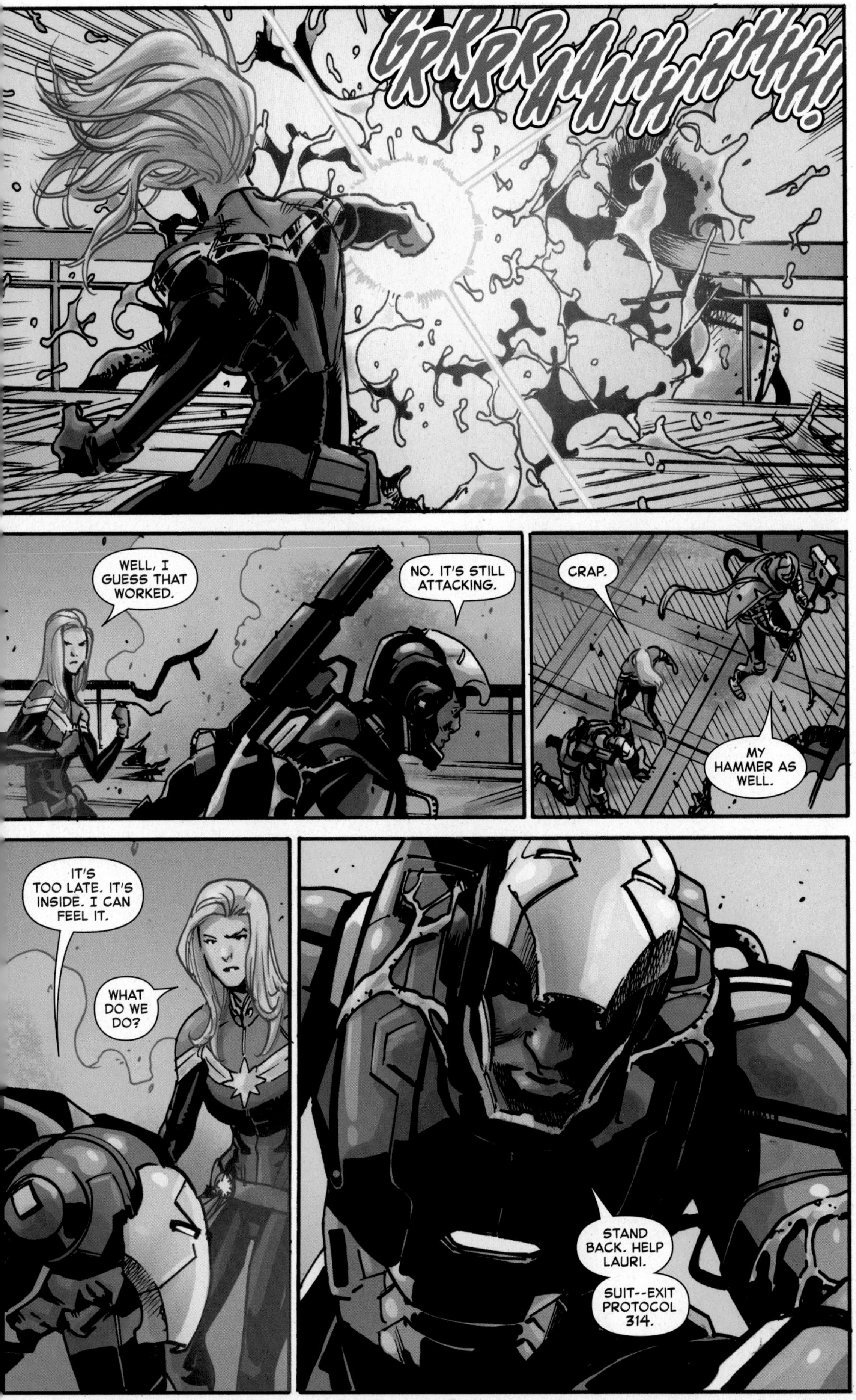
GRRRRAAAHHHHHHH!
WELL, I GUESS THAT WORKED.
NO. IT'S STILL ATTACKING.
CRAP.
MY HAMMER AS WELL.
IT'S TOO LATE. IT'S INSIDE. I CAN FEEL IT.
WHAT DO WE DO?
STAND BACK. HELP LAURI.
SUIT--EXIT PROTOCOL 314.

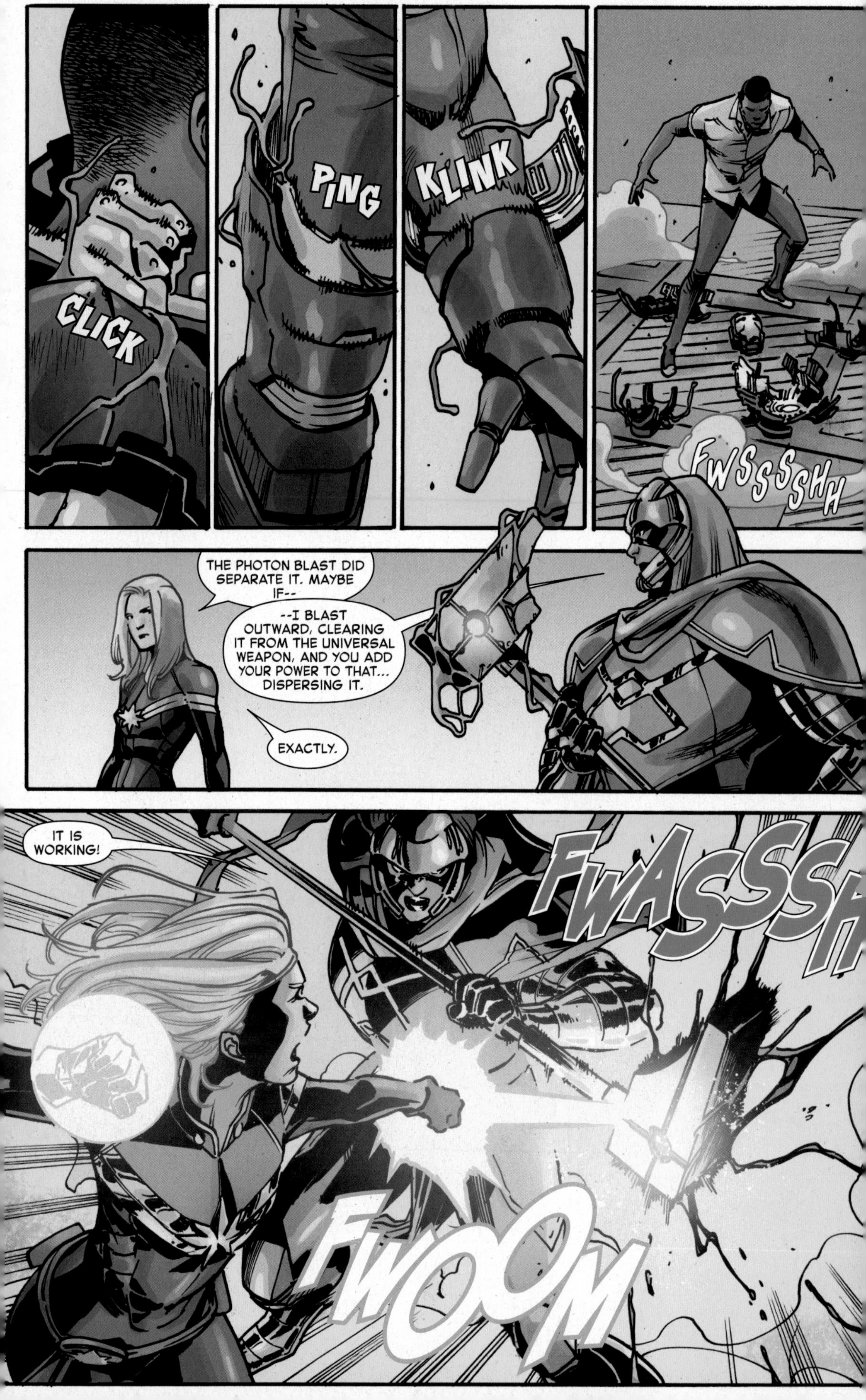
CLICK
PING
KLINK
FWSSSSHH
THE PHOTON BLAST DID SEPARATE IT. MAYBE IF--
--I BLAST OUTWARD, CLEARING IT FROM THE UNIVERSAL WEAPON, AND YOU ADD YOUR POWER TO THAT... DISPERSING IT.
EXACTLY.
IT IS WORKING!
FWASSSH
FWOOM

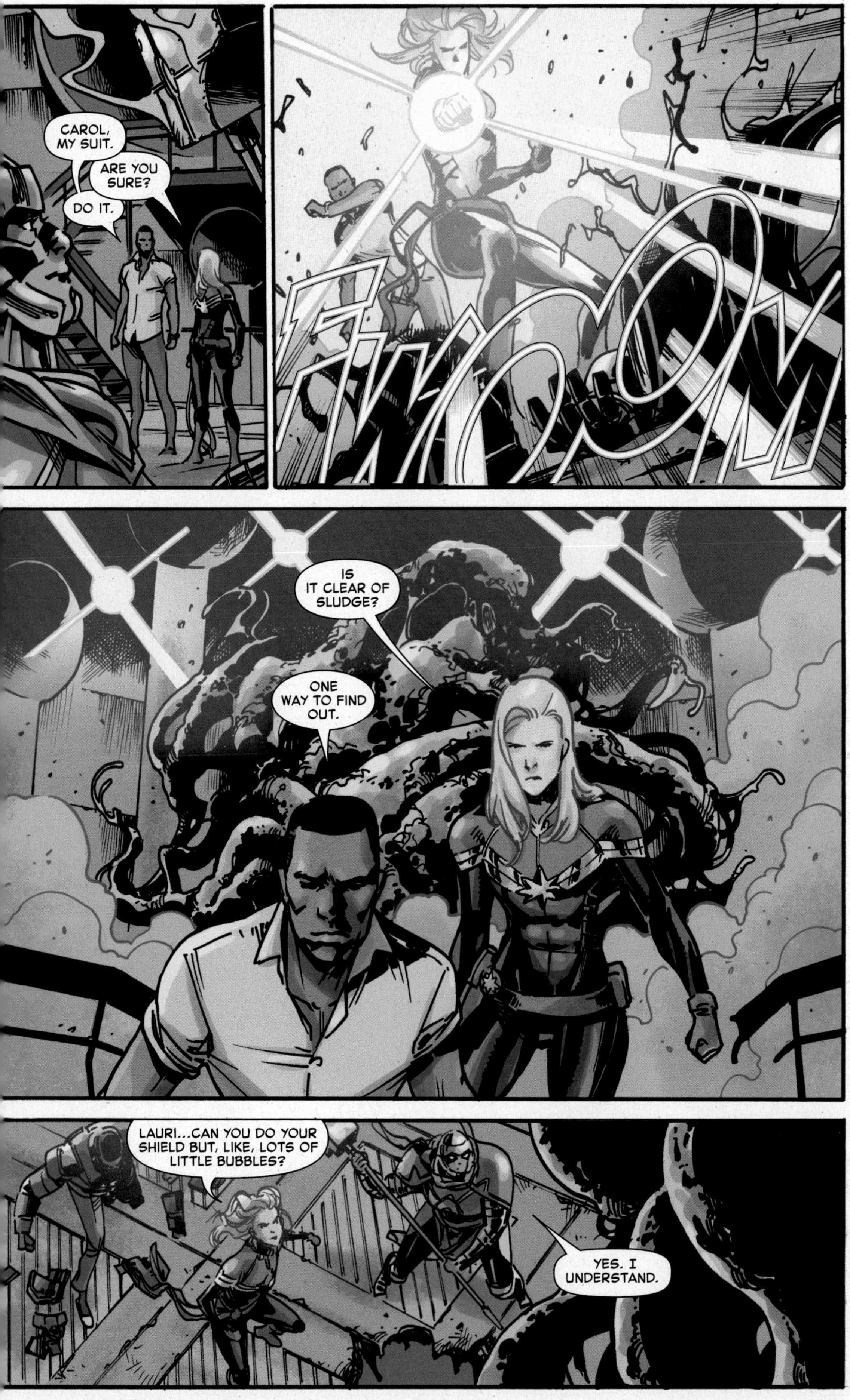
CAROL, MY SUIT.
ARE YOU SURE?
DO IT.
IS IT CLEAR OF SLUDGE?
ONE WAY TO FIND OUT.
LAURI...CAN YOU DO YOUR SHIELD BUT, LIKE, LOTS OF LITTLE BUBBLES?
YES. I UNDERSTAND.

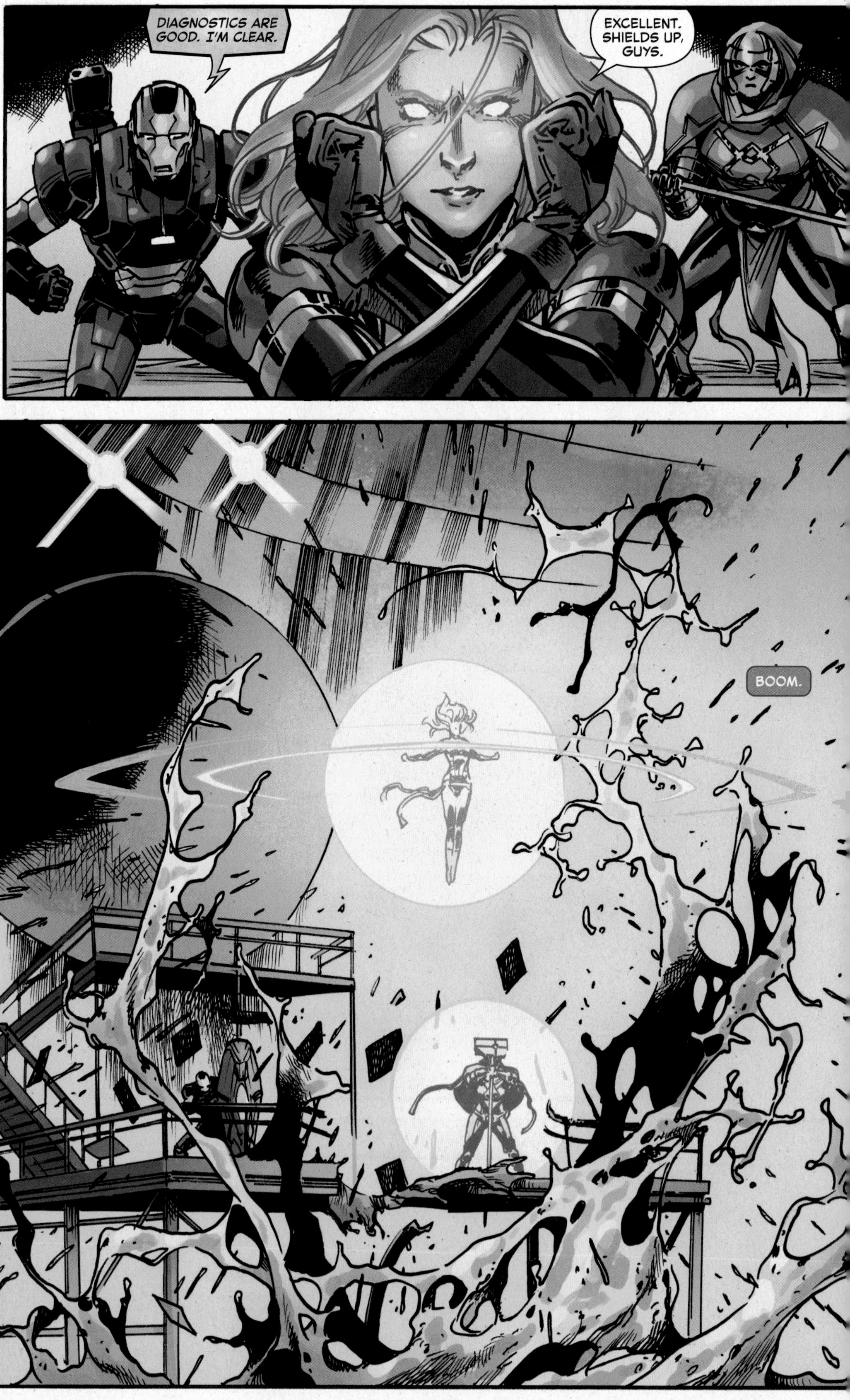
DIAGNOSTICS ARE GOOD. I'M CLEAR.
EXCELLENT. SHIELDS UP, GUYS.
BOOM.

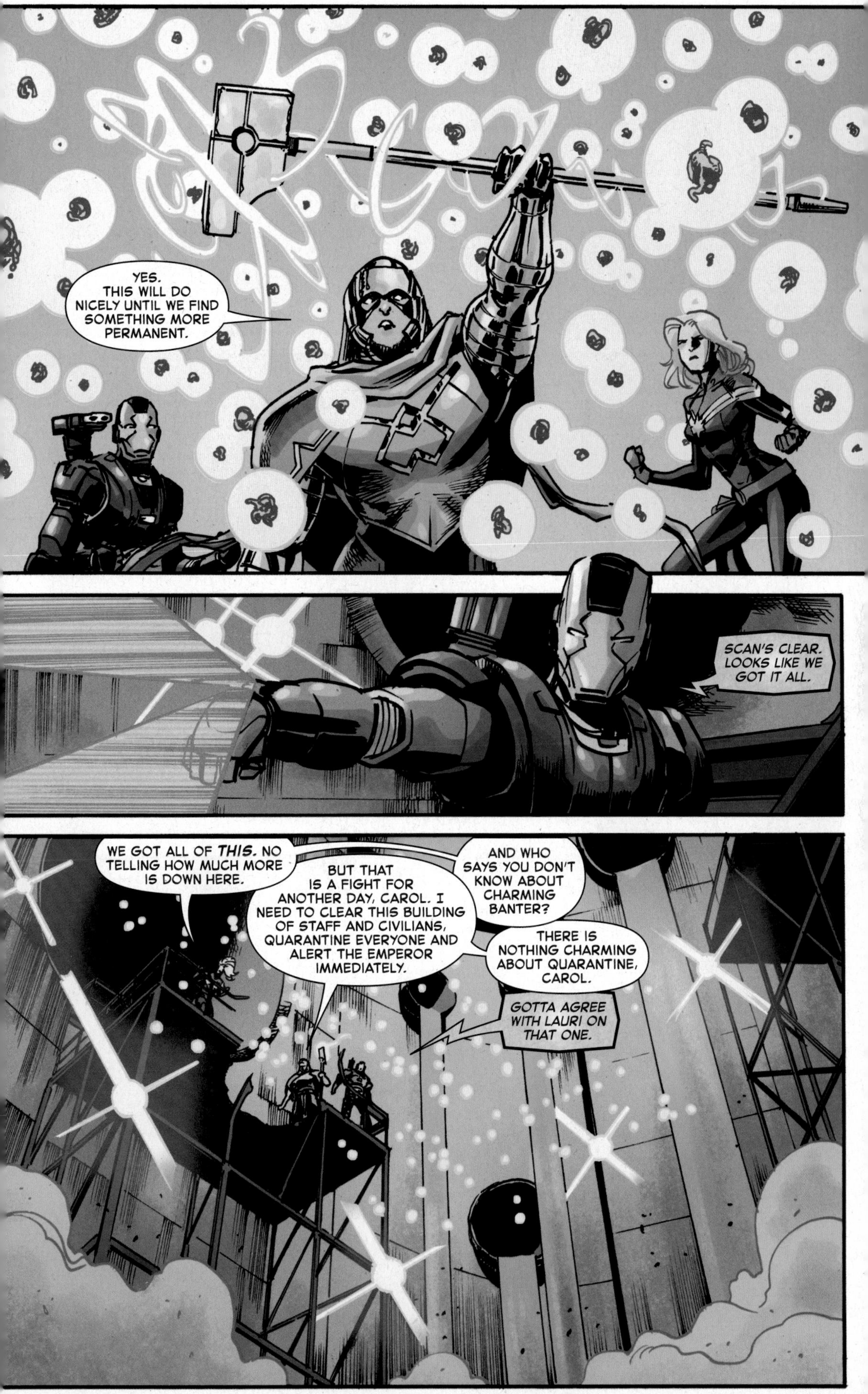
YES. THIS WILL DO NICELY UNTIL WE FIND SOMETHING MORE PERMANENT.
SCAN'S CLEAR. LOOKS LIKE WE GOT IT ALL.
WE GOT ALL OF *THIS.* NO TELLING HOW MUCH MORE IS DOWN HERE.
BUT THAT IS A FIGHT FOR ANOTHER DAY, CAROL. I NEED TO CLEAR THIS BUILDING OF STAFF AND CIVILIANS, QUARANTINE EVERYONE AND ALERT THE EMPEROR IMMEDIATELY.
AND WHO SAYS YOU DON'T KNOW ABOUT CHARMING BANTER?
THERE IS NOTHING CHARMING ABOUT QUARANTINE, CAROL.
GOTTA AGREE WITH LAURI ON THAT ONE.

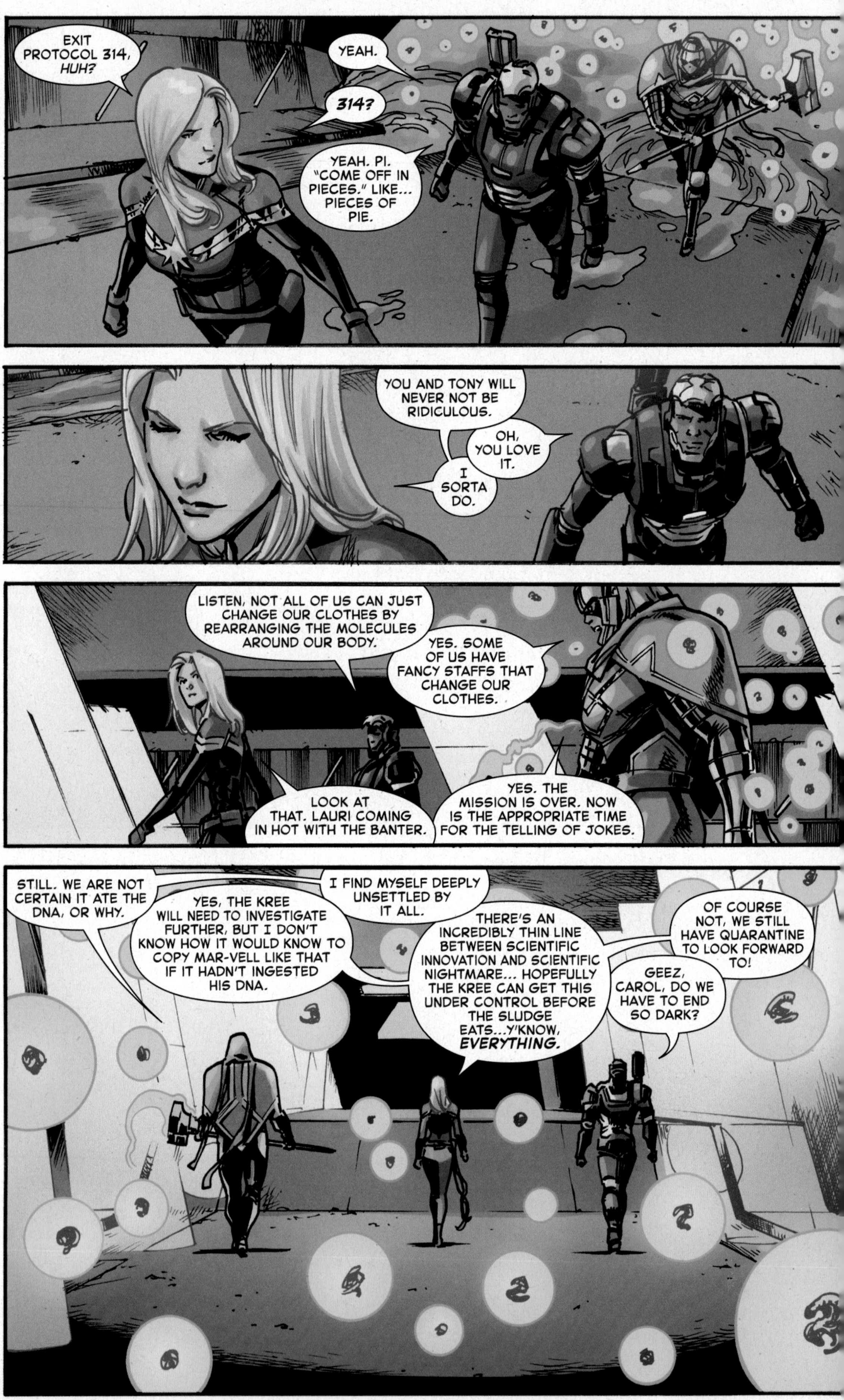
EXIT PROTOCOL 314, HUH?
YEAH.
314?
YEAH. PI. "COME OFF IN PIECES." LIKE... PIECES OF PIE.
YOU AND TONY WILL NEVER NOT BE RIDICULOUS.
OH, YOU LOVE IT.
I SORTA DO.
LISTEN, NOT ALL OF US CAN JUST CHANGE OUR CLOTHES BY REARRANGING THE MOLECULES AROUND OUR BODY.
YES. SOME OF US HAVE FANCY STAFFS THAT CHANGE OUR CLOTHES.
LOOK AT THAT. LAURI COMING IN HOT WITH THE BANTER.
YES. THE MISSION IS OVER. NOW IS THE APPROPRIATE TIME FOR THE TELLING OF JOKES.
STILL. WE ARE NOT CERTAIN IT ATE THE DNA, OR WHY.
I FIND MYSELF DEEPLY UNSETTLED BY IT ALL.
YES, THE KREE WILL NEED TO INVESTIGATE FURTHER, BUT I DON'T KNOW HOW IT WOULD KNOW TO COPY MAR-VELL LIKE THAT IF IT HADN'T INGESTED HIS DNA.
THERE'S AN INCREDIBLY THIN LINE BETWEEN SCIENTIFIC INNOVATION AND SCIENTIFIC NIGHTMARE... HOPEFULLY THE KREE CAN GET THIS UNDER CONTROL BEFORE THE SLUDGE EATS...Y'KNOW, EVERYTHING.
GEEZ, CAROL, DO WE HAVE TO END SO DARK?
OF COURSE NOT, WE STILL HAVE QUARANTINE TO LOOK FORWARD TO!

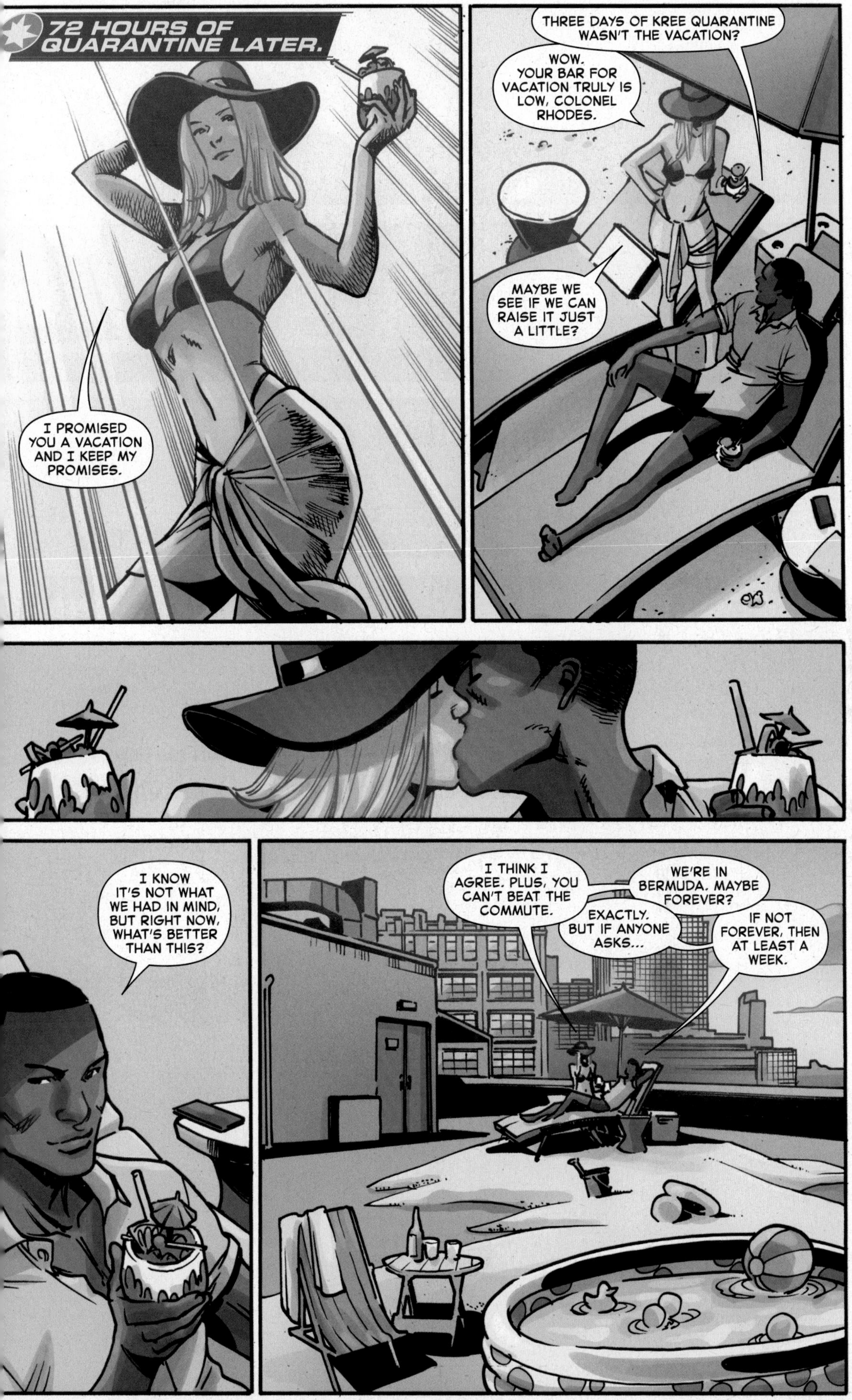
72 HOURS OF QUARANTINE LATER.
I PROMISED YOU A VACATION AND I KEEP MY PROMISES.
THREE DAYS OF KREE QUARANTINE WASN'T THE VACATION?
WOW. YOUR BAR FOR VACATION TRULY IS LOW, COLONEL RHODES.
MAYBE WE SEE IF WE CAN RAISE IT JUST A LITTLE?
I KNOW IT'S NOT WHAT WE HAD IN MIND, BUT RIGHT NOW, WHAT'S BETTER THAN THIS?
I THINK I AGREE. PLUS, YOU CAN'T BEAT THE COMMUTE.
WE'RE IN BERMUDA. MAYBE FOREVER?
EXACTLY. BUT IF ANYONE ASKS...
IF NOT FOREVER, THEN AT LEAST A WEEK.

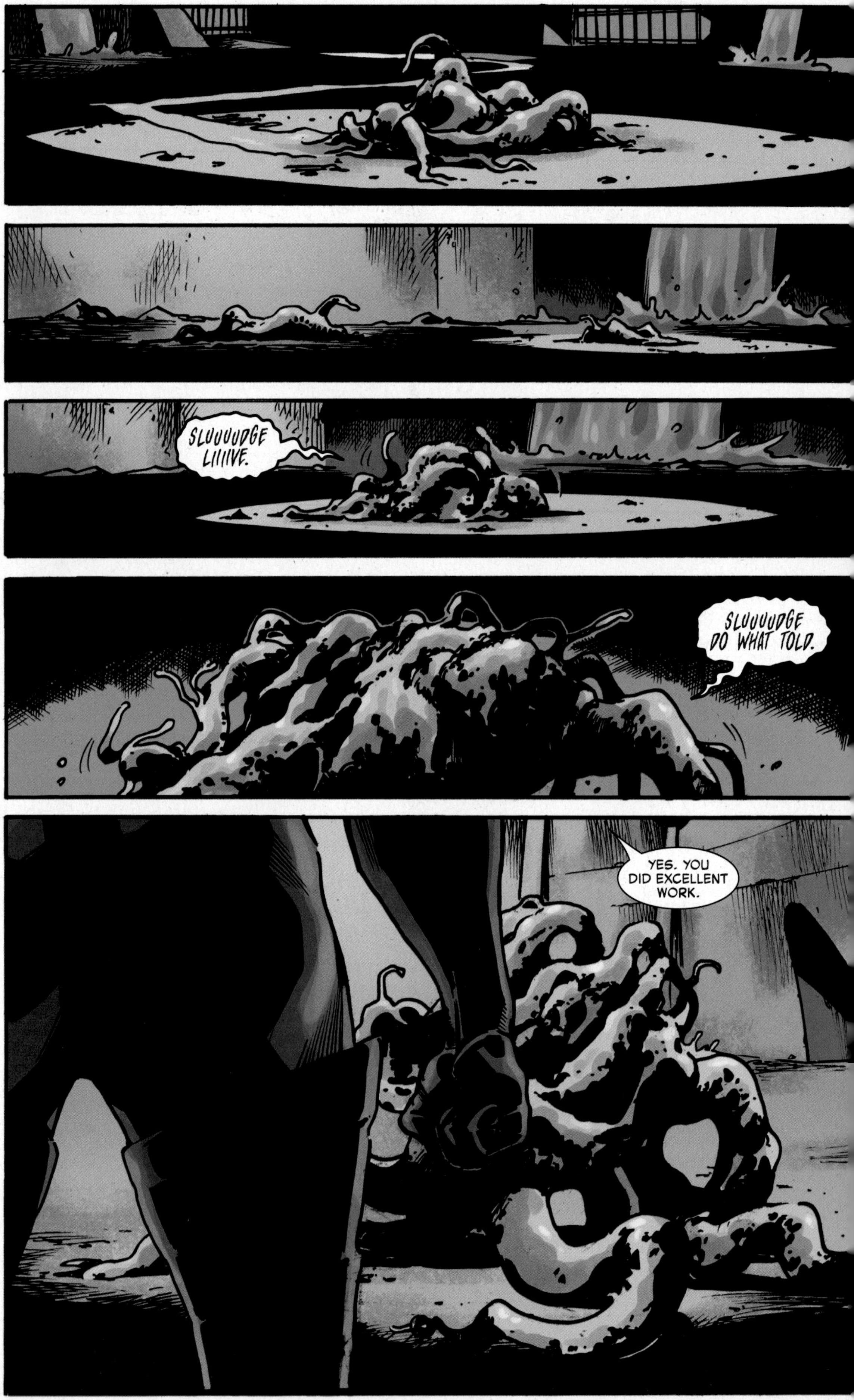
SLUUUUDGE LIIIIVE.
SLUUUUDGE DO WHAT TOLD.
YES. YOU DID EXCELLENT WORK.

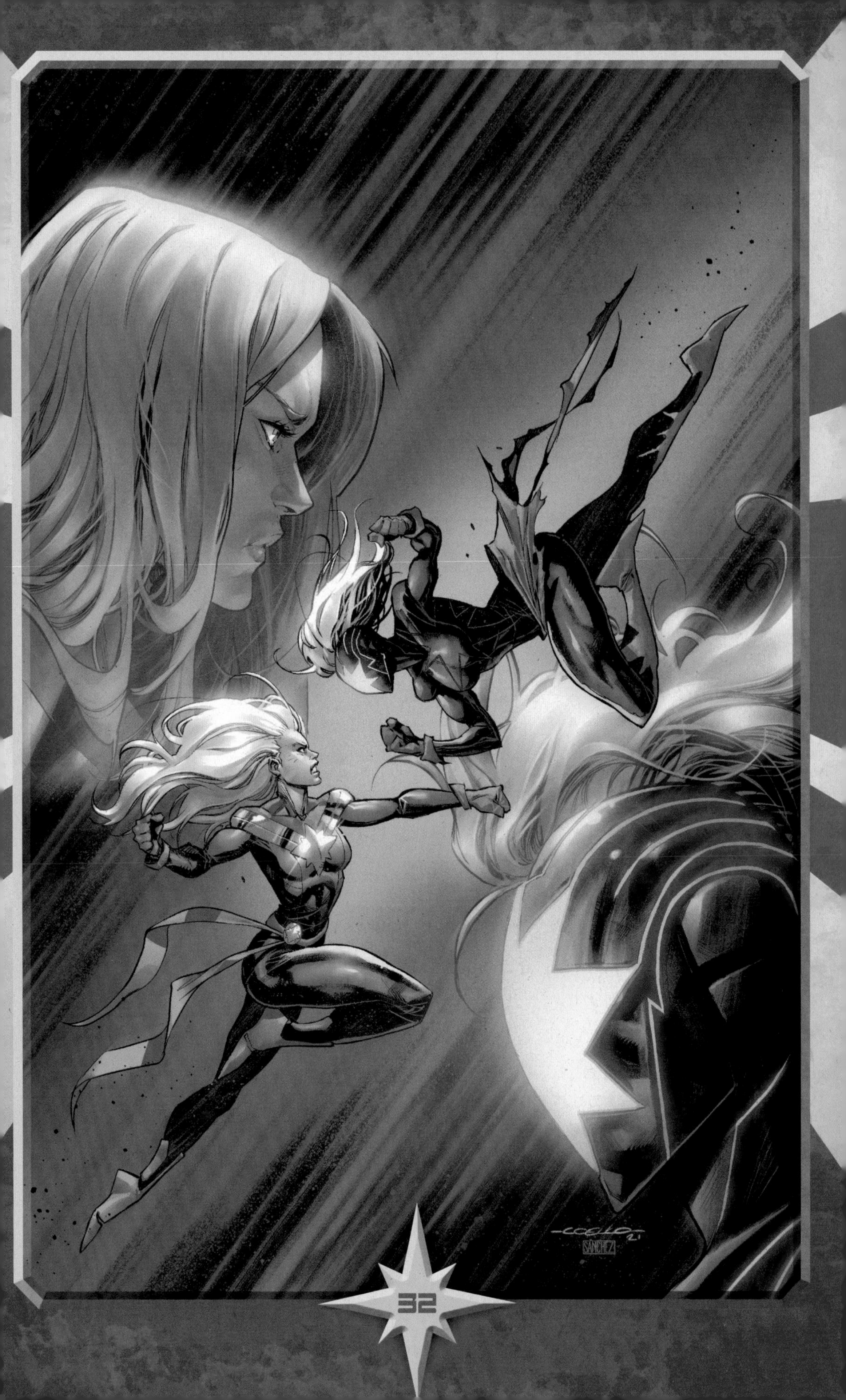
32

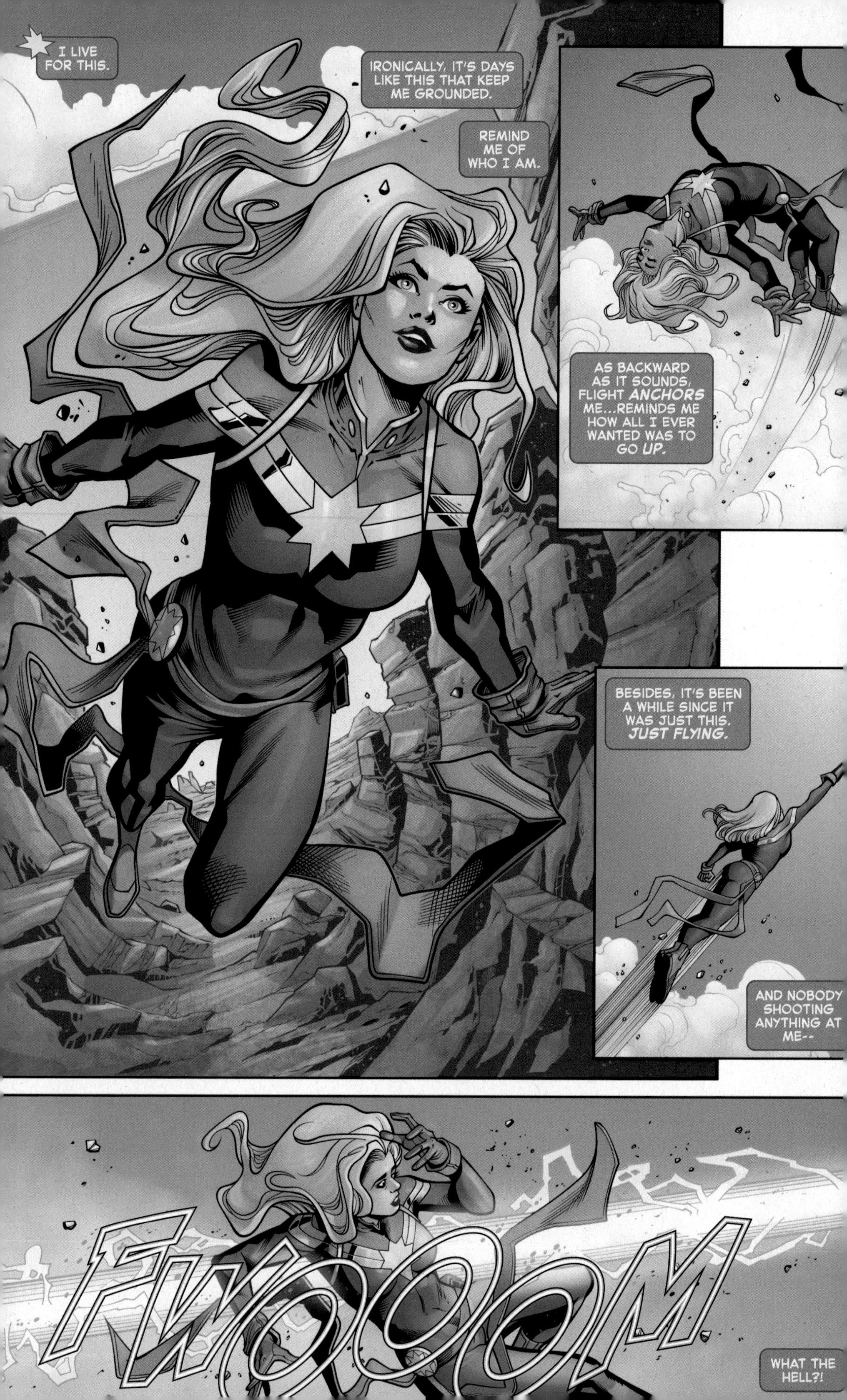
I LIVE FOR THIS.
IRONICALLY, IT'S DAYS LIKE THIS THAT KEEP ME GROUNDED.
REMIND ME OF WHO I AM.
AS BACKWARD AS IT SOUNDS, FLIGHT ANCHORS ME...REMINDS ME HOW ALL I EVER WANTED WAS TO GO UP.
BESIDES, IT'S BEEN A WHILE SINCE IT WAS JUST THIS. JUST FLYING.
AND NOBODY SHOOTING ANYTHING AT ME--
FWOOOM
WHAT THE HELL?!

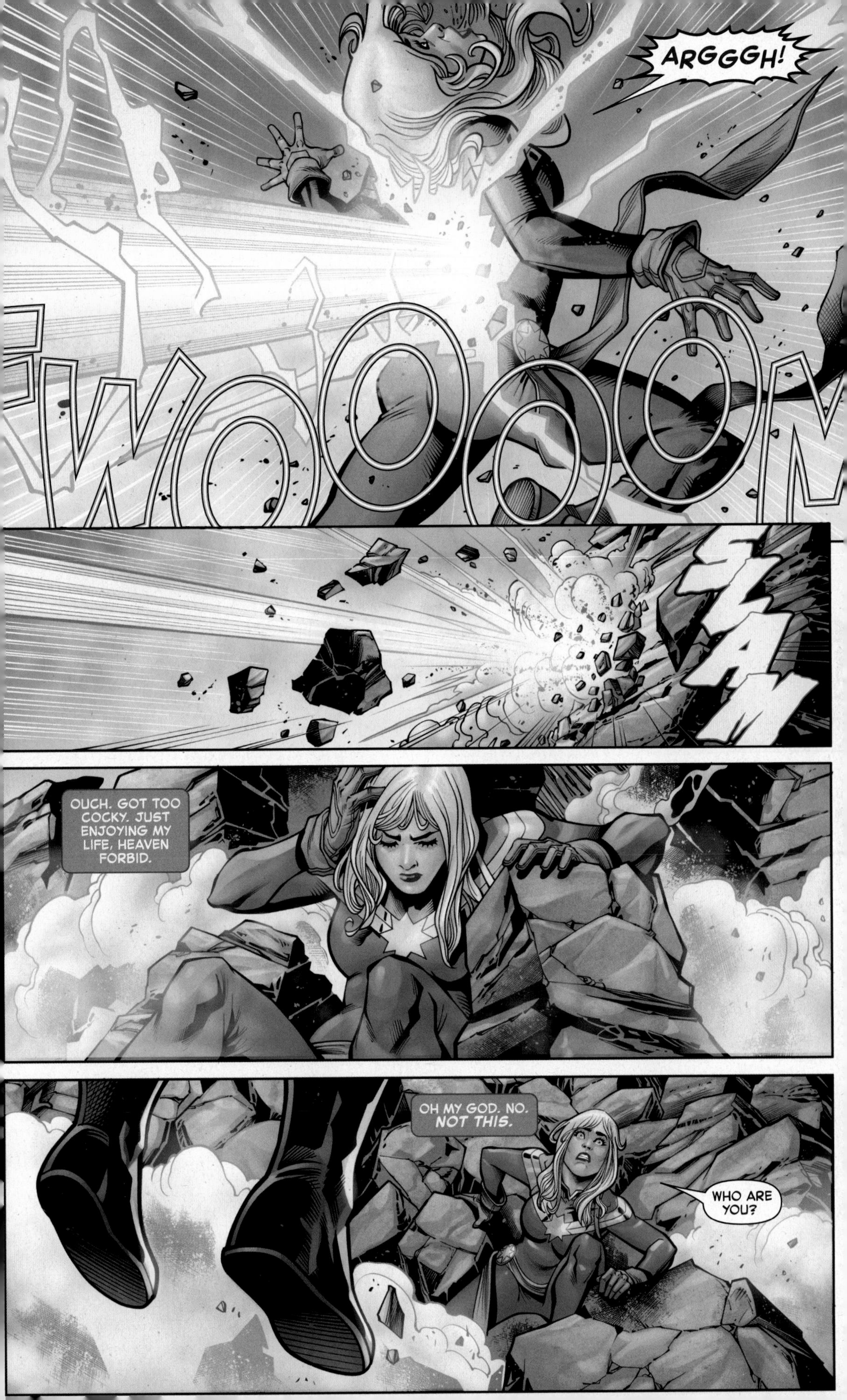
ARGGGH!
WOOOOOM
SLAM
OUCH. GOT TOO COCKY. JUST ENJOYING MY LIFE, HEAVEN FORBID.
OH MY GOD. NO. *NOT THIS.*
WHO ARE YOU?

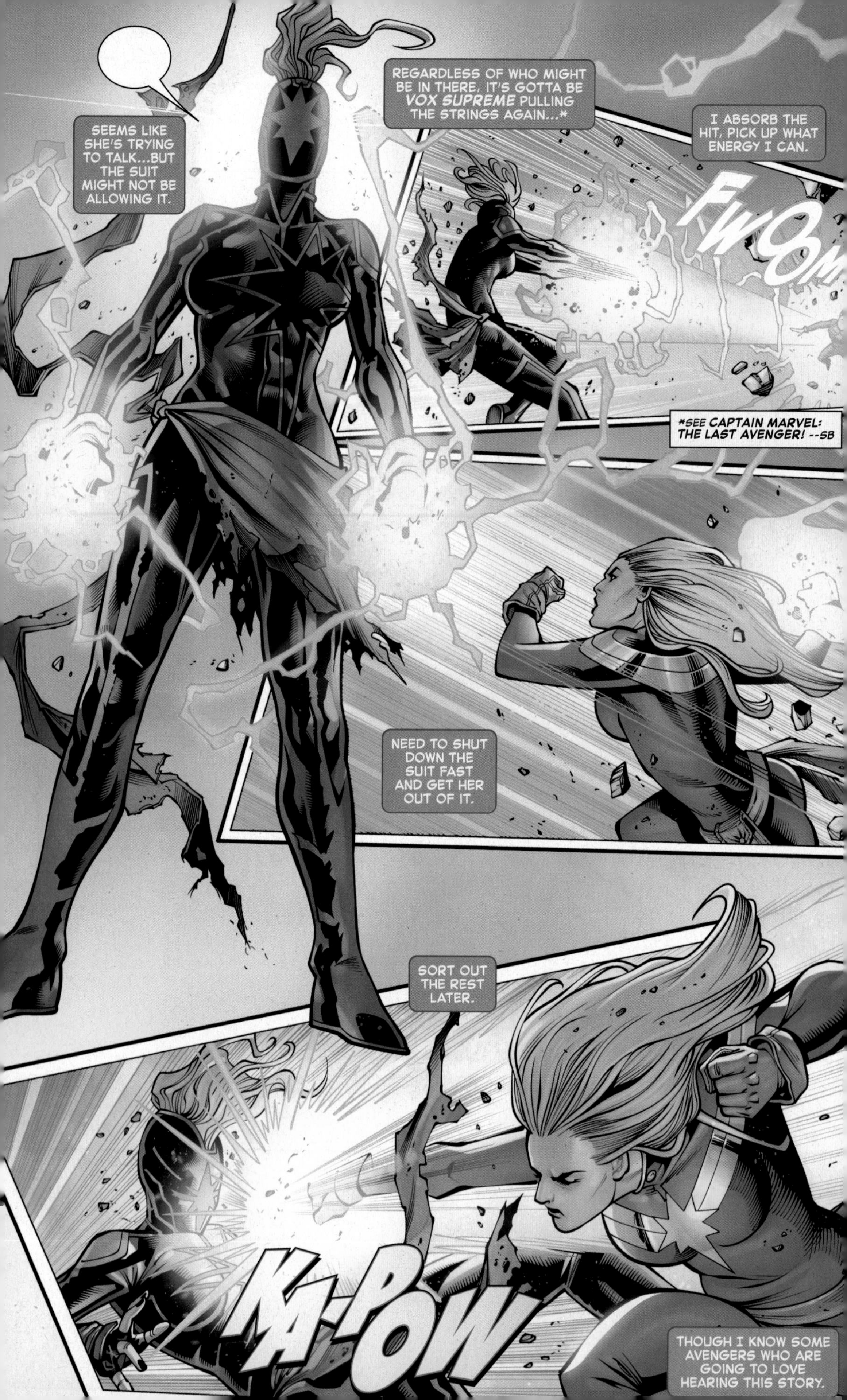
SEEMS LIKE SHE'S TRYING TO TALK...BUT THE SUIT MIGHT NOT BE ALLOWING IT.
REGARDLESS OF WHO MIGHT BE IN THERE, IT'S GOTTA BE VOX SUPREME PULLING THE STRINGS AGAIN...*
I ABSORB THE HIT, PICK UP WHAT ENERGY I CAN.
FWOOM
*SEE CAPTAIN MARVEL: THE LAST AVENGER! --SB
NEED TO SHUT DOWN THE SUIT FAST AND GET HER OUT OF IT.
SORT OUT THE REST LATER.
KA-POW
THOUGH I KNOW SOME AVENGERS WHO ARE GOING TO LOVE HEARING THIS STORY.

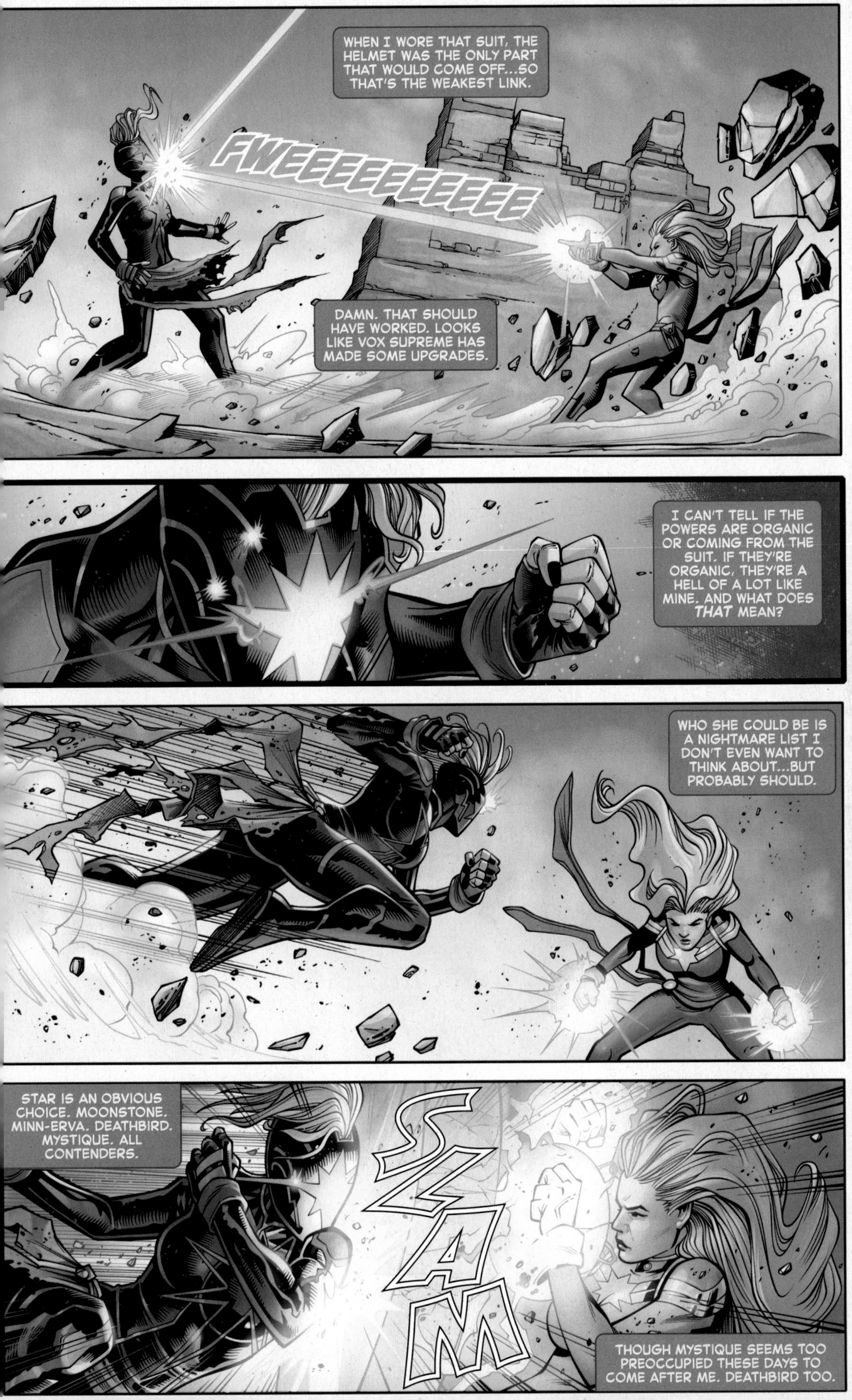

WHEN I WORE THAT SUIT, THE HELMET WAS THE ONLY PART THAT WOULD COME OFF...SO THAT'S THE WEAKEST LINK.
FWEEEEEEEEEEEE
DAMN. THAT SHOULD HAVE WORKED. LOOKS LIKE VOX SUPREME HAS MADE SOME UPGRADES.
I CAN'T TELL IF THE POWERS ARE ORGANIC OR COMING FROM THE SUIT. IF THEY'RE ORGANIC, THEY'RE A HELL OF A LOT LIKE MINE. AND WHAT DOES *THAT* MEAN?
WHO SHE COULD BE IS A NIGHTMARE LIST I DON'T EVEN WANT TO THINK ABOUT...BUT PROBABLY SHOULD.
STAR IS AN OBVIOUS CHOICE. MOONSTONE. MINN-ERVA. DEATHBIRD. MYSTIQUE. ALL CONTENDERS.
SLAM
THOUGH MYSTIQUE SEEMS TOO PREOCCUPIED THESE DAYS TO COME AFTER ME. DEATHBIRD TOO.

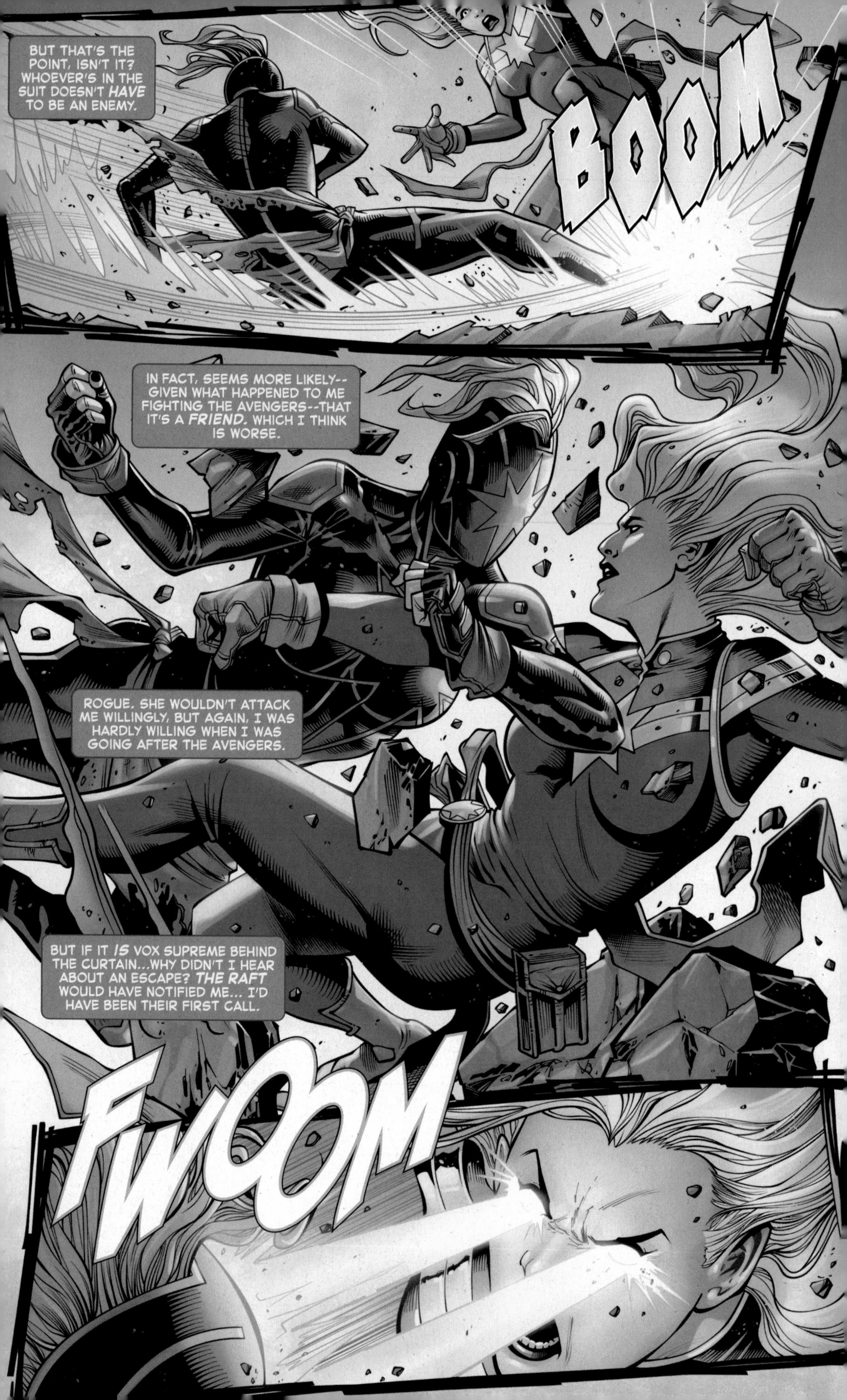
BUT THAT'S THE POINT, ISN'T IT? WHOEVER'S IN THE SUIT DOESN'T *HAVE* TO BE AN ENEMY.
BOOM
IN FACT, SEEMS MORE LIKELY--GIVEN WHAT HAPPENED TO ME FIGHTING THE AVENGERS--THAT IT'S A *FRIEND.* WHICH I THINK IS WORSE.
ROGUE. SHE WOULDN'T ATTACK ME WILLINGLY, BUT AGAIN, I WAS HARDLY WILLING WHEN I WAS GOING AFTER THE AVENGERS.
BUT IF IT *IS* VOX SUPREME BEHIND THE CURTAIN...WHY DIDN'T I HEAR ABOUT AN ESCAPE? *THE RAFT* WOULD HAVE NOTIFIED ME... I'D HAVE BEEN THEIR FIRST CALL.
FWOOM

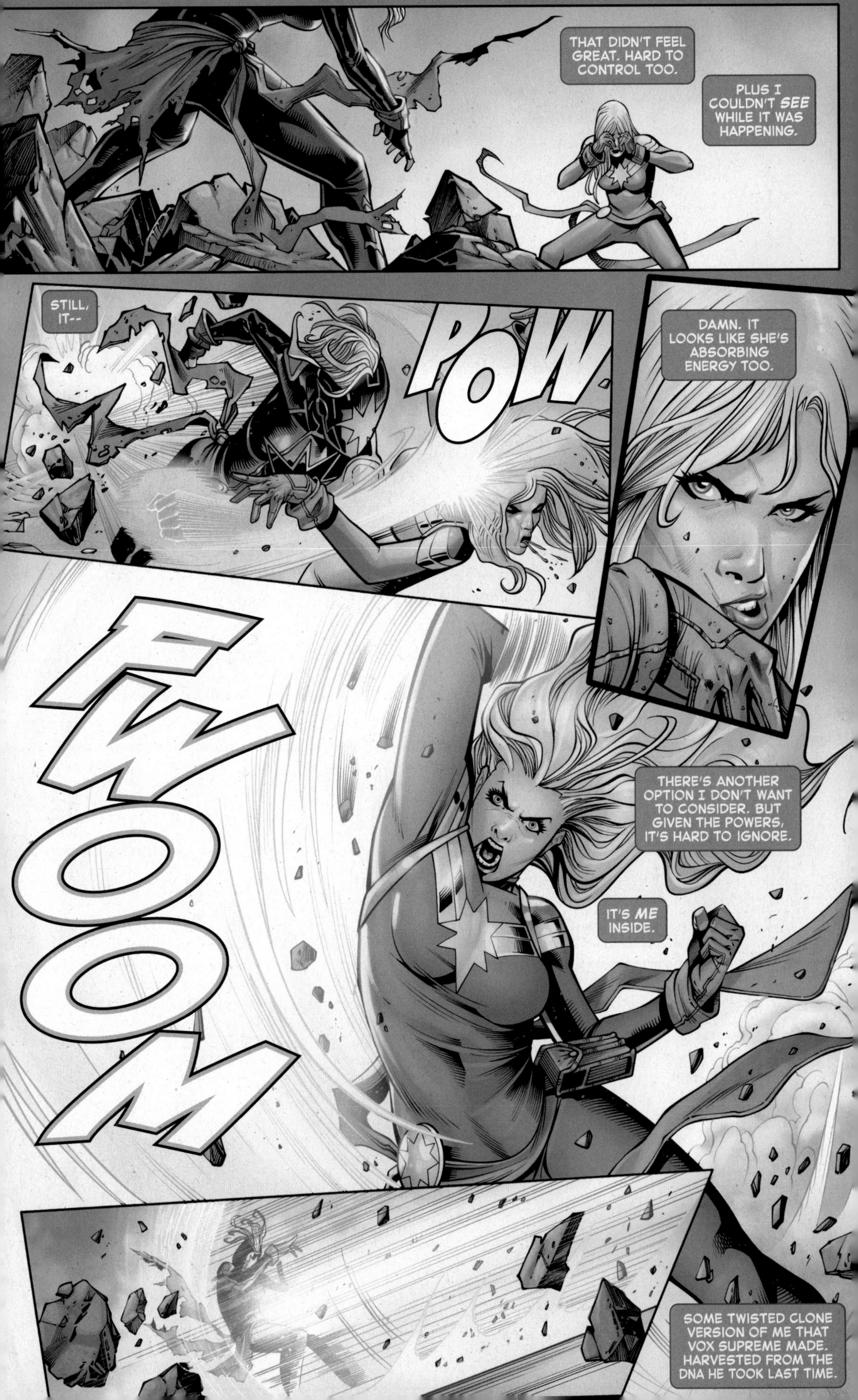
THAT DIDN'T FEEL GREAT. HARD TO CONTROL TOO.
PLUS I COULDN'T *SEE* WHILE IT WAS HAPPENING.
STILL, IT--
POW
DAMN. IT LOOKS LIKE SHE'S ABSORBING ENERGY TOO.
FWOOOM
THERE'S ANOTHER OPTION I DON'T WANT TO CONSIDER. BUT GIVEN THE POWERS, IT'S HARD TO IGNORE.
IT'S *ME* INSIDE.
SOME TWISTED CLONE VERSION OF ME THAT VOX SUPREME MADE. HARVESTED FROM THE DNA HE TOOK LAST TIME.

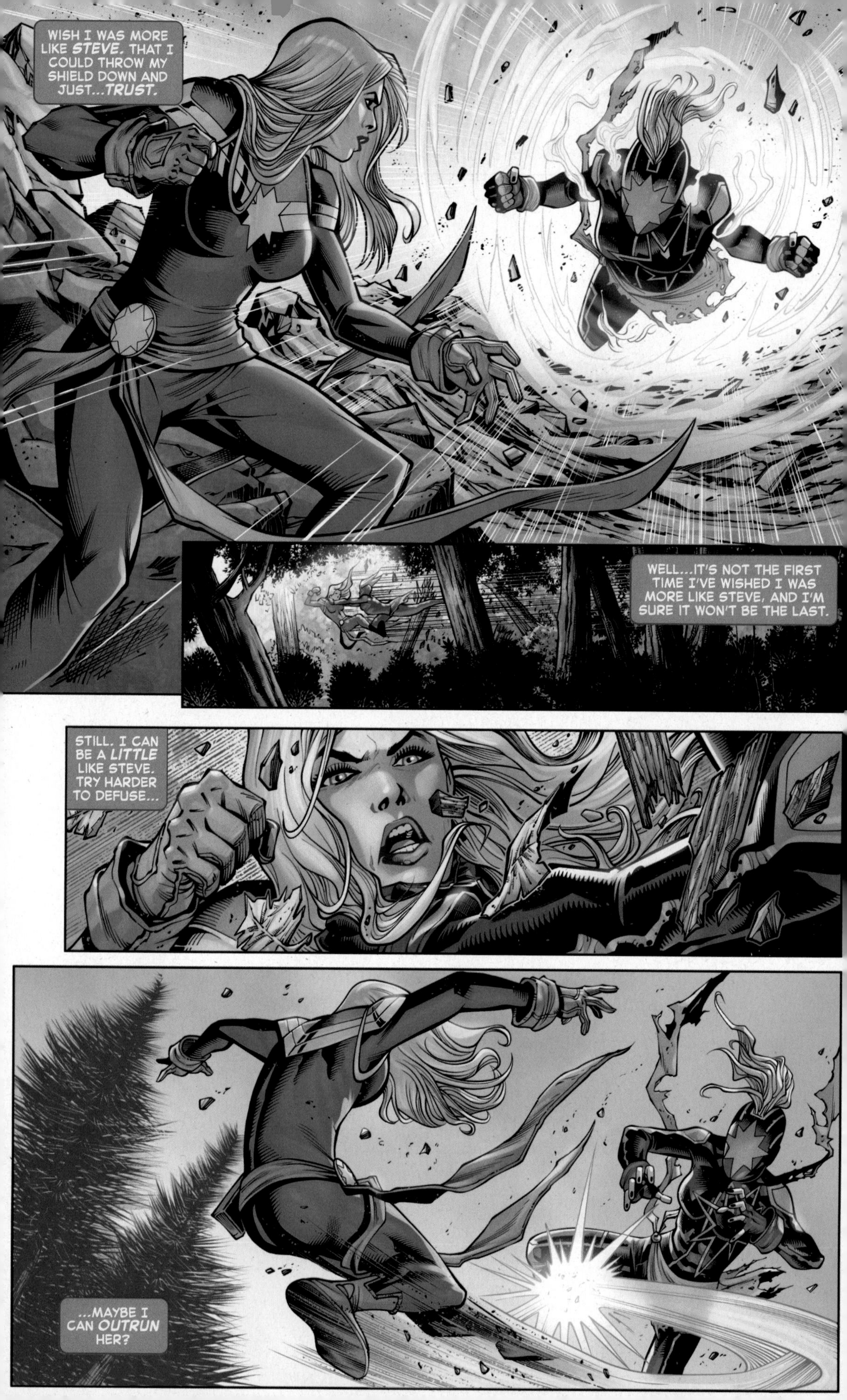
WISH I WAS MORE LIKE STEVE. THAT I COULD THROW MY SHIELD DOWN AND JUST...TRUST.
WELL...IT'S NOT THE FIRST TIME I'VE WISHED I WAS MORE LIKE STEVE, AND I'M SURE IT WON'T BE THE LAST.
STILL. I CAN BE A LITTLE LIKE STEVE. TRY HARDER TO DEFUSE...
...MAYBE I CAN OUTRUN HER?

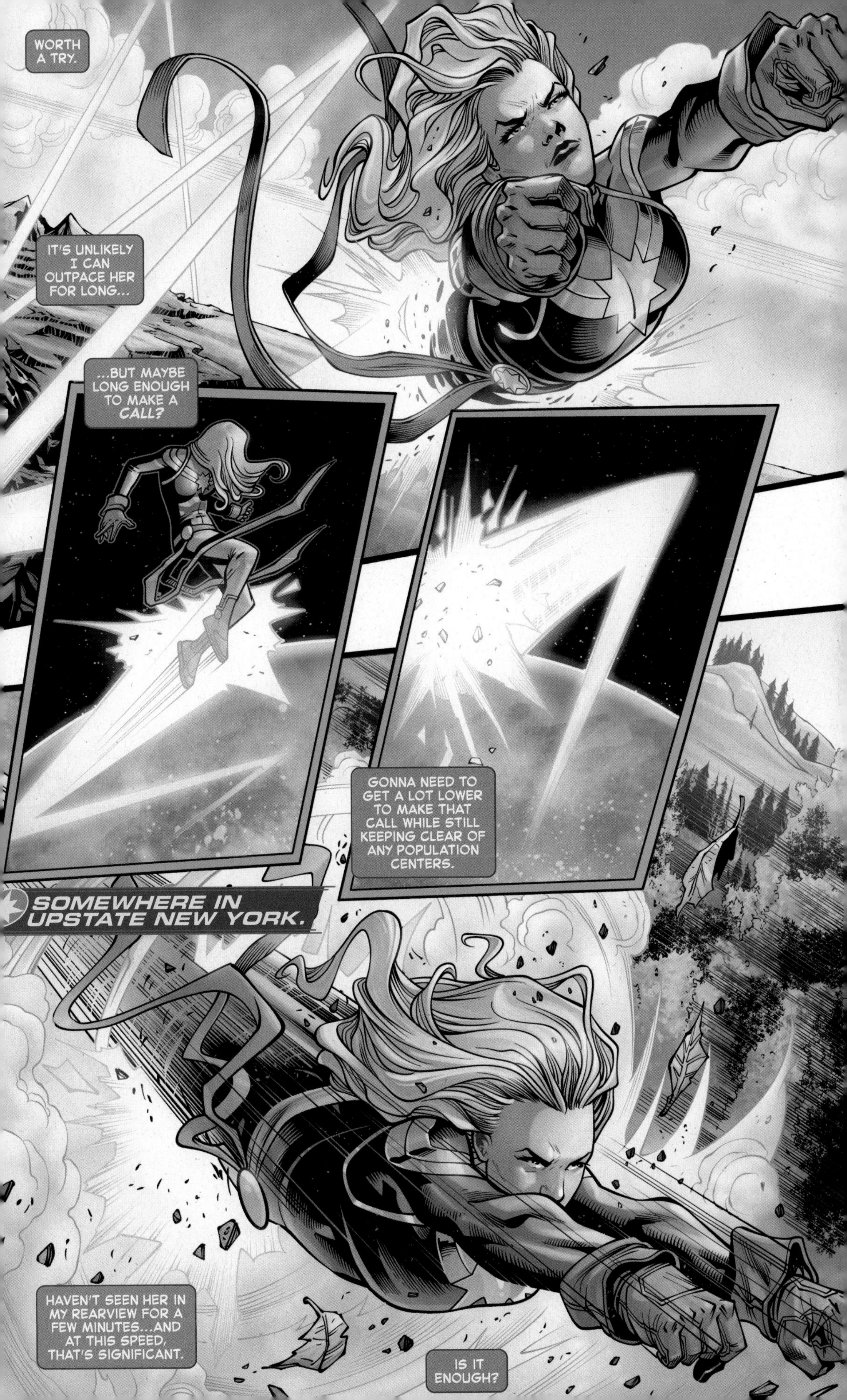
WORTH A TRY.
IT'S UNLIKELY I CAN OUTPACE HER FOR LONG...
...BUT MAYBE LONG ENOUGH TO MAKE A CALL?
GONNA NEED TO GET A LOT LOWER TO MAKE THAT CALL WHILE STILL KEEPING CLEAR OF ANY POPULATION CENTERS.
SOMEWHERE IN UPSTATE NEW YORK.
HAVEN'T SEEN HER IN MY REARVIEW FOR A FEW MINUTES...AND AT THIS SPEED, THAT'S SIGNIFICANT.
IS IT ENOUGH?

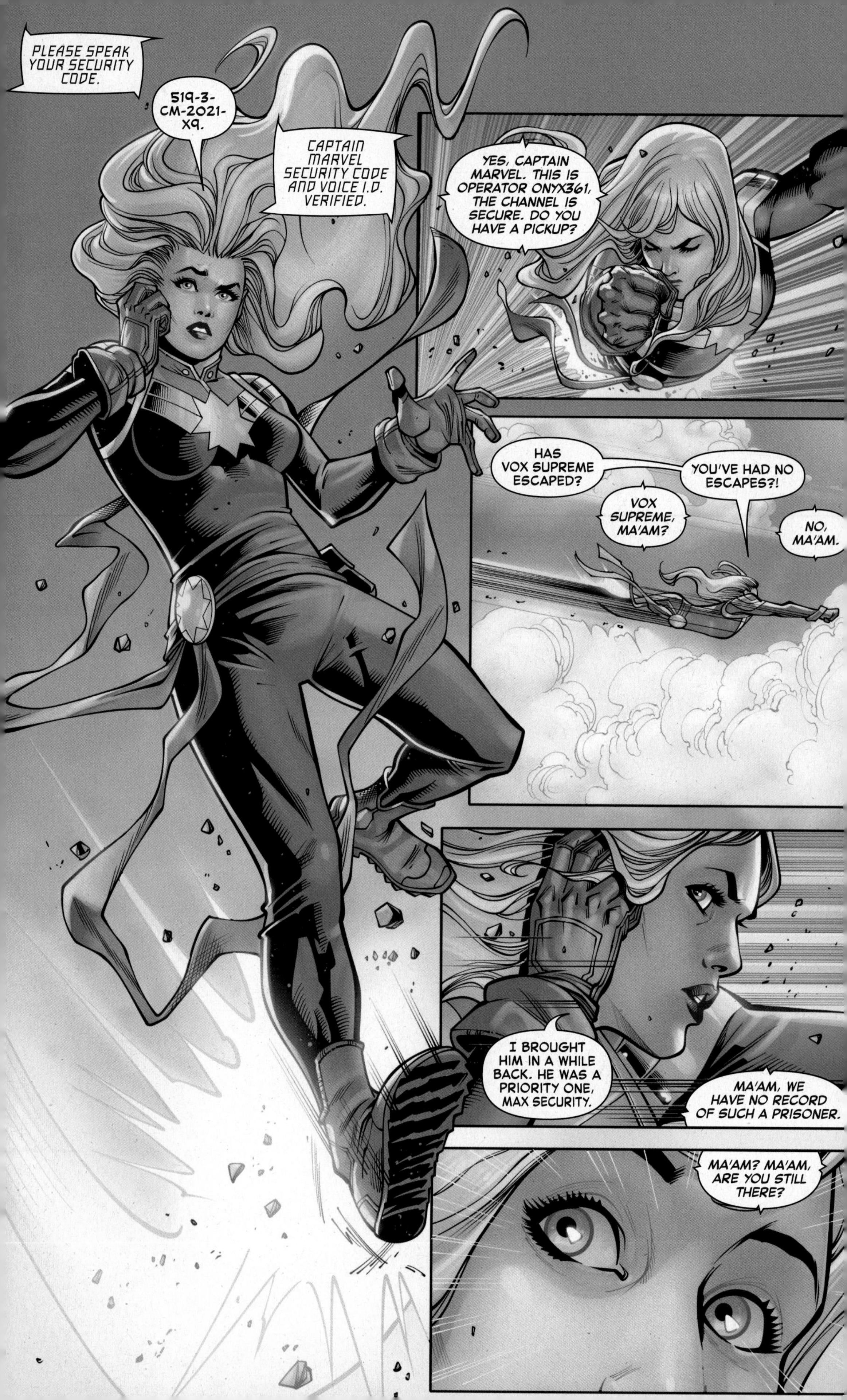
PLEASE SPEAK YOUR SECURITY CODE.
519-3-CM-2021-X9.
CAPTAIN MARVEL SECURITY CODE AND VOICE I.D. VERIFIED.
YES, CAPTAIN MARVEL. THIS IS OPERATOR ONYX361, THE CHANNEL IS SECURE. DO YOU HAVE A PICKUP?
HAS VOX SUPREME ESCAPED?
VOX SUPREME, MA'AM?
YOU'VE HAD NO ESCAPES?!
NO, MA'AM.
I BROUGHT HIM IN A WHILE BACK. HE WAS A PRIORITY ONE, MAX SECURITY.
MA'AM, WE HAVE NO RECORD OF SUCH A PRISONER.
MA'AM? MA'AM, ARE YOU STILL THERE?

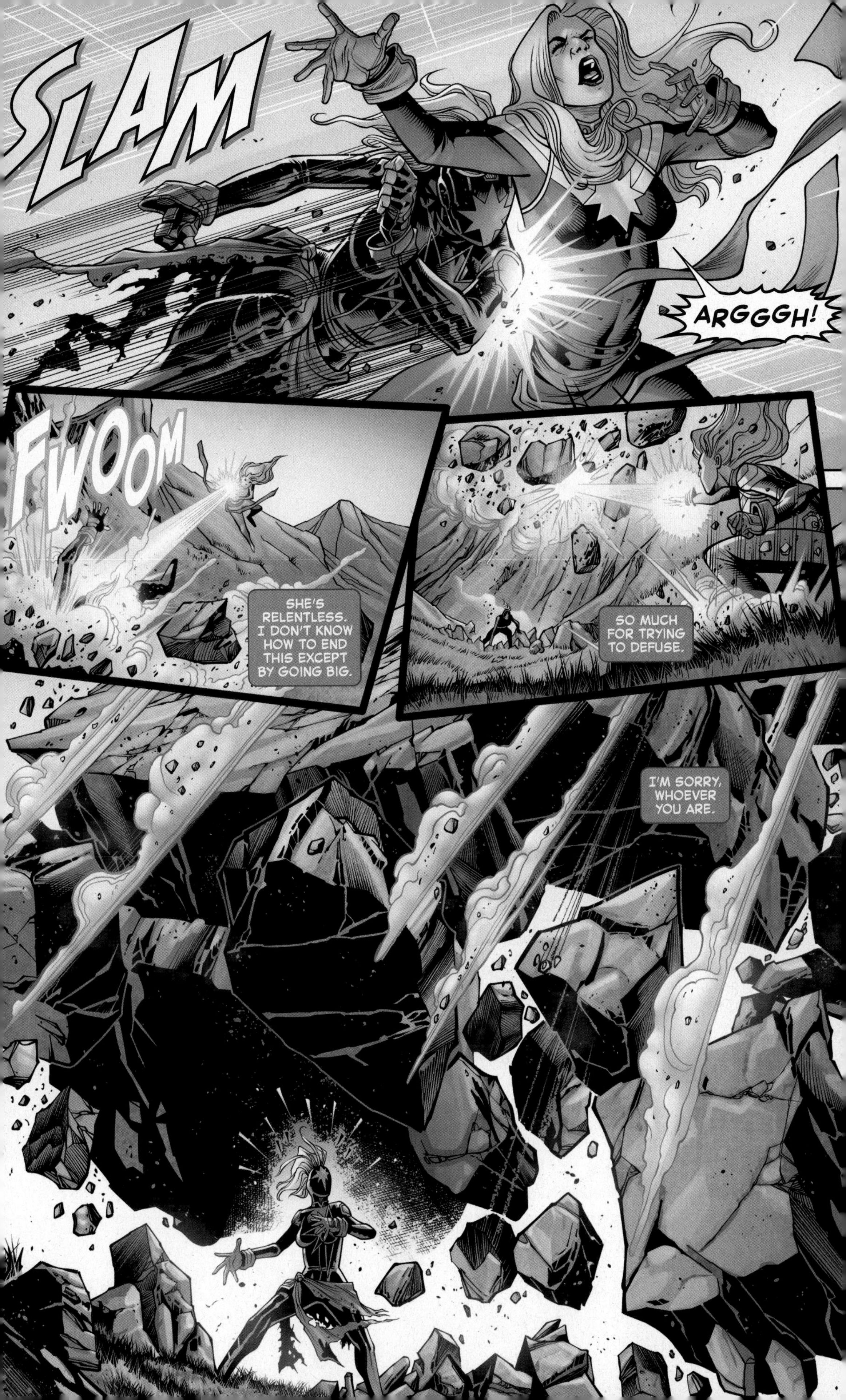
SLAM
ARGGGH!
FWOOM
SHE'S RELENTLESS. I DON'T KNOW HOW TO END THIS EXCEPT BY GOING BIG.
SO MUCH FOR TRYING TO DEFUSE.
I'M SORRY, WHOEVER YOU ARE.

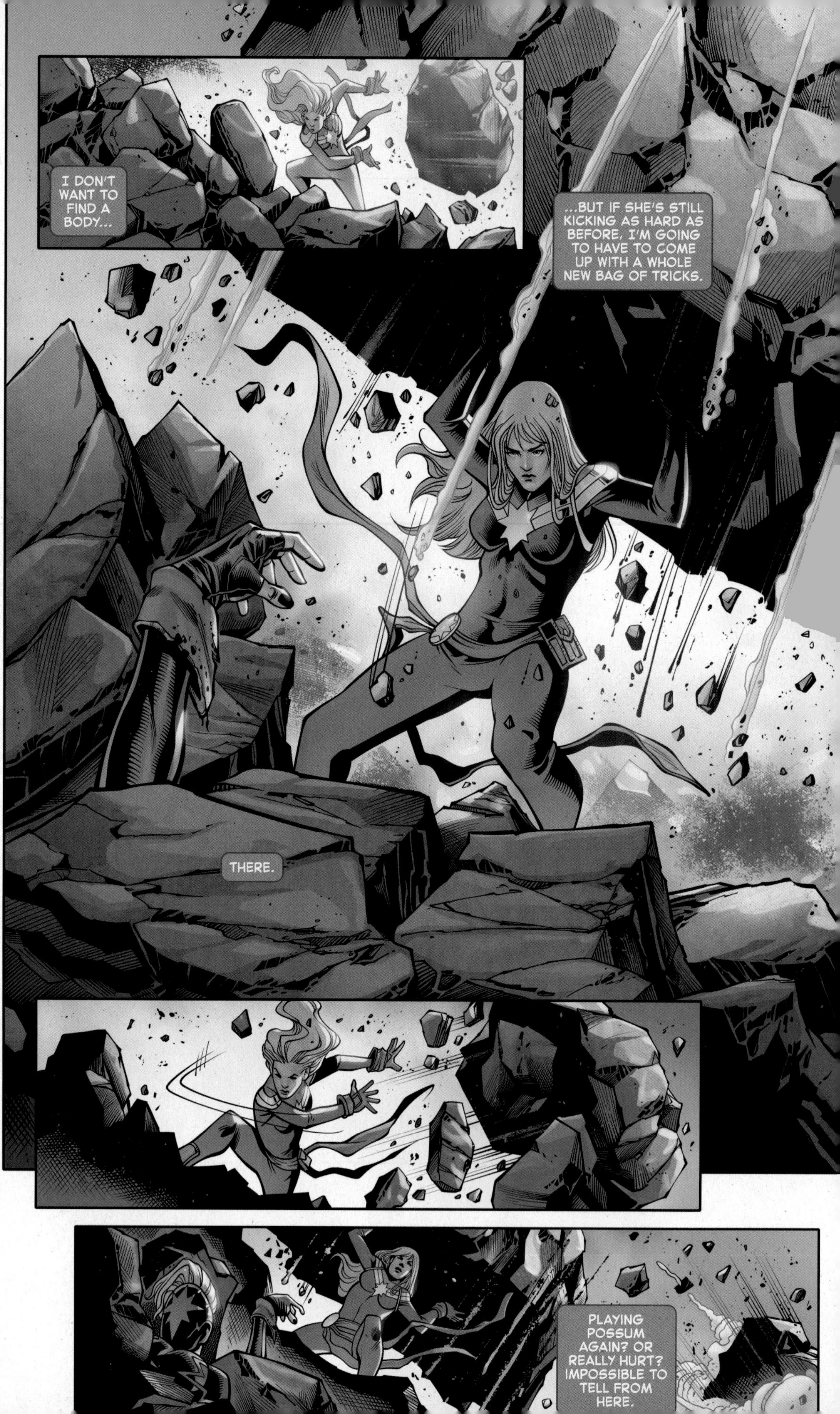
I DON'T WANT TO FIND A BODY...
...BUT IF SHE'S STILL KICKING AS HARD AS BEFORE, I'M GOING TO HAVE TO COME UP WITH A WHOLE NEW BAG OF TRICKS.
THERE.
PLAYING POSSUM AGAIN? OR REALLY HURT? IMPOSSIBLE TO TELL FROM HERE.

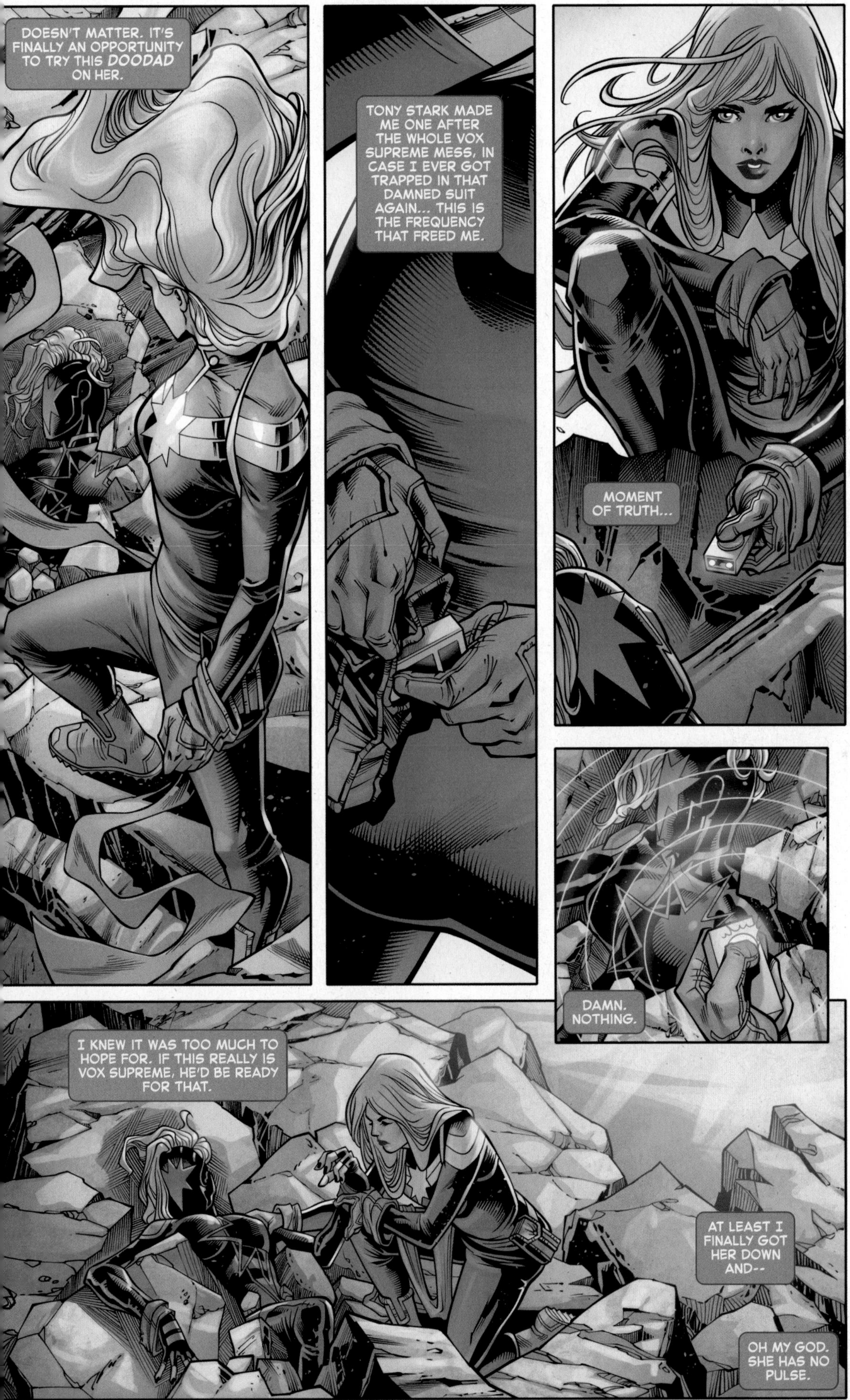
DOESN'T MATTER. IT'S FINALLY AN OPPORTUNITY TO TRY THIS *DOODAD* ON HER.
TONY STARK MADE ME ONE AFTER THE WHOLE VOX SUPREME MESS, IN CASE I EVER GOT TRAPPED IN THAT DAMNED SUIT AGAIN... THIS IS THE FREQUENCY THAT FREED ME.
MOMENT OF TRUTH...
DAMN. NOTHING.
I KNEW IT WAS TOO MUCH TO HOPE FOR. IF THIS REALLY IS VOX SUPREME, HE'D BE READY FOR THAT.
AT LEAST I FINALLY GOT HER DOWN AND--
OH MY GOD. SHE HAS NO PULSE.

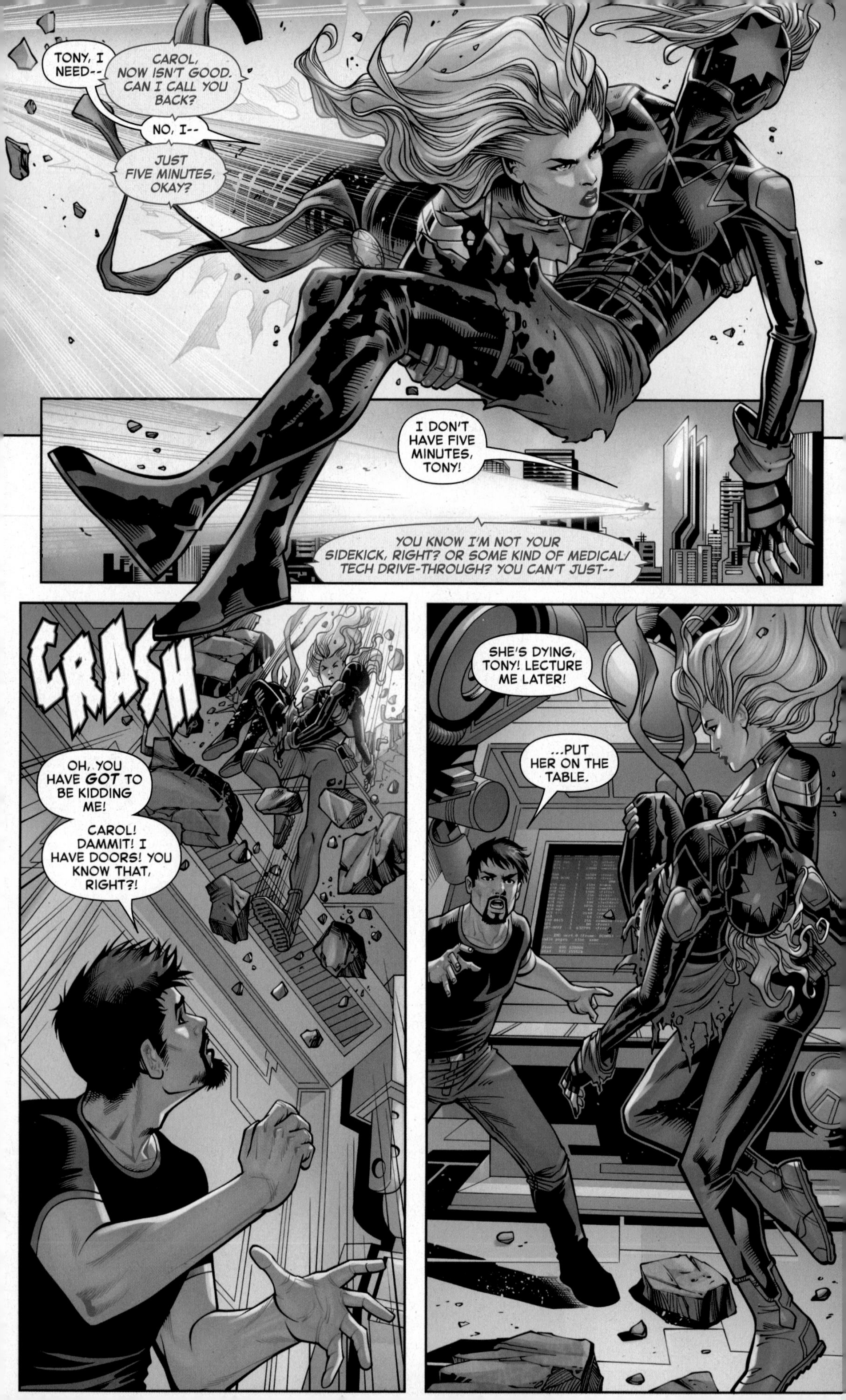
TONY, I NEED--
CAROL, NOW ISN'T GOOD. CAN I CALL YOU BACK?
NO, I--
JUST FIVE MINUTES, OKAY?
I DON'T HAVE FIVE MINUTES, TONY!
YOU KNOW I'M NOT YOUR SIDEKICK, RIGHT? OR SOME KIND OF MEDICAL/ TECH DRIVE-THROUGH? YOU CAN'T JUST--
CRASH
OH, YOU HAVE GOT TO BE KIDDING ME!
CAROL! DAMMIT! I HAVE DOORS! YOU KNOW THAT, RIGHT?!
SHE'S DYING, TONY! LECTURE ME LATER!
...PUT HER ON THE TABLE.

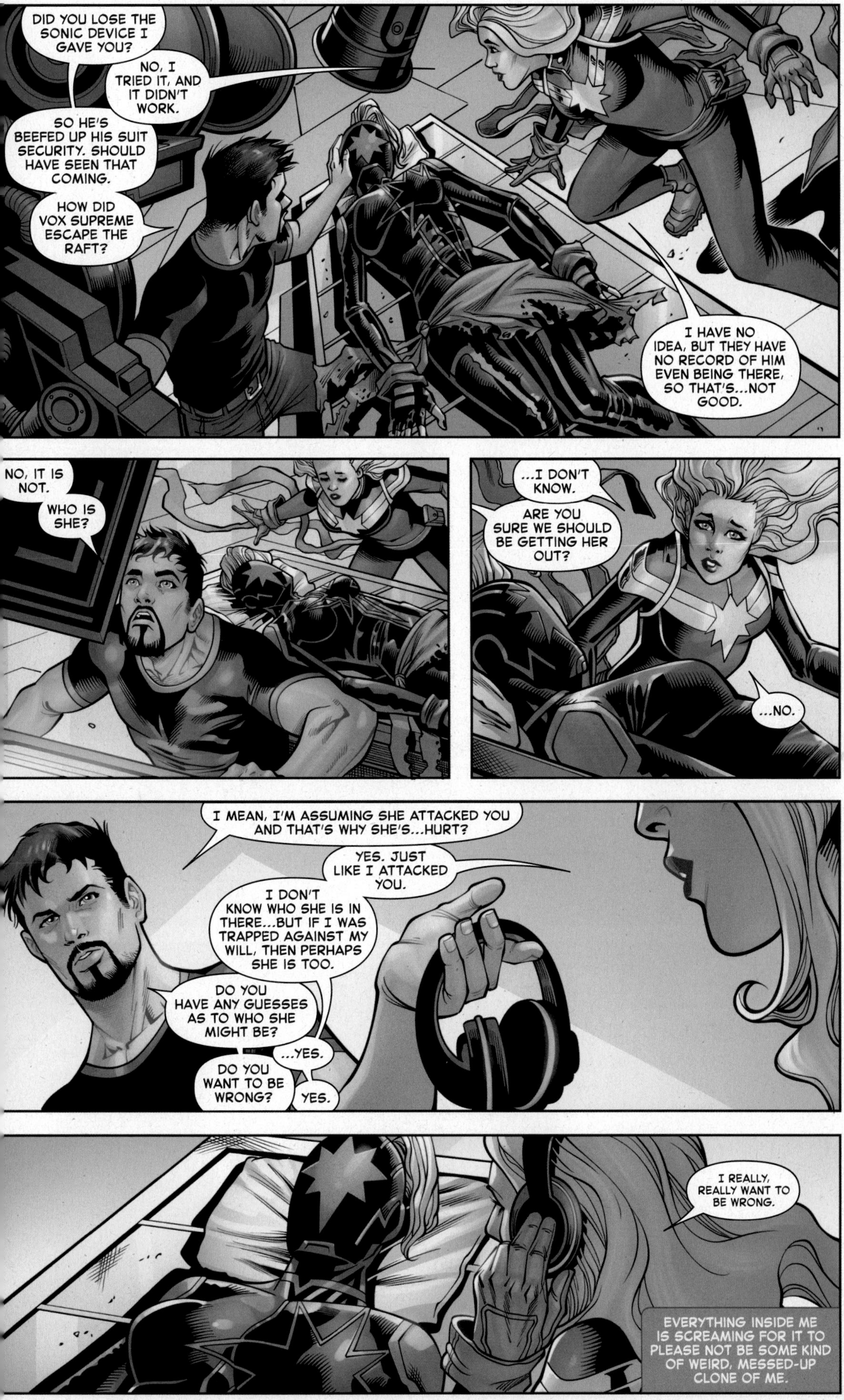
DID YOU LOSE THE SONIC DEVICE I GAVE YOU?
NO, I TRIED IT, AND IT DIDN'T WORK.
SO HE'S BEEFED UP HIS SUIT SECURITY. SHOULD HAVE SEEN THAT COMING.
HOW DID VOX SUPREME ESCAPE THE RAFT?
I HAVE NO IDEA, BUT THEY HAVE NO RECORD OF HIM EVEN BEING THERE, SO THAT'S...NOT GOOD.
NO, IT IS NOT.
WHO IS SHE?
...I DON'T KNOW.
ARE YOU SURE WE SHOULD BE GETTING HER OUT?
...NO.
I MEAN, I'M ASSUMING SHE ATTACKED YOU AND THAT'S WHY SHE'S...HURT?
YES. JUST LIKE I ATTACKED YOU.
I DON'T KNOW WHO SHE IS IN THERE...BUT IF I WAS TRAPPED AGAINST MY WILL, THEN PERHAPS SHE IS TOO.
DO YOU HAVE ANY GUESSES AS TO WHO SHE MIGHT BE?
...YES.
DO YOU WANT TO BE WRONG?
YES.
I REALLY, REALLY WANT TO BE WRONG.
EVERYTHING INSIDE ME IS SCREAMING FOR IT TO PLEASE NOT BE SOME KIND OF WEIRD, MESSED-UP CLONE OF ME.

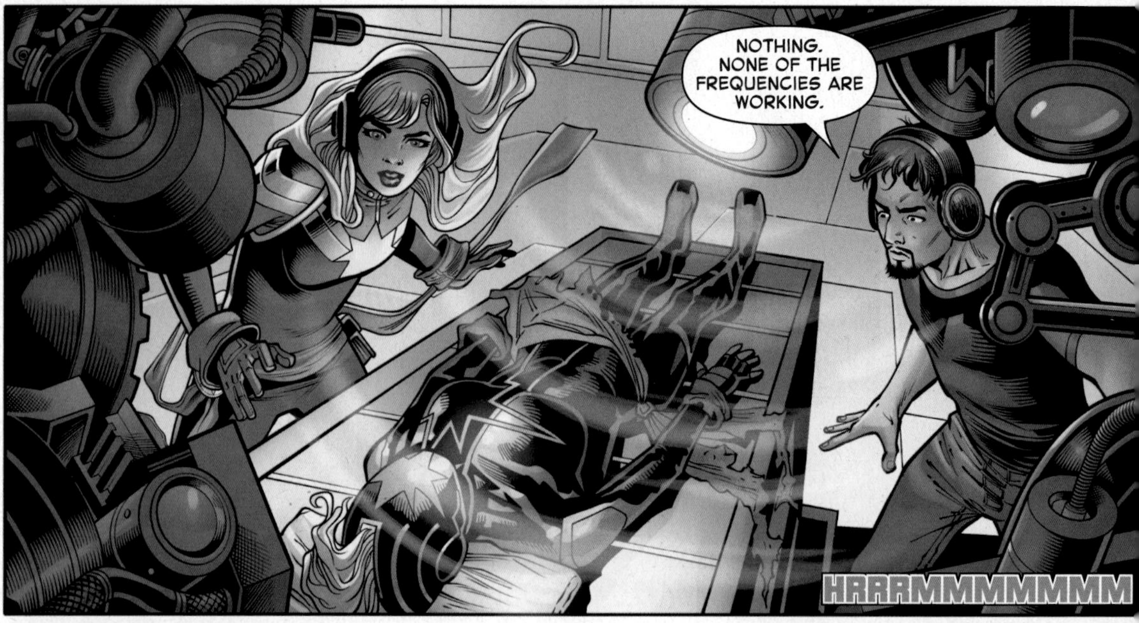
NOTHING. NONE OF THE FREQUENCIES ARE WORKING.
HRRRMMMMMMMM

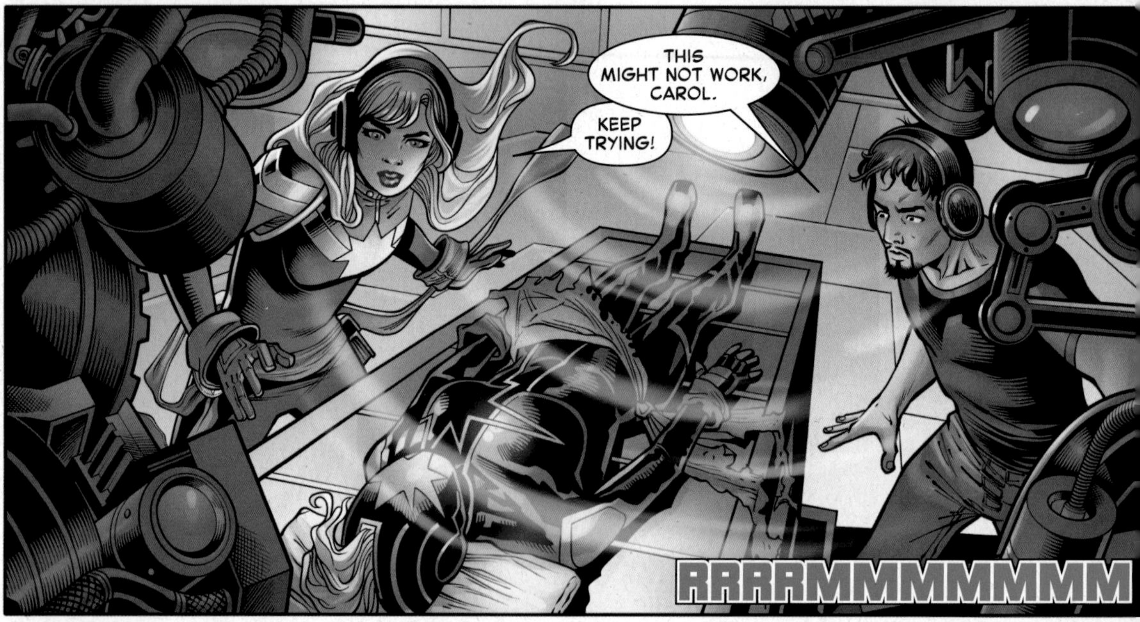
THIS MIGHT NOT WORK, CAROL.
KEEP TRYING!
RRRRMMMMMMMM

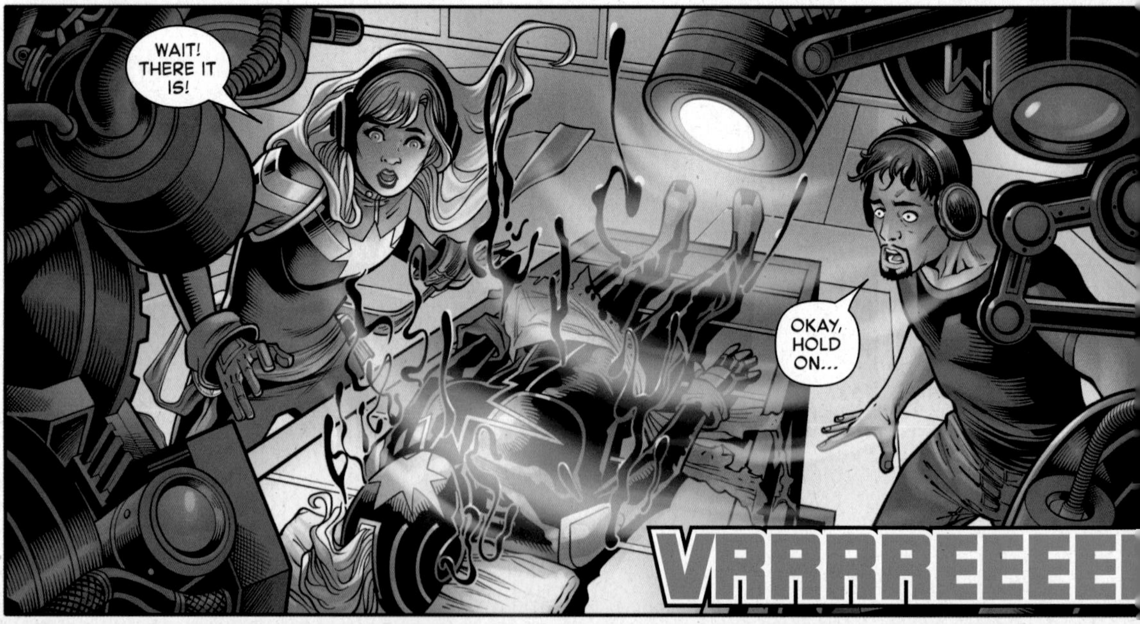
WAIT! THERE IT IS!
OKAY, HOLD ON...

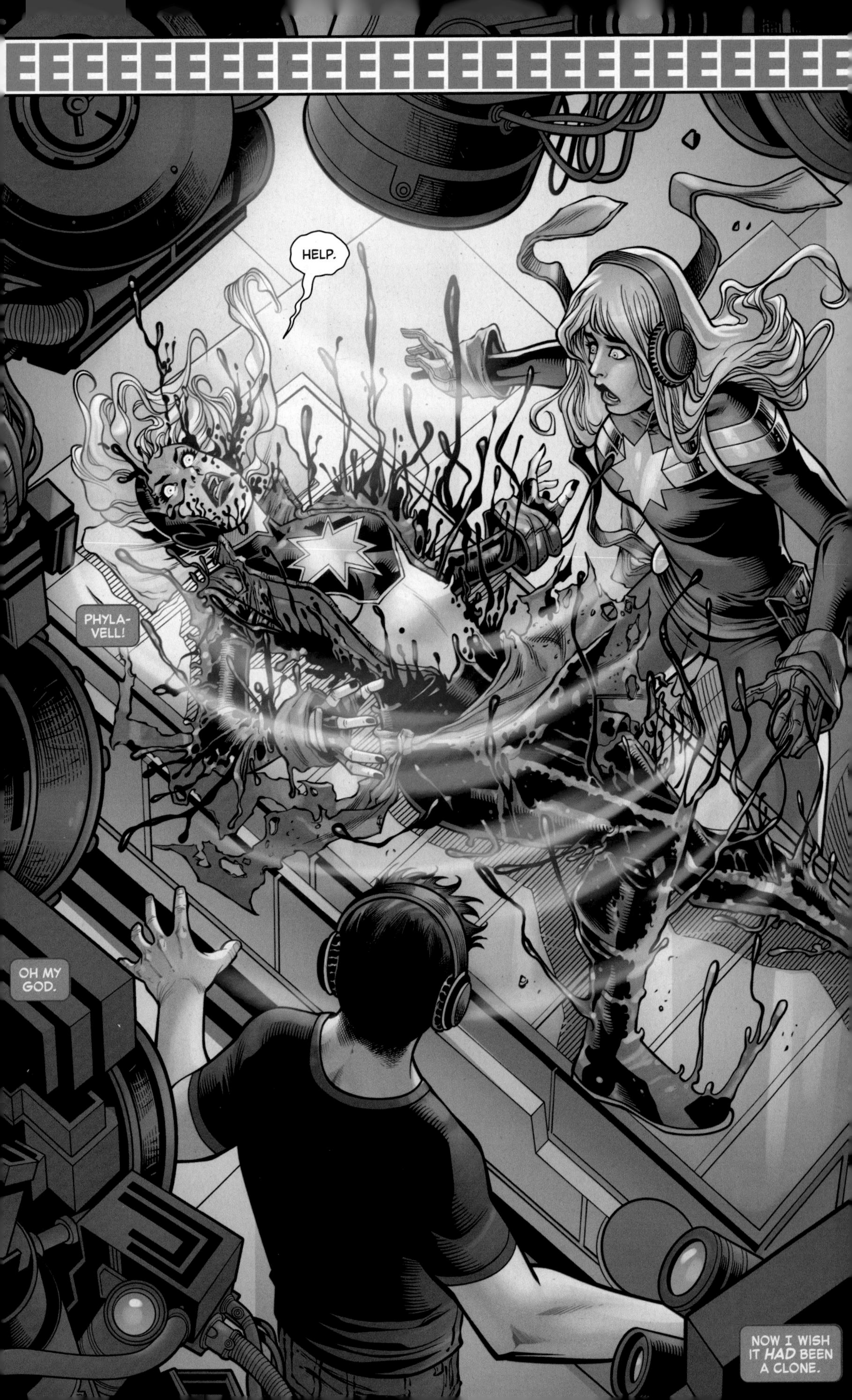
EEEEEEEEEEEEEEEEEEEEEEE
HELP.
PHYLA-VELL!
OH MY GOD.
NOW I WISH IT *HAD* BEEN A CLONE.

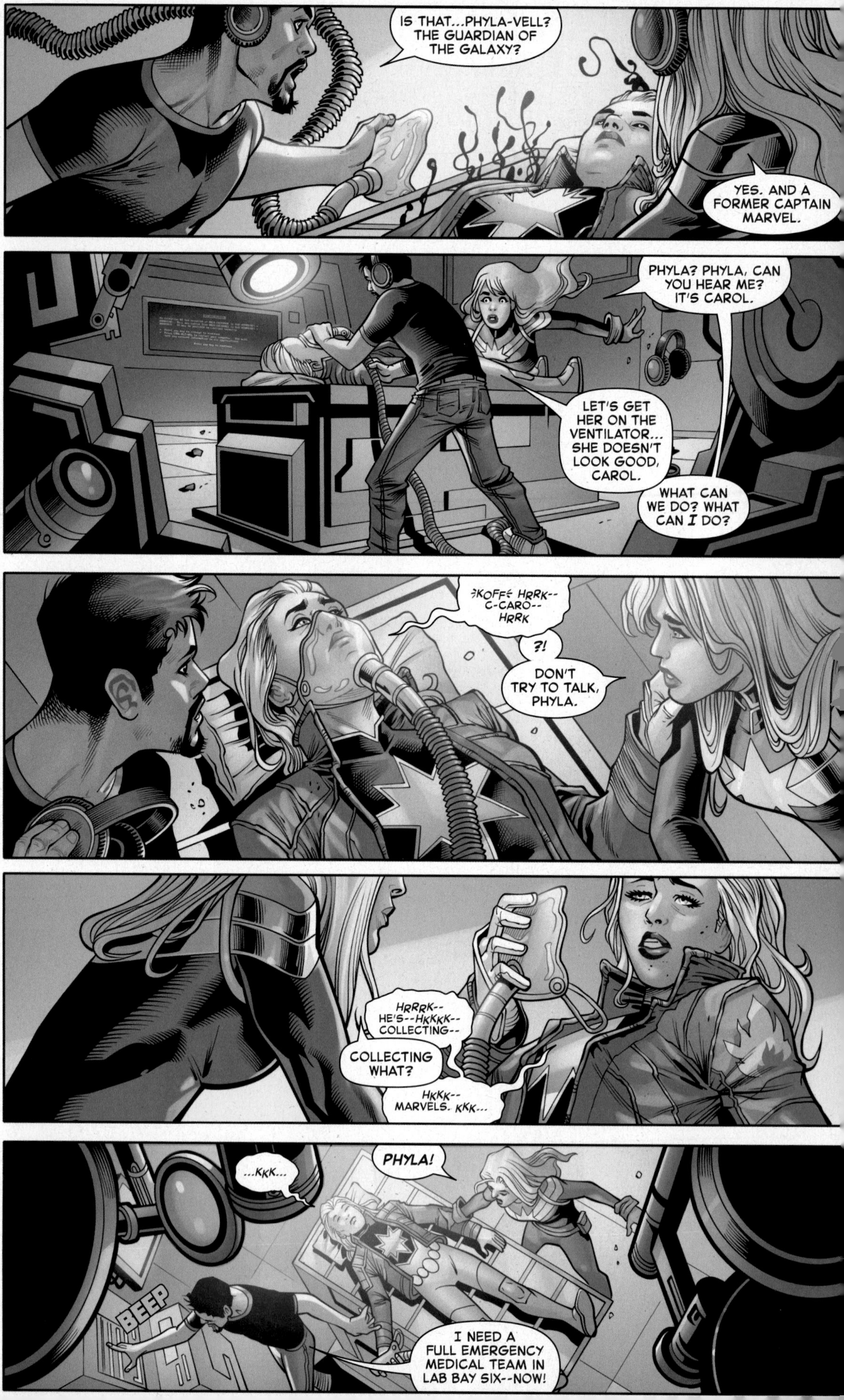
IS THAT...PHYLA-VELL? THE GUARDIAN OF THE GALAXY?
YES. AND A FORMER CAPTAIN MARVEL.
PHYLA? PHYLA, CAN YOU HEAR ME? IT'S CAROL.
LET'S GET HER ON THE VENTILATOR... SHE DOESN'T LOOK GOOD, CAROL.
WHAT CAN WE DO? WHAT CAN *I* DO?
KOFF HRRK-- C-CARO-- HRRK
?!
DON'T TRY TO TALK, PHYLA.
HRRRK-- HE'S--HKKKK-- COLLECTING--
COLLECTING WHAT?
HKKK-- MARVELS. KKK...
...KKK...
PHYLA!
BEEP
I NEED A FULL EMERGENCY MEDICAL TEAM IN LAB BAY SIX--NOW!

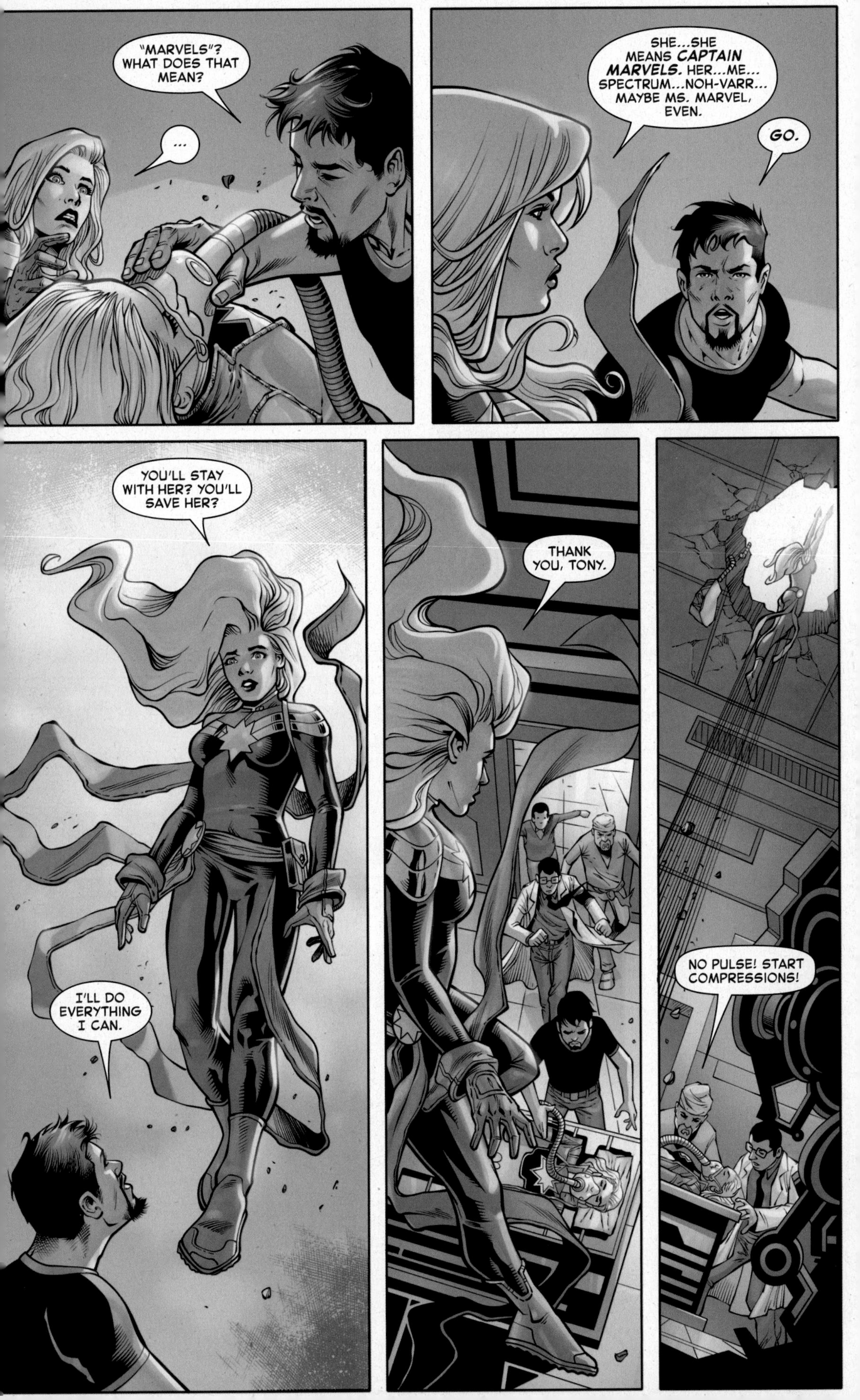
"MARVELS"? WHAT DOES THAT MEAN?
...
SHE...SHE MEANS CAPTAIN MARVELS. HER...ME... SPECTRUM...NOH-VARR... MAYBE MS. MARVEL, EVEN.
GO.
YOU'LL STAY WITH HER? YOU'LL SAVE HER?
I'LL DO EVERYTHING I CAN.
THANK YOU, TONY.
NO PULSE! START COMPRESSIONS!

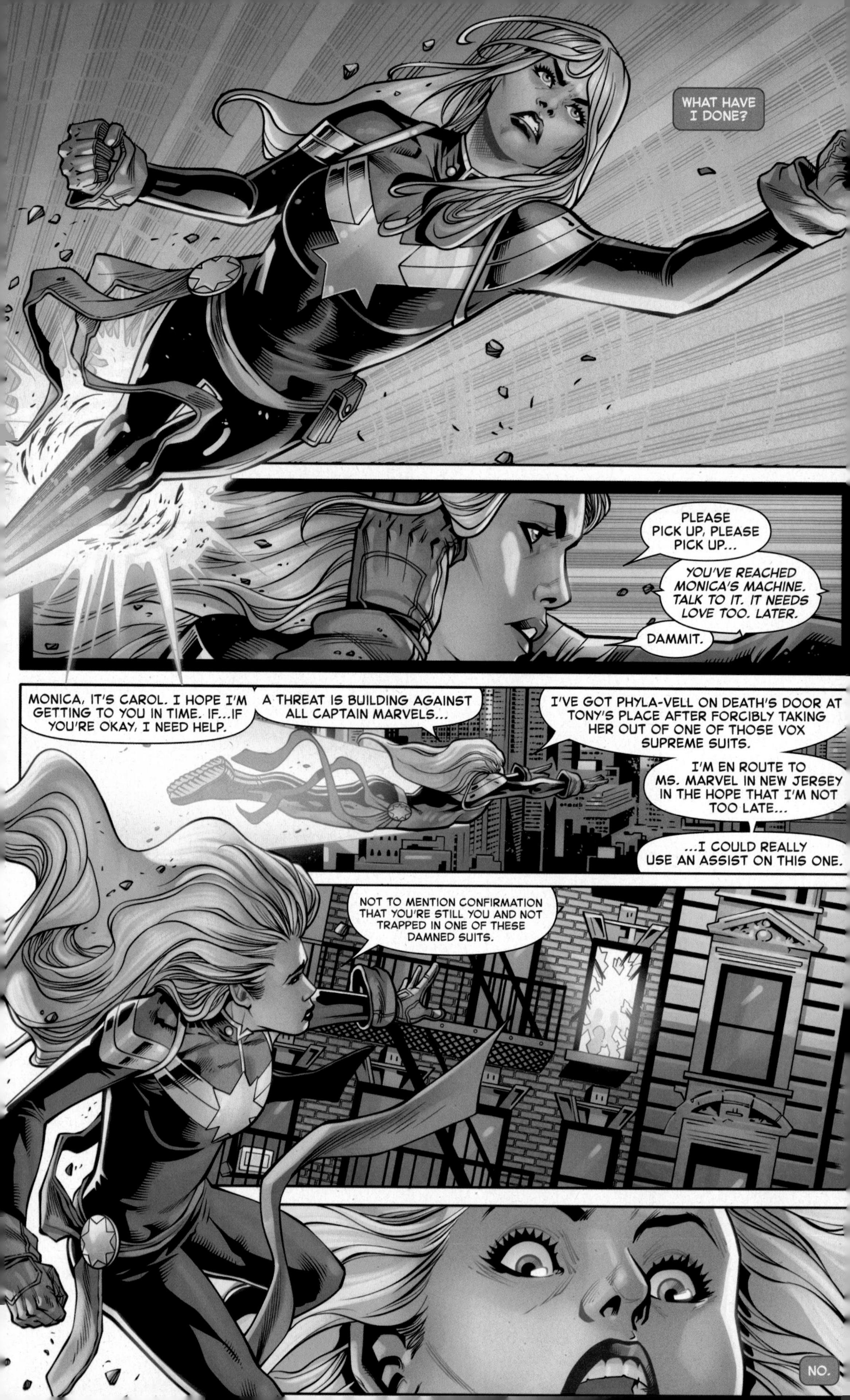
WHAT HAVE I DONE?
PLEASE PICK UP, PLEASE PICK UP...
YOU'VE REACHED MONICA'S MACHINE. TALK TO IT. IT NEEDS LOVE TOO. LATER.
DAMMIT.
MONICA, IT'S CAROL. I HOPE I'M GETTING TO YOU IN TIME. IF...IF YOU'RE OKAY, I NEED HELP.
A THREAT IS BUILDING AGAINST ALL CAPTAIN MARVELS...
I'VE GOT PHYLA-VELL ON DEATH'S DOOR AT TONY'S PLACE AFTER FORCIBLY TAKING HER OUT OF ONE OF THOSE VOX SUPREME SUITS.
I'M EN ROUTE TO MS. MARVEL IN NEW JERSEY IN THE HOPE THAT I'M NOT TOO LATE...
...I COULD REALLY USE AN ASSIST ON THIS ONE.
NOT TO MENTION CONFIRMATION THAT YOU'RE STILL YOU AND NOT TRAPPED IN ONE OF THESE DAMNED SUITS.
NO.

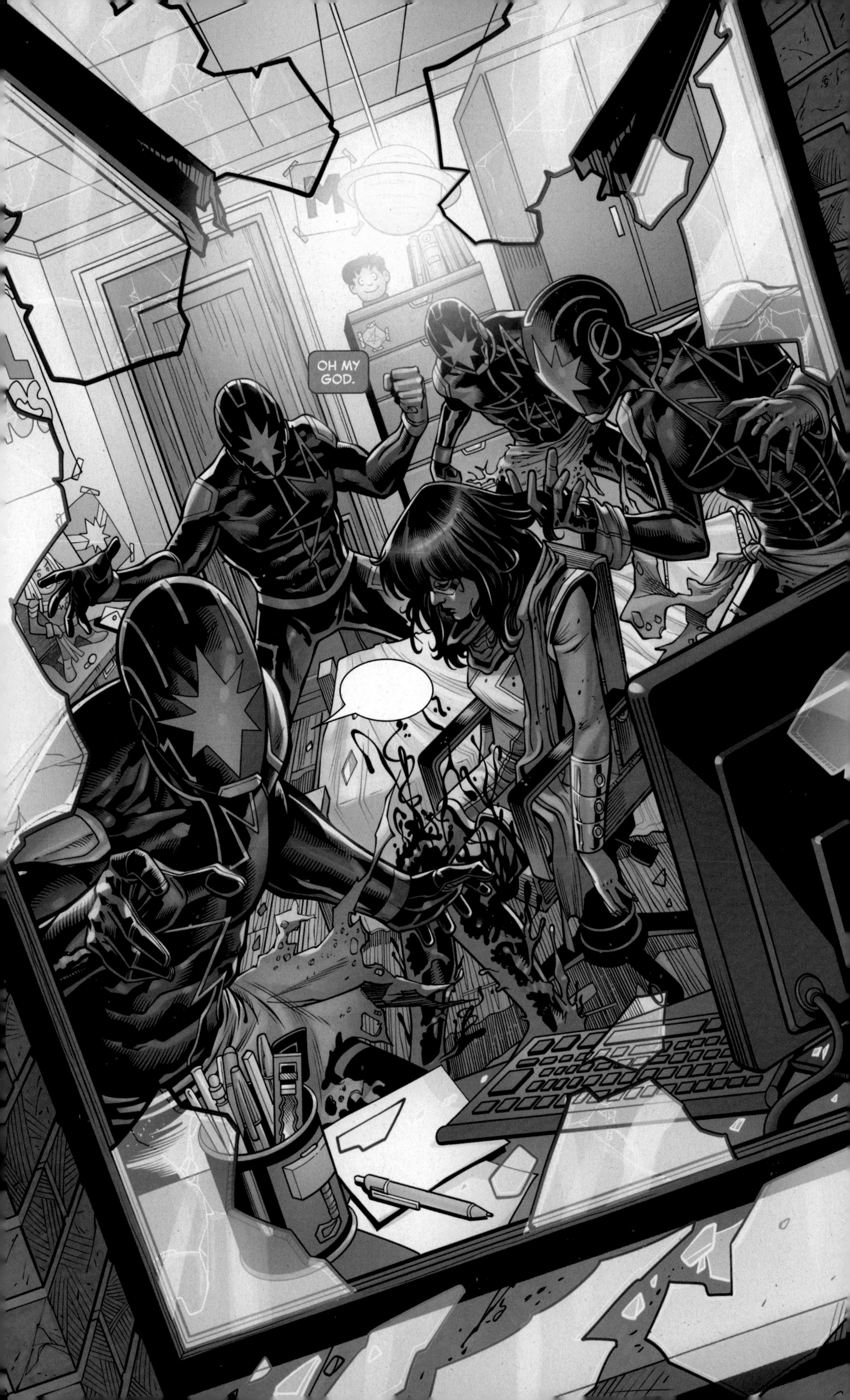
OH MY GOD.

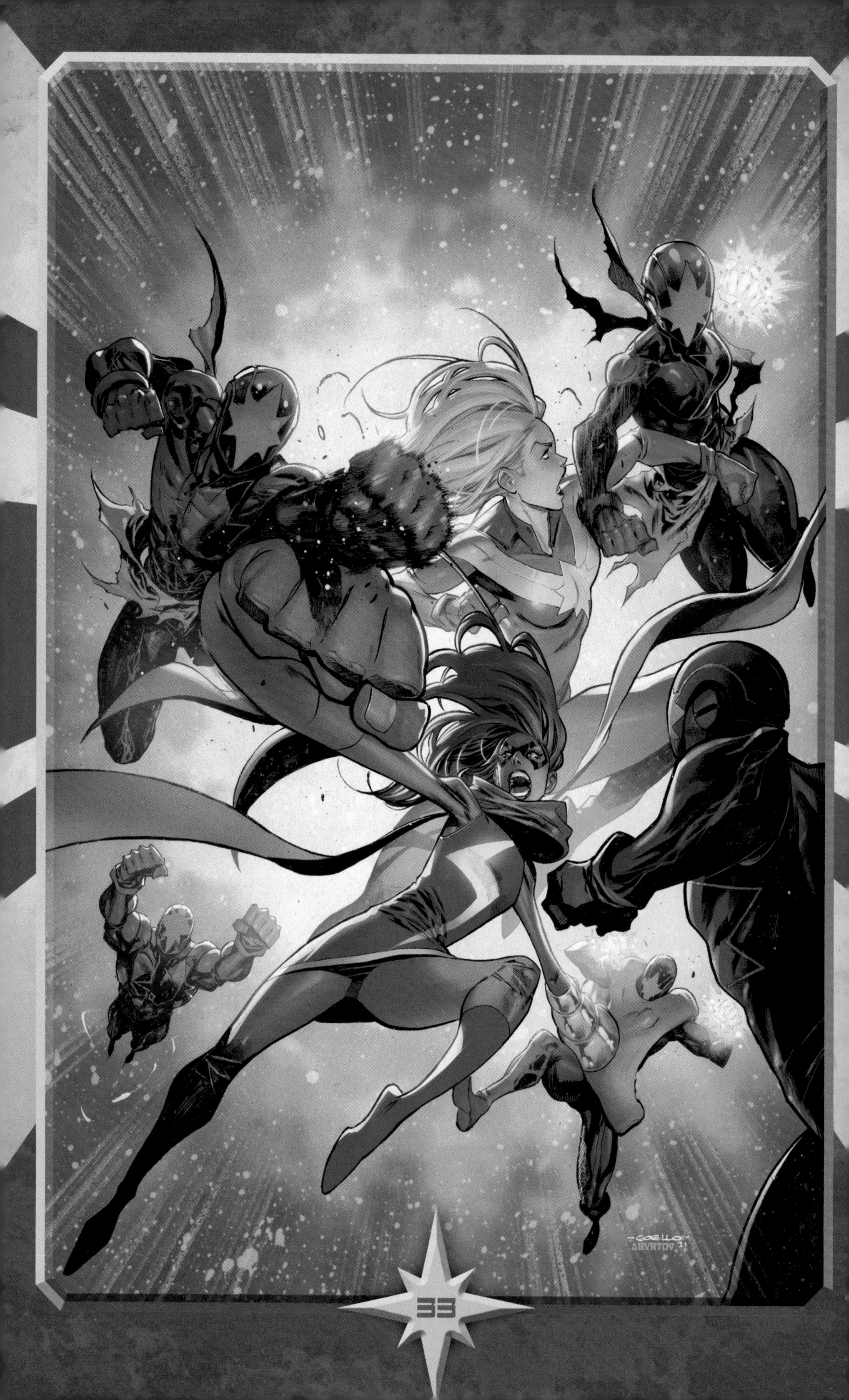
33

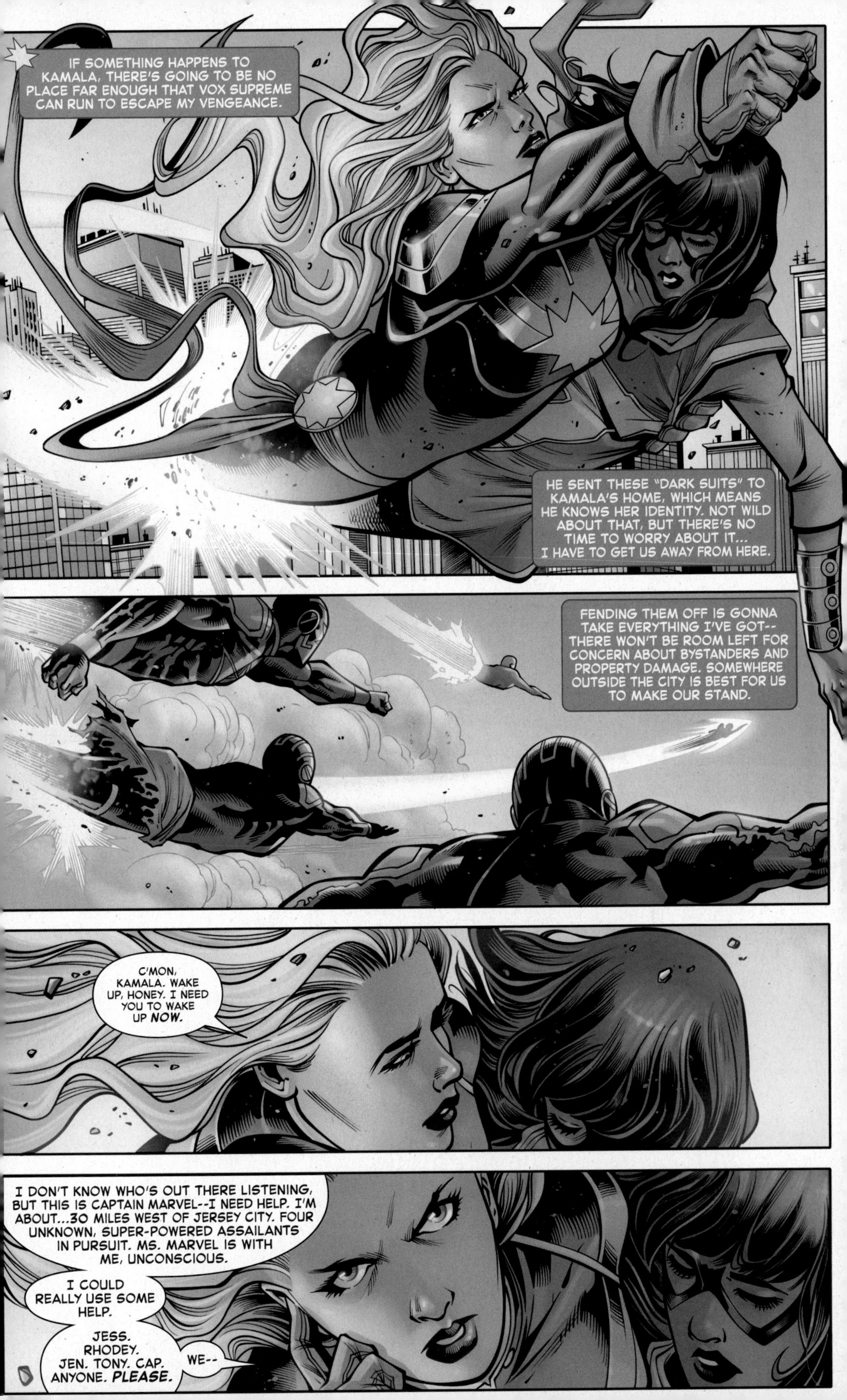
IF SOMETHING HAPPENS TO KAMALA, THERE'S GOING TO BE NO PLACE FAR ENOUGH THAT VOX SUPREME CAN RUN TO ESCAPE MY VENGEANCE.
HE SENT THESE "DARK SUITS" TO KAMALA'S HOME, WHICH MEANS HE KNOWS HER IDENTITY. NOT WILD ABOUT THAT, BUT THERE'S NO TIME TO WORRY ABOUT IT... I HAVE TO GET US AWAY FROM HERE.
FENDING THEM OFF IS GONNA TAKE EVERYTHING I'VE GOT-- THERE WON'T BE ROOM LEFT FOR CONCERN ABOUT BYSTANDERS AND PROPERTY DAMAGE. SOMEWHERE OUTSIDE THE CITY IS BEST FOR US TO MAKE OUR STAND.
C'MON, KAMALA. WAKE UP, HONEY. I NEED YOU TO WAKE UP *NOW.*
I DON'T KNOW WHO'S OUT THERE LISTENING, BUT THIS IS CAPTAIN MARVEL--I NEED HELP. I'M ABOUT...30 MILES WEST OF JERSEY CITY. FOUR UNKNOWN, SUPER-POWERED ASSAILANTS IN PURSUIT. MS. MARVEL IS WITH ME, UNCONSCIOUS.
I COULD REALLY USE SOME HELP.
JESS. RHODEY. JEN. TONY. CAP. ANYONE. *PLEASE.*
WE--

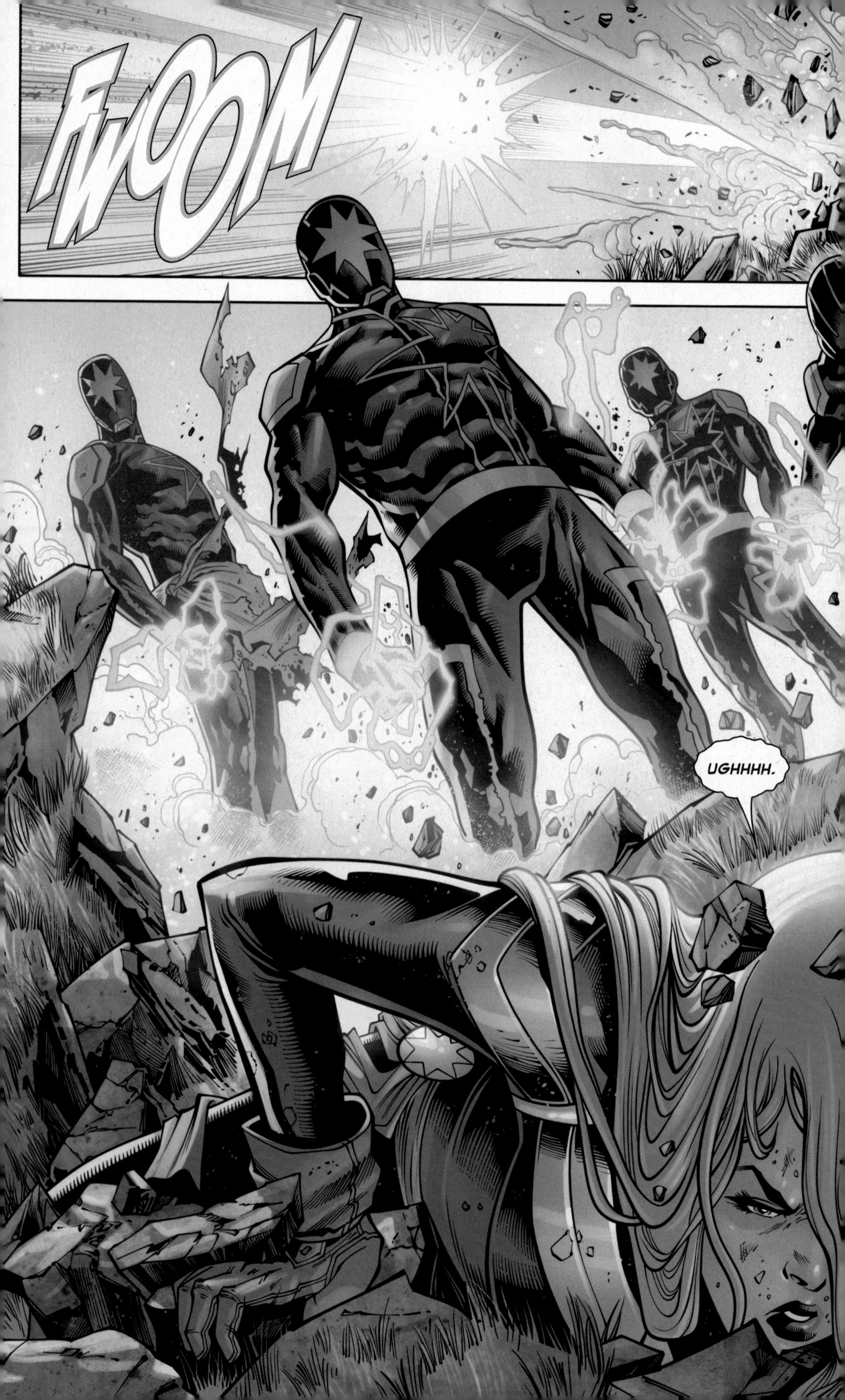
FWOOM
UGHHHH.

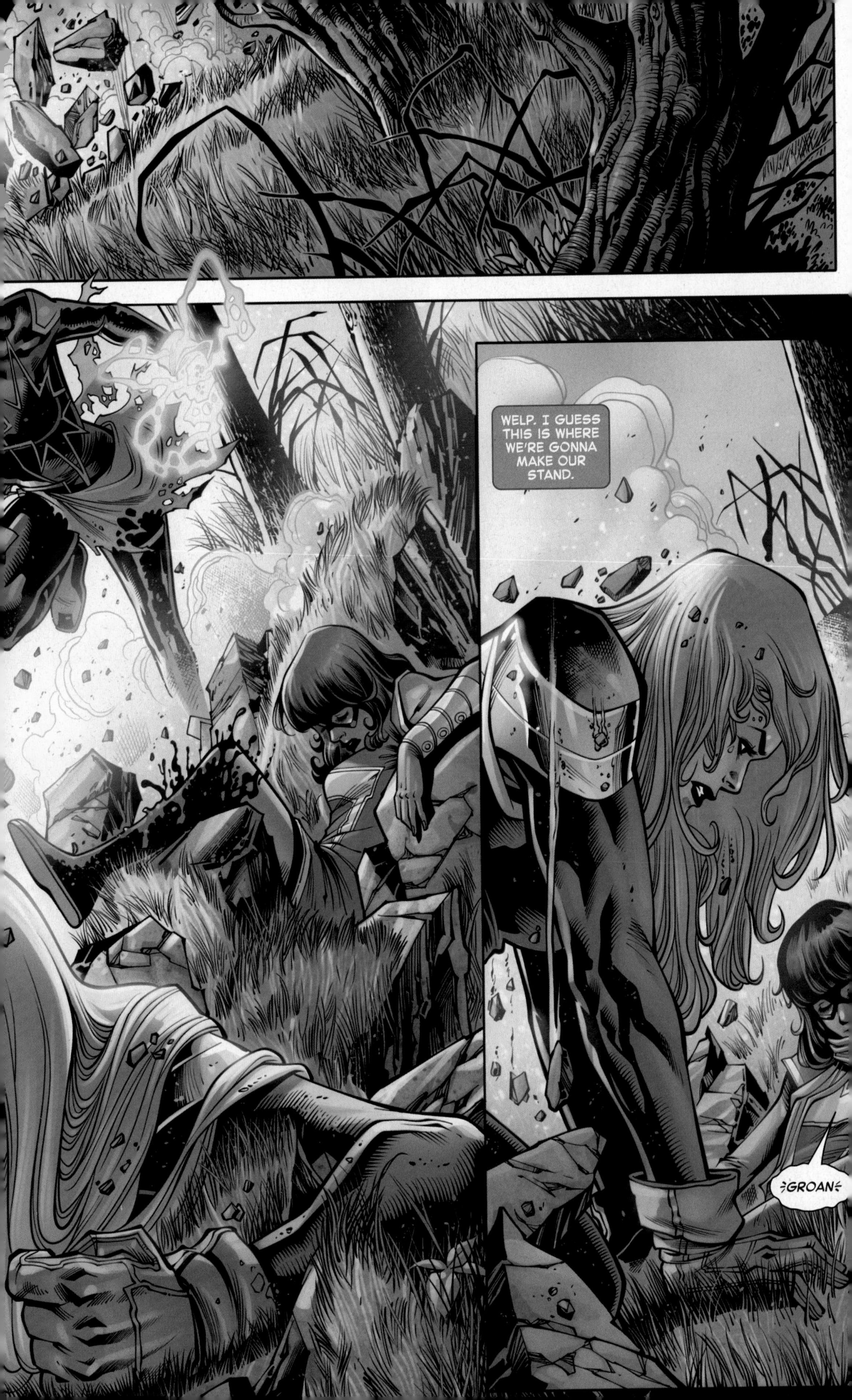
WELP. I GUESS THIS IS WHERE WE'RE GONNA MAKE OUR STAND.
GROAN

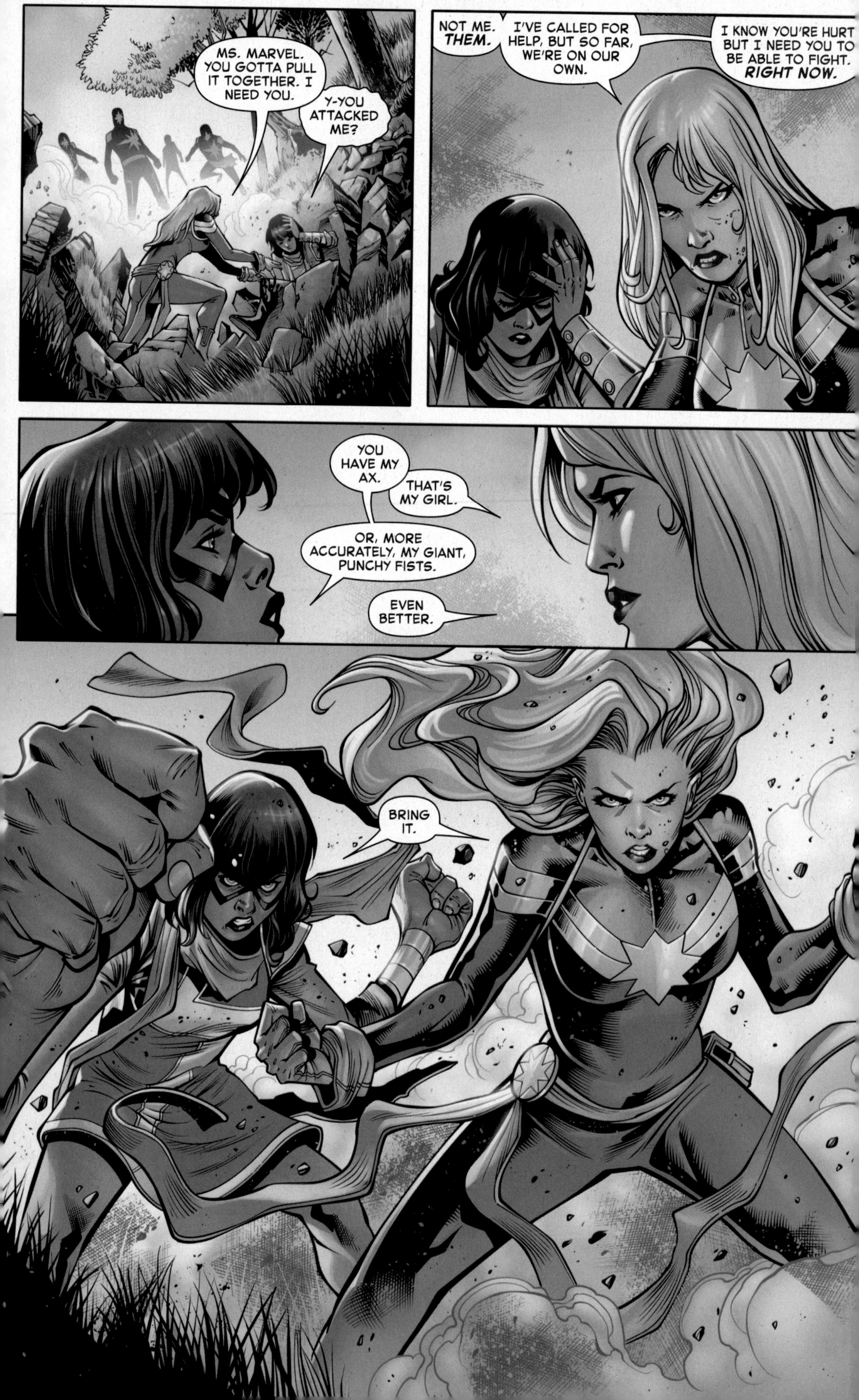
MS. MARVEL. YOU GOTTA PULL IT TOGETHER. I NEED YOU.
Y-YOU ATTACKED ME?
NOT ME. THEM.
I'VE CALLED FOR HELP, BUT SO FAR, WE'RE ON OUR OWN.
I KNOW YOU'RE HURT BUT I NEED YOU TO BE ABLE TO FIGHT. RIGHT NOW.
YOU HAVE MY AX.
THAT'S MY GIRL.
OR, MORE ACCURATELY, MY GIANT, PUNCHY FISTS.
EVEN BETTER.
BRING IT.

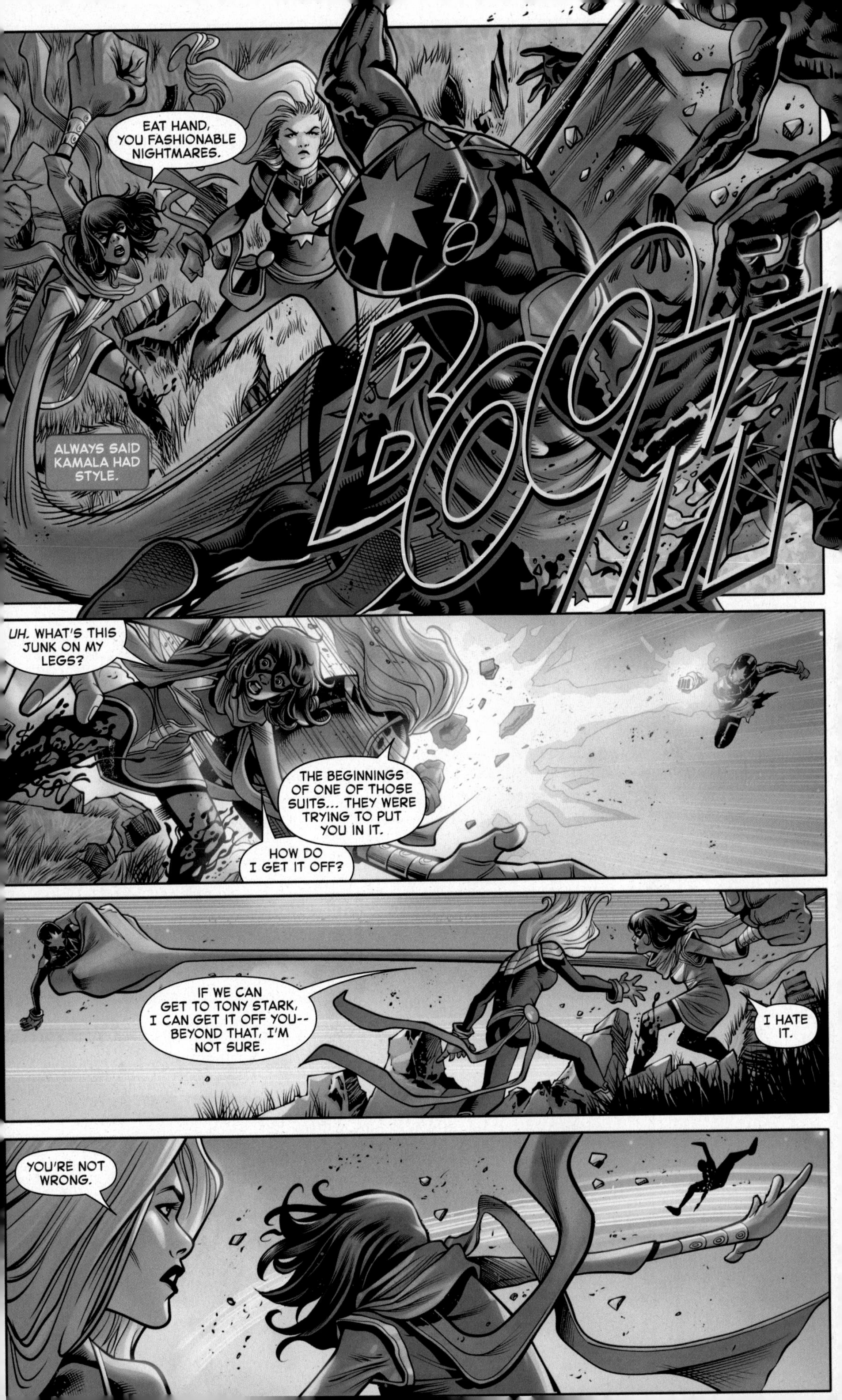
EAT HAND, YOU FASHIONABLE NIGHTMARES.
ALWAYS SAID KAMALA HAD STYLE.
BOOM
UH. WHAT'S THIS JUNK ON MY LEGS?
THE BEGINNINGS OF ONE OF THOSE SUITS... THEY WERE TRYING TO PUT YOU IN IT.
HOW DO I GET IT OFF?
IF WE CAN GET TO TONY STARK, I CAN GET IT OFF YOU-- BEYOND THAT, I'M NOT SURE.
I HATE IT.
YOU'RE NOT WRONG.

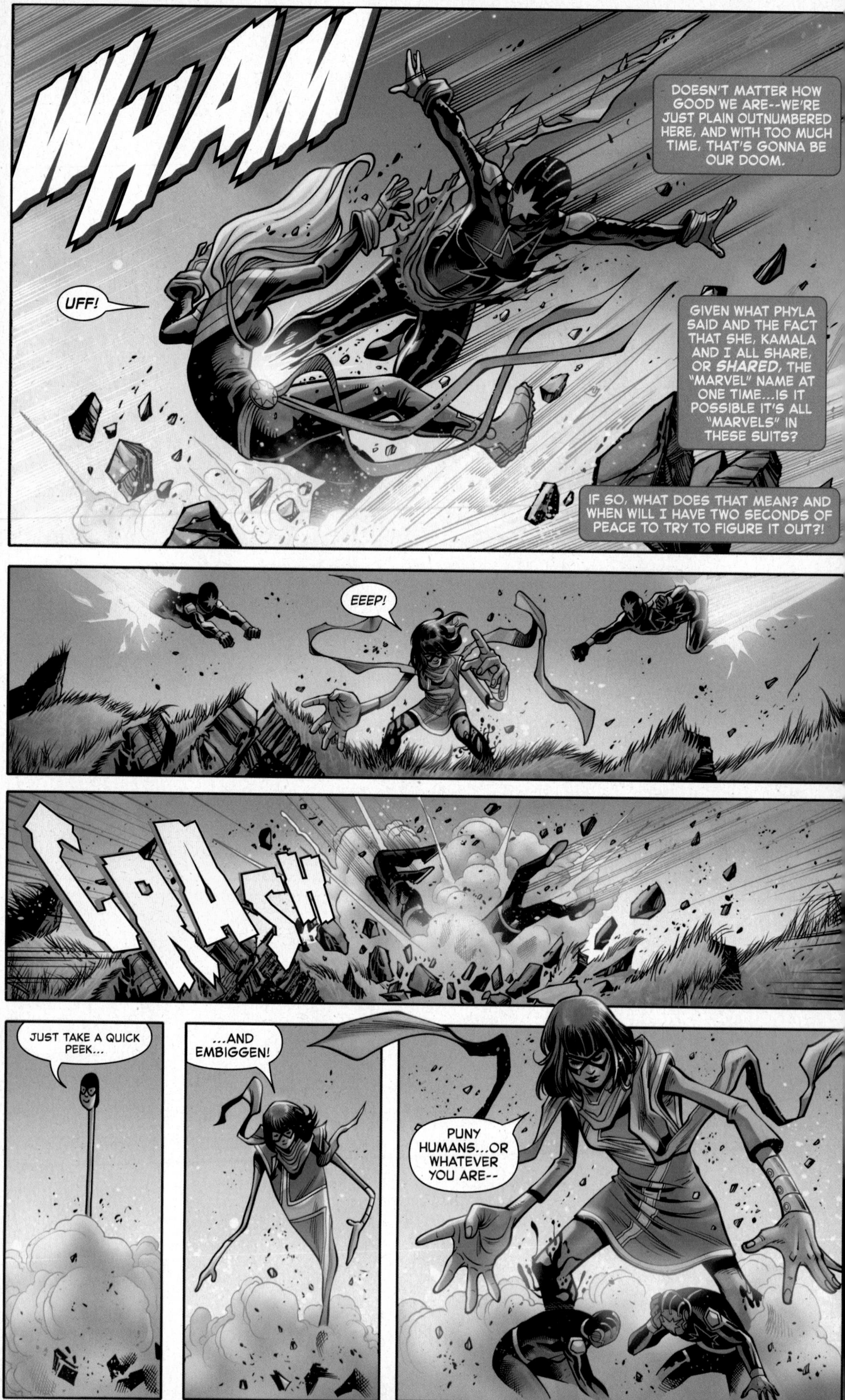
WHAM
DOESN'T MATTER HOW GOOD WE ARE--WE'RE JUST PLAIN OUTNUMBERED HERE, AND WITH TOO MUCH TIME, THAT'S GONNA BE OUR DOOM.
UFF!
GIVEN WHAT PHYLA SAID AND THE FACT THAT SHE, KAMALA AND I ALL SHARE, OR *SHARED*, THE "MARVEL" NAME AT ONE TIME...IS IT POSSIBLE IT'S ALL "MARVELS" IN THESE SUITS?
IF SO, WHAT DOES THAT MEAN? AND WHEN WILL I HAVE TWO SECONDS OF PEACE TO TRY TO FIGURE IT OUT?!
EEEP!
CRASH
JUST TAKE A QUICK PEEK...
...AND EMBIGGEN!
PUNY HUMANS...OR WHATEVER YOU ARE--

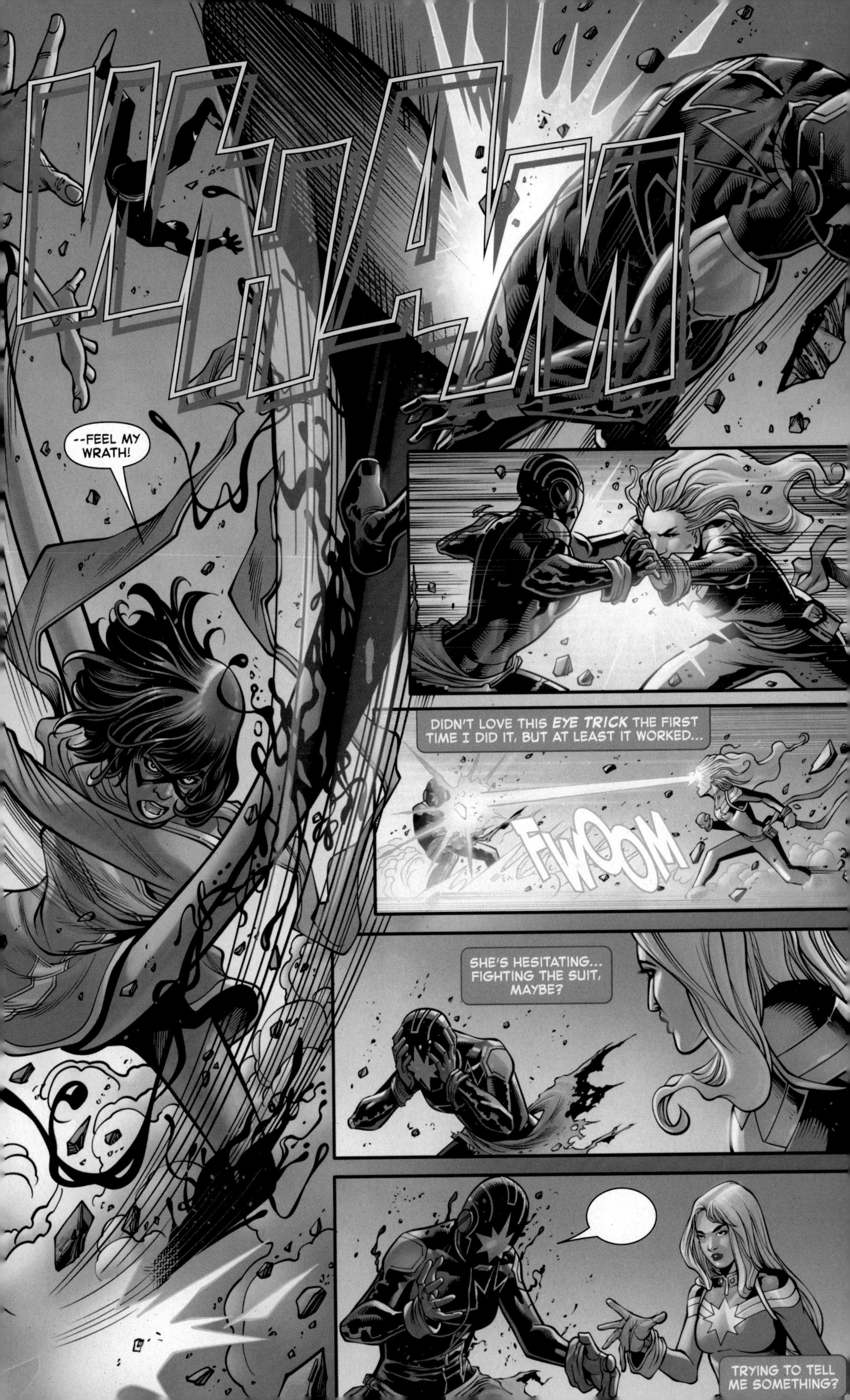

--FEEL MY WRATH!
DIDN'T LOVE THIS *EYE TRICK* THE FIRST TIME I DID IT, BUT AT LEAST IT WORKED...
FWOOM
SHE'S HESITATING... FIGHTING THE SUIT, MAYBE?
TRYING TO TELL ME SOMETHING?

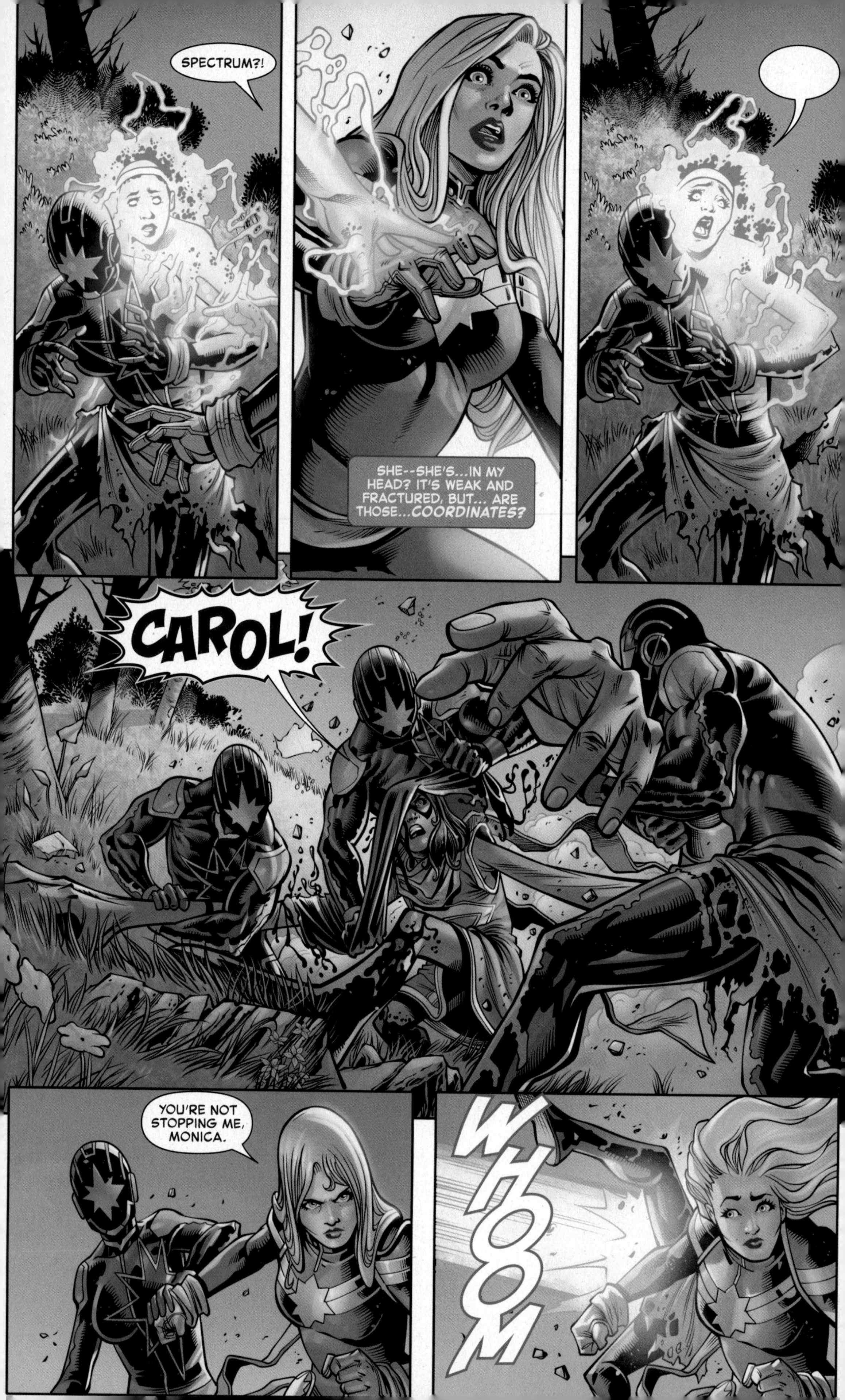
SPECTRUM?!
SHE--SHE'S...IN MY HEAD? IT'S WEAK AND FRACTURED, BUT... ARE THOSE...COORDINATES?
CAROL!
YOU'RE NOT STOPPING ME, MONICA.
WHOOM

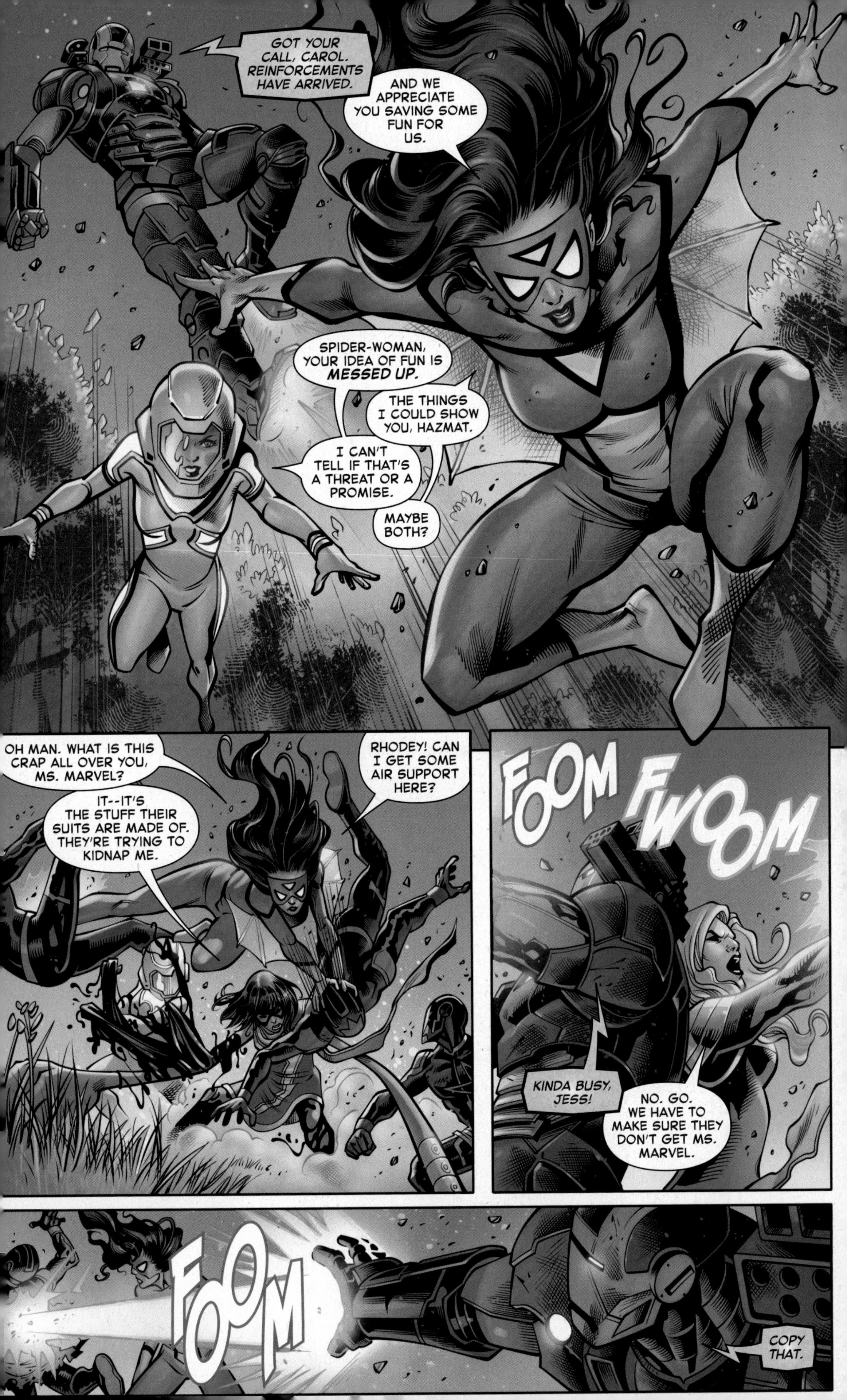
GOT YOUR CALL, CAROL. REINFORCEMENTS HAVE ARRIVED.
AND WE APPRECIATE YOU SAVING SOME FUN FOR US.
SPIDER-WOMAN, YOUR IDEA OF FUN IS *MESSED UP.*
THE THINGS I COULD SHOW YOU, HAZMAT.
I CAN'T TELL IF THAT'S A THREAT OR A PROMISE.
MAYBE BOTH?
OH MAN. WHAT IS THIS CRAP ALL OVER YOU, MS. MARVEL?
IT--IT'S THE STUFF THEIR SUITS ARE MADE OF. THEY'RE TRYING TO KIDNAP ME.
RHODEY! CAN I GET SOME AIR SUPPORT HERE?
FOOM
FWOOM
KINDA BUSY, JESS!
NO. GO. WE HAVE TO MAKE SURE THEY DON'T GET MS. MARVEL.
FOOM
COPY THAT.

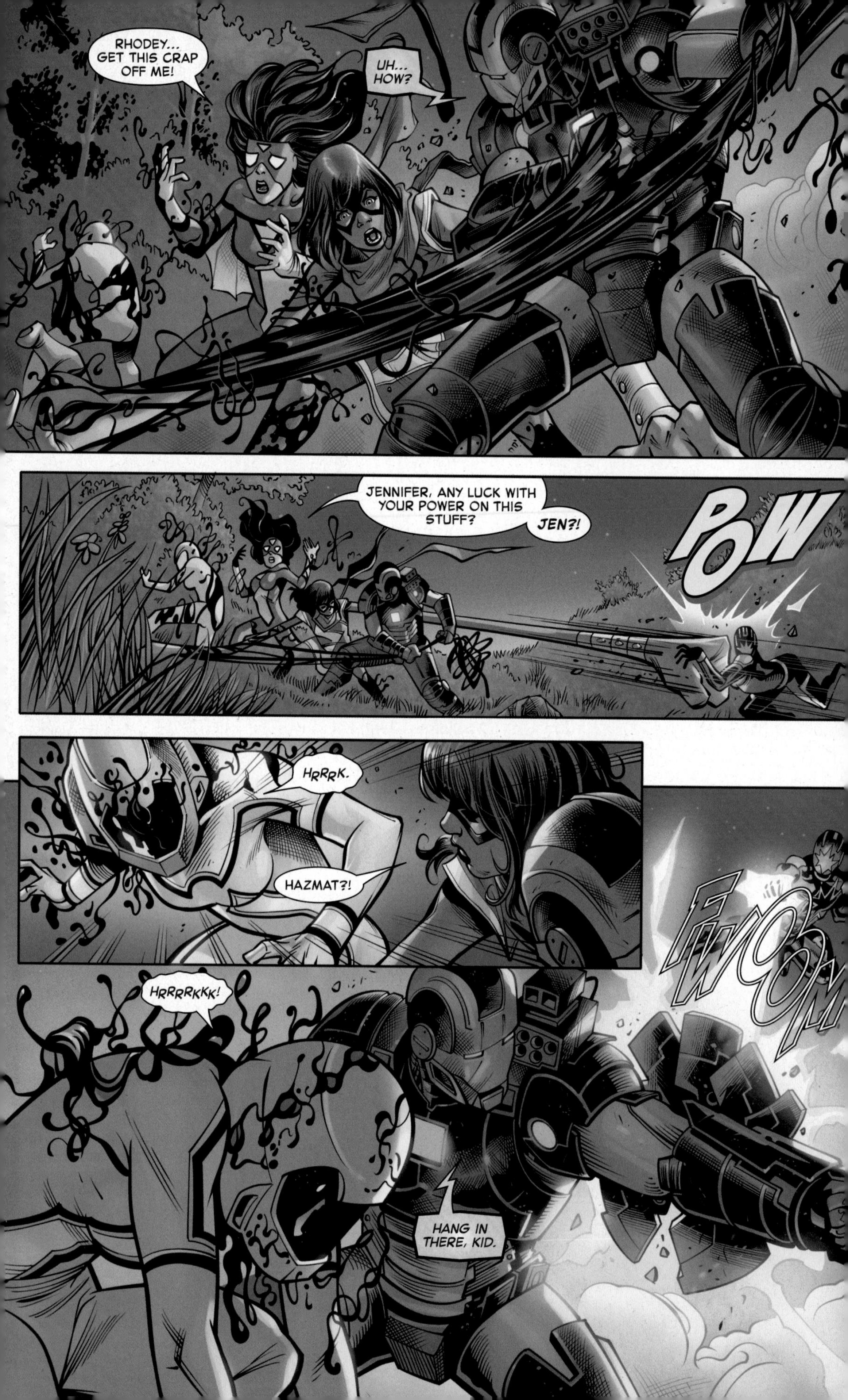
RHODEY... GET THIS CRAP OFF ME!
UH... HOW?
JENNIFER, ANY LUCK WITH YOUR POWER ON THIS STUFF?
JEN?!
POW
HRRRK.
HAZMAT?!
FWOOM
HRRRRKKK!
HANG IN THERE, KID.

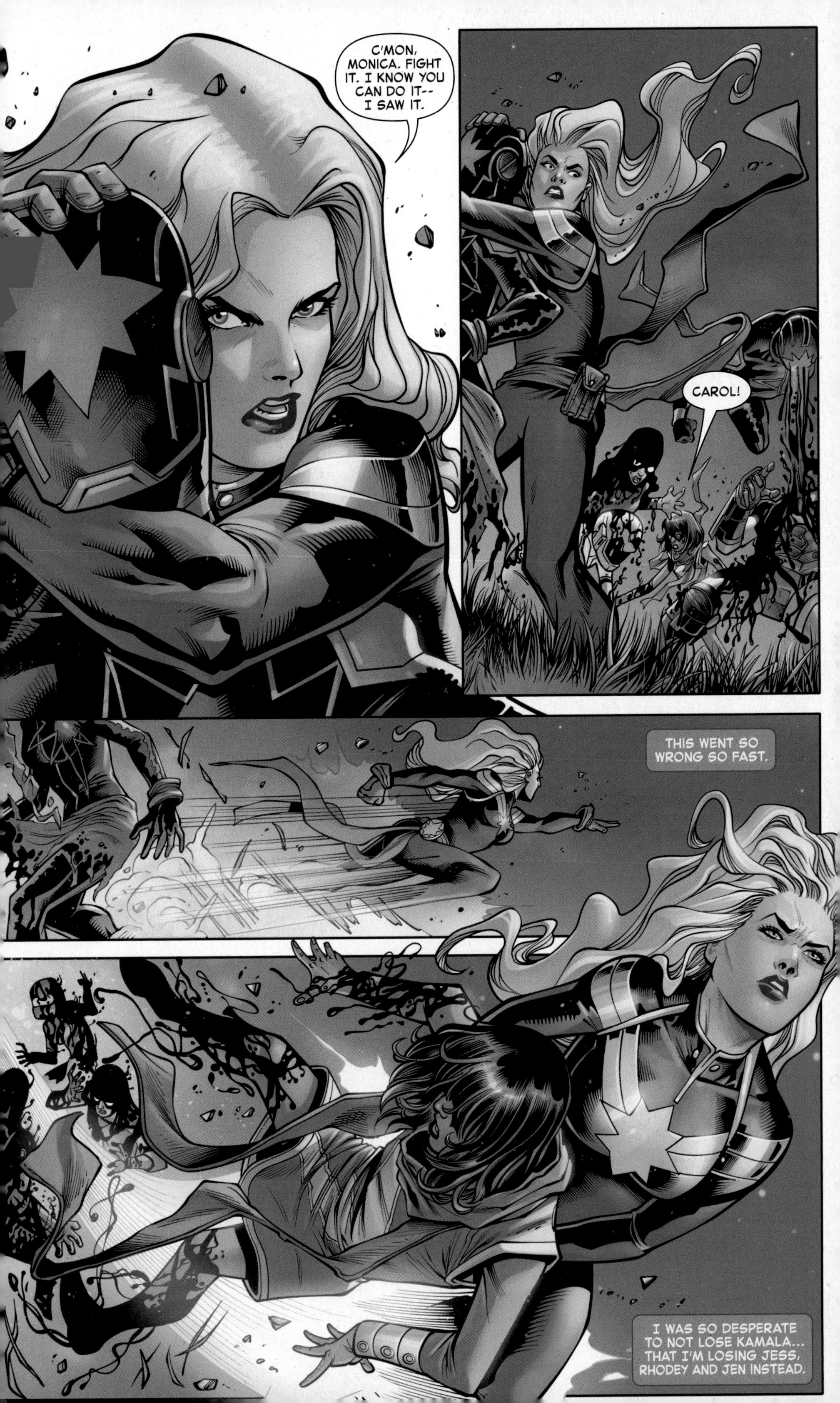
C'MON, MONICA. FIGHT IT. I KNOW YOU CAN DO IT-- I SAW IT.
CAROL!
THIS WENT SO WRONG SO FAST.
I WAS SO DESPERATE TO NOT LOSE KAMALA... THAT I'M LOSING JESS, RHODEY AND JEN INSTEAD.

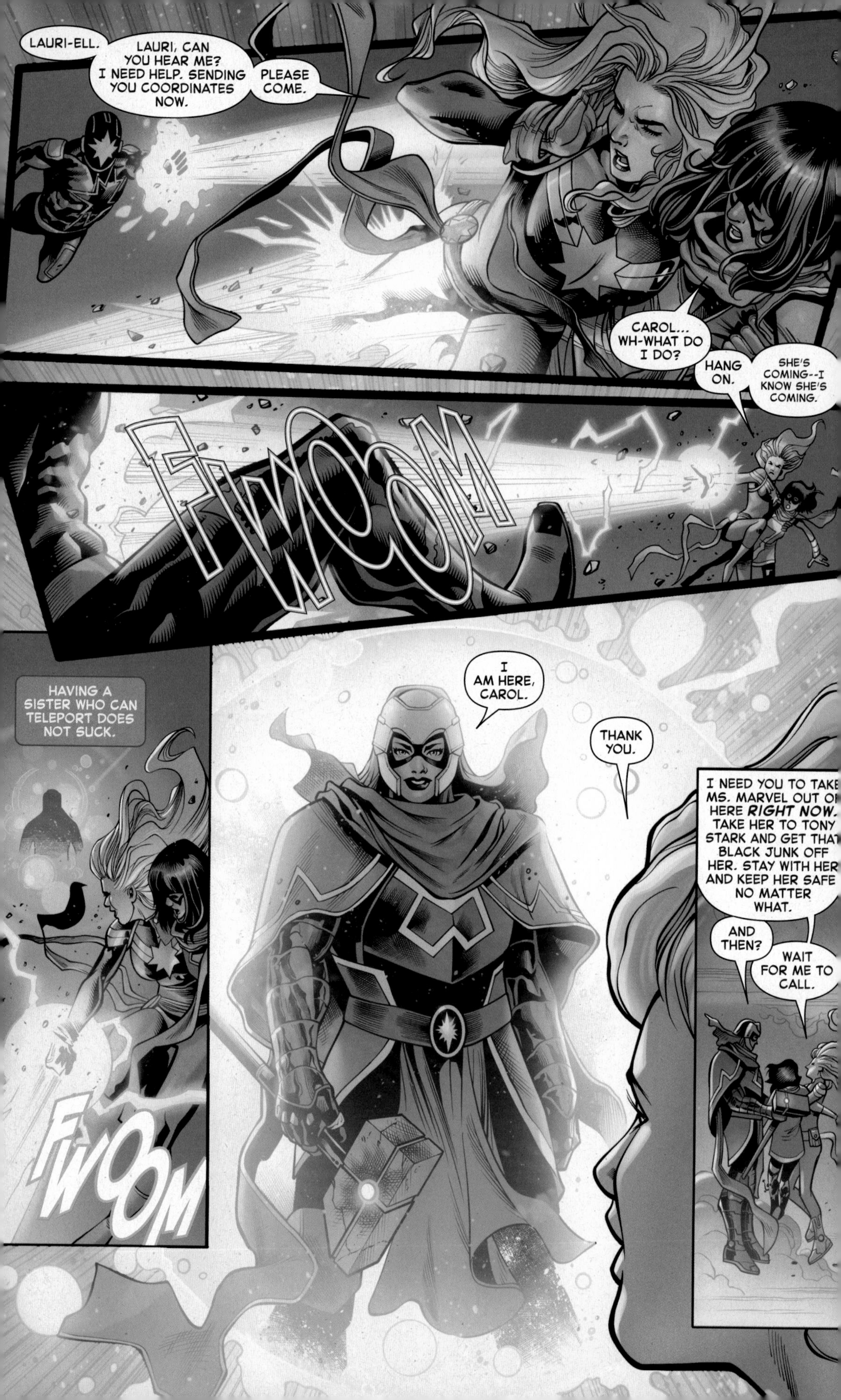

LAURI-ELL.
LAURI, CAN YOU HEAR ME? I NEED HELP. SENDING YOU COORDINATES NOW.
PLEASE COME.
CAROL... WH-WHAT DO I DO?
HANG ON.
SHE'S COMING--I KNOW SHE'S COMING.
FWOOM
HAVING A SISTER WHO CAN TELEPORT DOES NOT SUCK.
FWOOM
I AM HERE, CAROL.
THANK YOU.
I NEED YOU TO TAKE MS. MARVEL OUT OF HERE RIGHT NOW. TAKE HER TO TONY STARK AND GET THAT BLACK JUNK OFF HER. STAY WITH HER AND KEEP HER SAFE NO MATTER WHAT.
AND THEN?
WAIT FOR ME TO CALL.

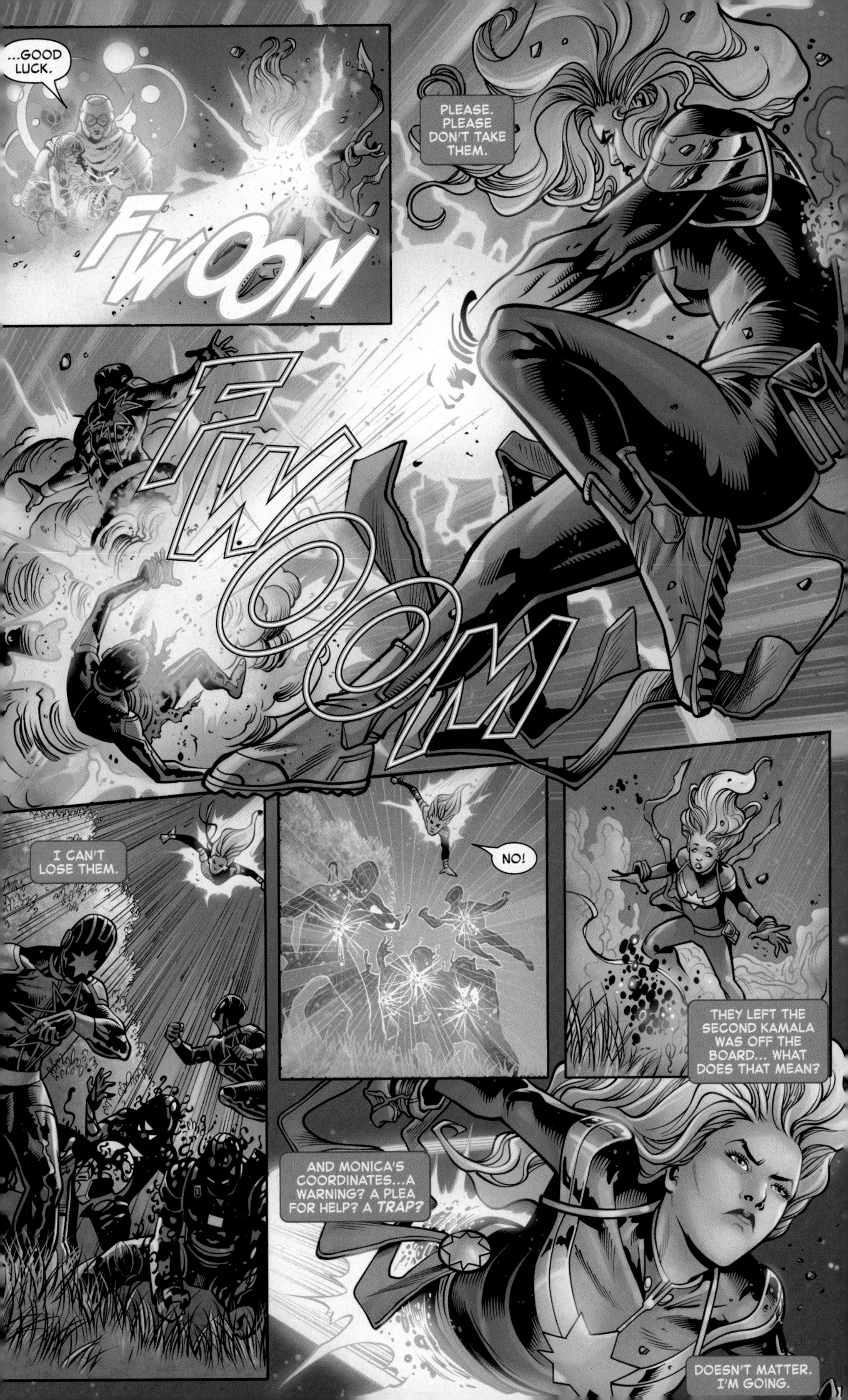
...GOOD LUCK.
FWOOM
PLEASE. PLEASE DON'T TAKE THEM.
FWOOM
I CAN'T LOSE THEM.
NO!
THEY LEFT THE SECOND KAMALA WAS OFF THE BOARD... WHAT DOES THAT MEAN?
AND MONICA'S COORDINATES...A WARNING? A PLEA FOR HELP? A TRAP?
DOESN'T MATTER. I'M GOING.

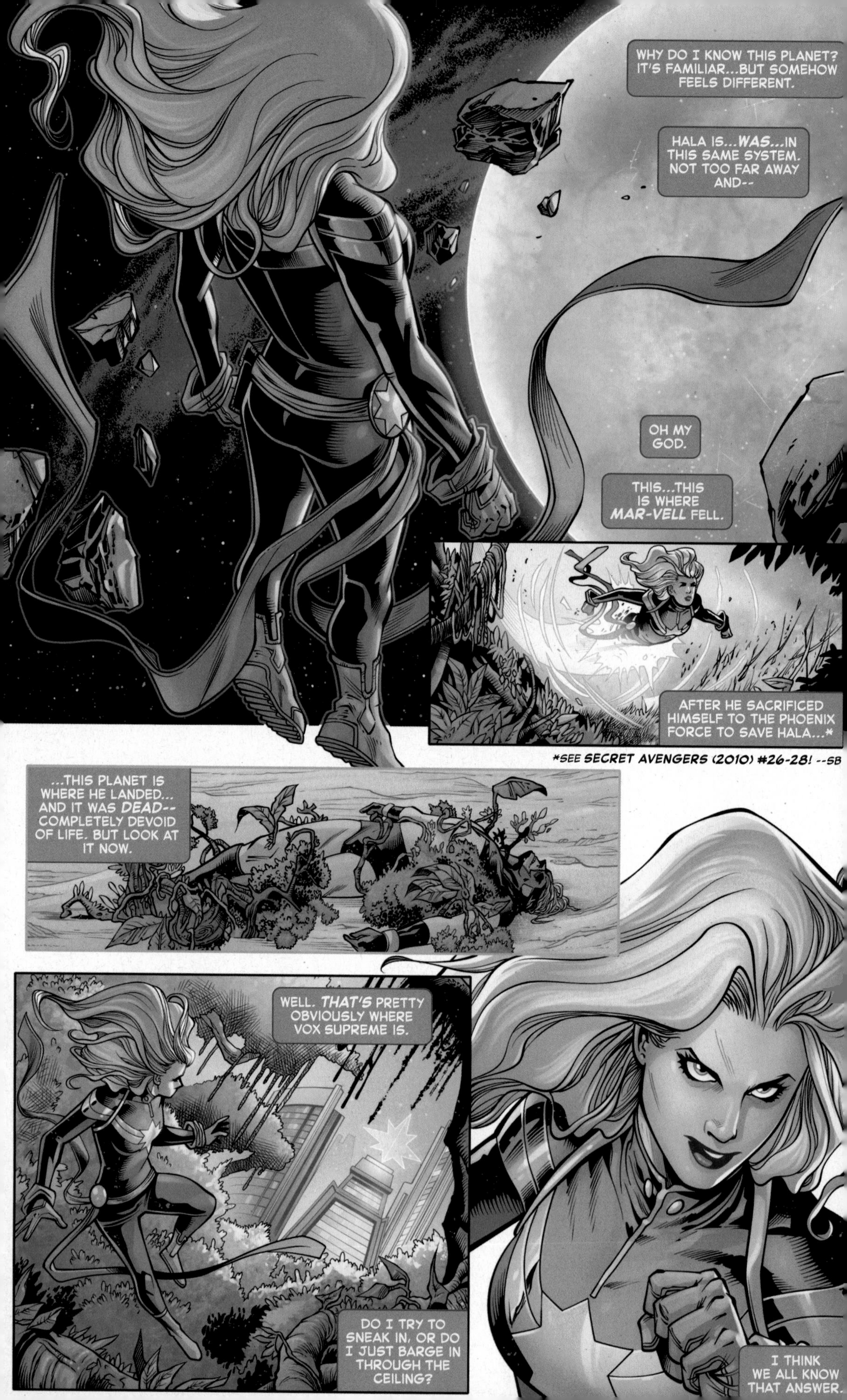
WHY DO I KNOW THIS PLANET? IT'S FAMILIAR...BUT SOMEHOW FEELS DIFFERENT.
HALA IS...WAS...IN THIS SAME SYSTEM. NOT TOO FAR AWAY AND--
OH MY GOD.
THIS...THIS IS WHERE MAR-VELL FELL.
AFTER HE SACRIFICED HIMSELF TO THE PHOENIX FORCE TO SAVE HALA...*
*SEE SECRET AVENGERS (2010) #26-28! --SB
...THIS PLANET IS WHERE HE LANDED... AND IT WAS DEAD-- COMPLETELY DEVOID OF LIFE. BUT LOOK AT IT NOW.
WELL. THAT'S PRETTY OBVIOUSLY WHERE VOX SUPREME IS.
DO I TRY TO SNEAK IN, OR DO I JUST BARGE IN THROUGH THE CEILING?
I THINK WE ALL KNOW THAT ANSWER.

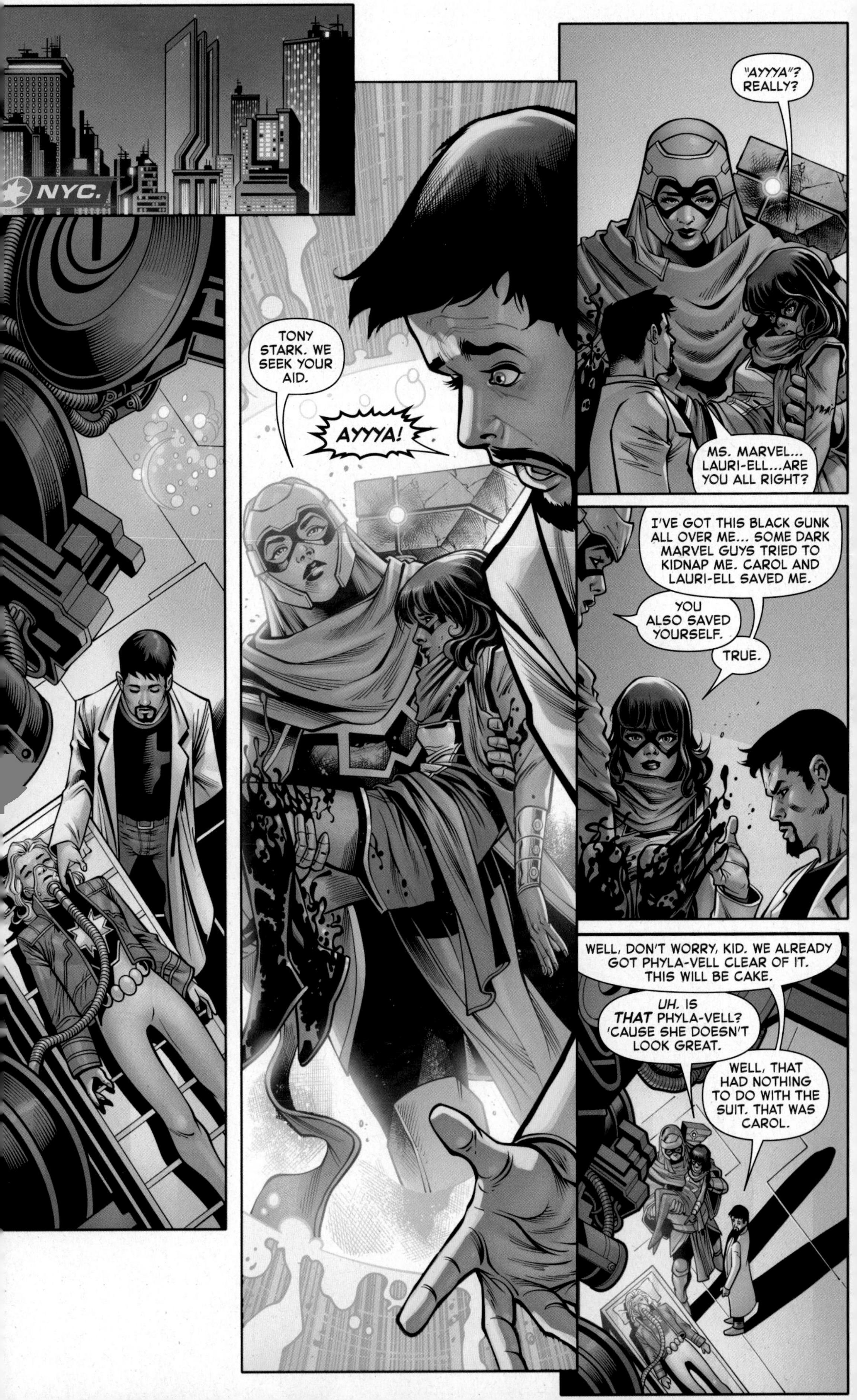

NYC.
TONY STARK. WE SEEK YOUR AID.
AYYYA!
"AYYYA"? REALLY?
MS. MARVEL... LAURI-ELL...ARE YOU ALL RIGHT?
I'VE GOT THIS BLACK GUNK ALL OVER ME... SOME DARK MARVEL GUYS TRIED TO KIDNAP ME. CAROL AND LAURI-ELL SAVED ME.
YOU ALSO SAVED YOURSELF.
TRUE.
WELL, DON'T WORRY, KID. WE ALREADY GOT PHYLA-VELL CLEAR OF IT. THIS WILL BE CAKE.
UH. IS THAT PHYLA-VELL? 'CAUSE SHE DOESN'T LOOK GREAT.
WELL, THAT HAD NOTHING TO DO WITH THE SUIT. THAT WAS CAROL.

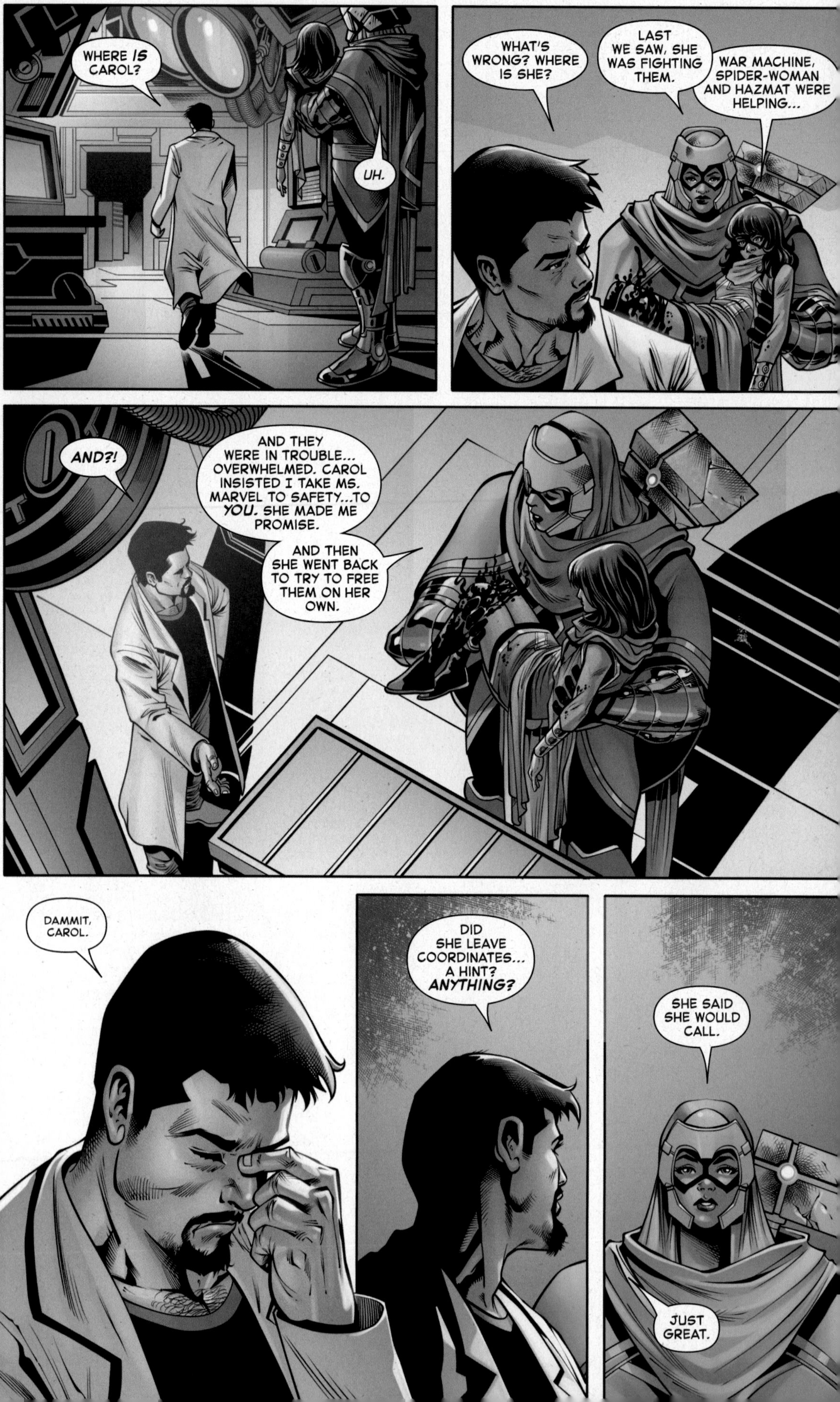
WHERE IS CAROL?
UH.
WHAT'S WRONG? WHERE IS SHE?
LAST WE SAW, SHE WAS FIGHTING THEM.
WAR MACHINE, SPIDER-WOMAN AND HAZMAT WERE HELPING...
AND?!
AND THEY WERE IN TROUBLE... OVERWHELMED. CAROL INSISTED I TAKE MS. MARVEL TO SAFETY...TO YOU. SHE MADE ME PROMISE.
AND THEN SHE WENT BACK TO TRY TO FREE THEM ON HER OWN.
DAMMIT, CAROL.
DID SHE LEAVE COORDINATES... A HINT? ANYTHING?
SHE SAID SHE WOULD CALL.
JUST GREAT.

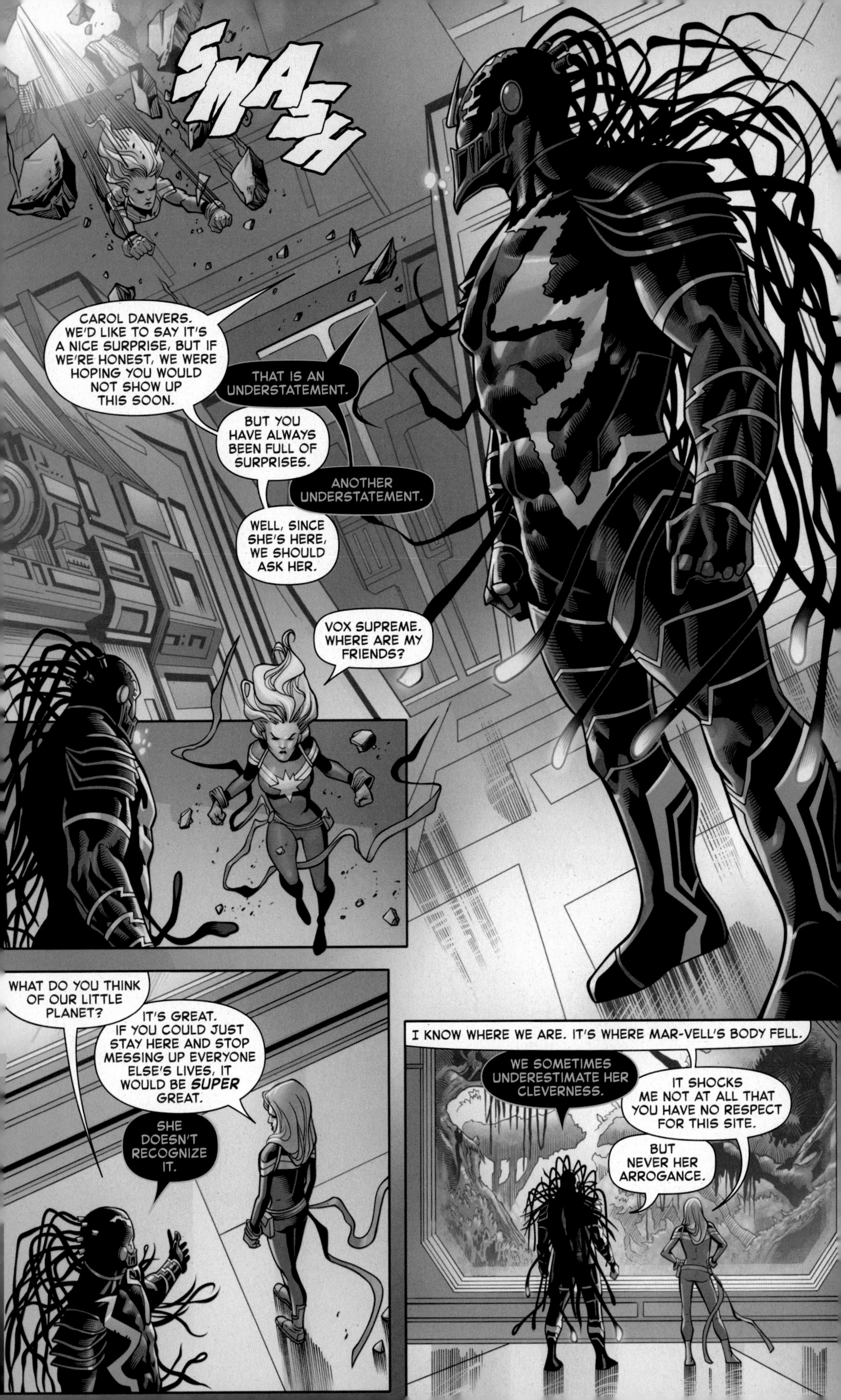
SMASH
CAROL DANVERS. WE'D LIKE TO SAY IT'S A NICE SURPRISE, BUT IF WE'RE HONEST, WE WERE HOPING YOU WOULD NOT SHOW UP THIS SOON.
THAT IS AN UNDERSTATEMENT.
BUT YOU HAVE ALWAYS BEEN FULL OF SURPRISES.
ANOTHER UNDERSTATEMENT.
WELL, SINCE SHE'S HERE, WE SHOULD ASK HER.
VOX SUPREME. WHERE ARE MY FRIENDS?
WHAT DO YOU THINK OF OUR LITTLE PLANET?
IT'S GREAT. IF YOU COULD JUST STAY HERE AND STOP MESSING UP EVERYONE ELSE'S LIVES, IT WOULD BE SUPER GREAT.
SHE DOESN'T RECOGNIZE IT.
I KNOW WHERE WE ARE. IT'S WHERE MAR-VELL'S BODY FELL.
WE SOMETIMES UNDERESTIMATE HER CLEVERNESS.
IT SHOCKS ME NOT AT ALL THAT YOU HAVE NO RESPECT FOR THIS SITE.
BUT NEVER HER ARROGANCE.

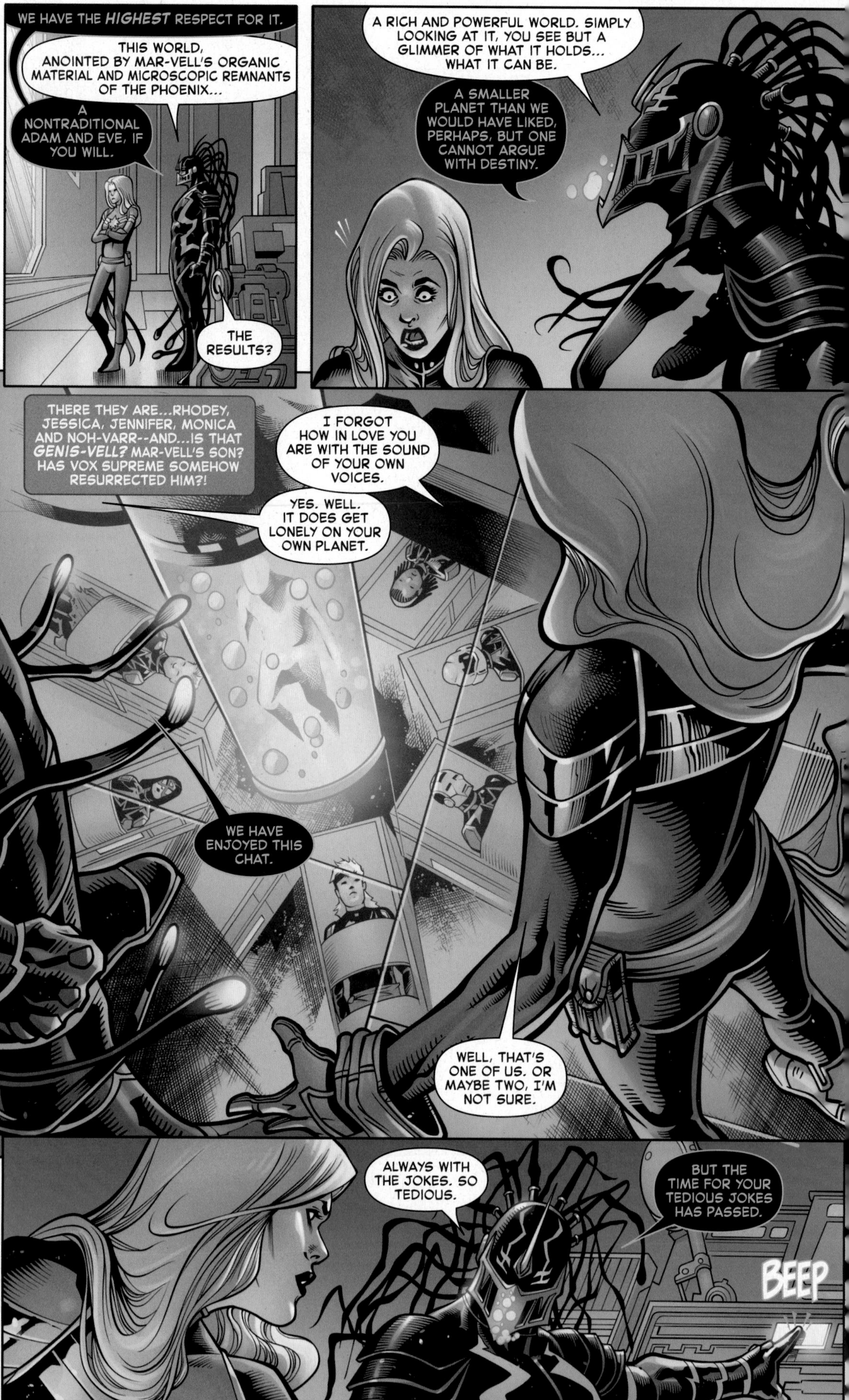
WE HAVE THE HIGHEST RESPECT FOR IT.
THIS WORLD, ANOINTED BY MAR-VELL'S ORGANIC MATERIAL AND MICROSCOPIC REMNANTS OF THE PHOENIX...
A NONTRADITIONAL ADAM AND EVE, IF YOU WILL.
THE RESULTS?
A RICH AND POWERFUL WORLD. SIMPLY LOOKING AT IT, YOU SEE BUT A GLIMMER OF WHAT IT HOLDS... WHAT IT CAN BE.
A SMALLER PLANET THAN WE WOULD HAVE LIKED, PERHAPS, BUT ONE CANNOT ARGUE WITH DESTINY.
THERE THEY ARE...RHODEY, JESSICA, JENNIFER, MONICA AND NOH-VARR--AND...IS THAT GENIS-VELL? MAR-VELL'S SON? HAS VOX SUPREME SOMEHOW RESURRECTED HIM?!
I FORGOT HOW IN LOVE YOU ARE WITH THE SOUND OF YOUR OWN VOICES.
YES. WELL. IT DOES GET LONELY ON YOUR OWN PLANET.
WE HAVE ENJOYED THIS CHAT.
WELL, THAT'S ONE OF US. OR MAYBE TWO, I'M NOT SURE.
ALWAYS WITH THE JOKES. SO TEDIOUS.
BUT THE TIME FOR YOUR TEDIOUS JOKES HAS PASSED.
BEEP

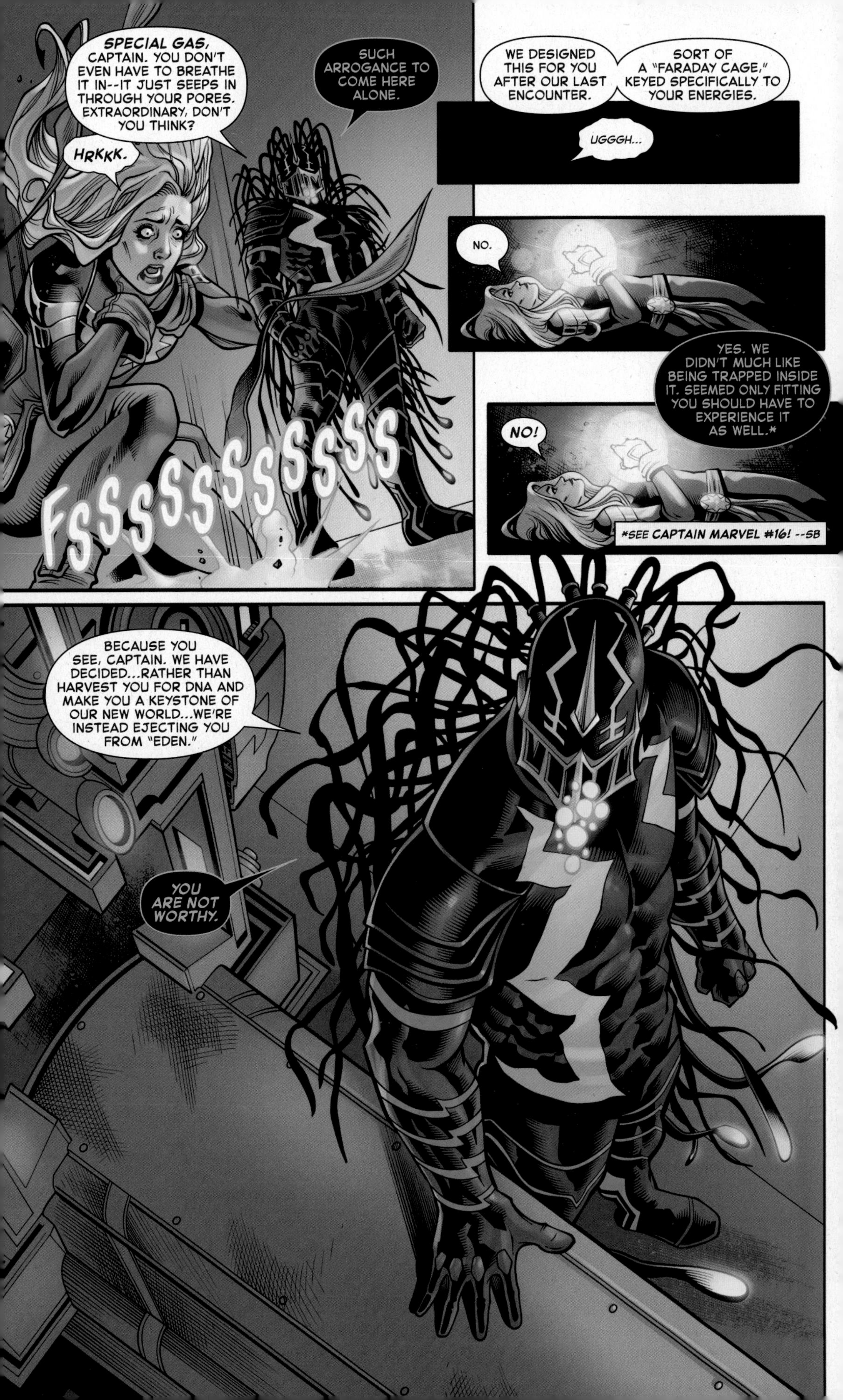
SPECIAL GAS, CAPTAIN. YOU DON'T EVEN HAVE TO BREATHE IT IN--IT JUST SEEPS IN THROUGH YOUR PORES. EXTRAORDINARY, DON'T YOU THINK?
HRKKK.
SUCH ARROGANCE TO COME HERE ALONE.
FSSSSSSSSSSSS
WE DESIGNED THIS FOR YOU AFTER OUR LAST ENCOUNTER.
SORT OF A "FARADAY CAGE," KEYED SPECIFICALLY TO YOUR ENERGIES.
UGGGH...
NO.
YES. WE DIDN'T MUCH LIKE BEING TRAPPED INSIDE IT. SEEMED ONLY FITTING YOU SHOULD HAVE TO EXPERIENCE IT AS WELL.*
NO!
*SEE CAPTAIN MARVEL #16! --SB
BECAUSE YOU SEE, CAPTAIN. WE HAVE DECIDED...RATHER THAN HARVEST YOU FOR DNA AND MAKE YOU A KEYSTONE OF OUR NEW WORLD...WE'RE INSTEAD EJECTING YOU FROM "EDEN."
YOU ARE NOT WORTHY.

STAY CALM. THERE'S NO WAY THIS CAN HOLD YOU.

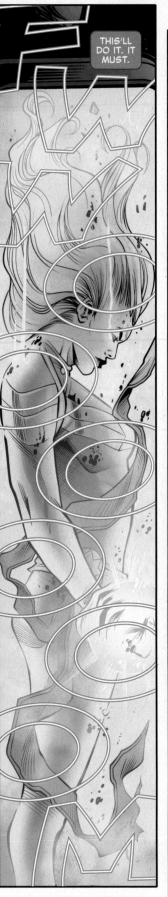

THIS'LL DO IT. IT MUST.

...NOTHING.

...ABSOLUTELY NOTHING.

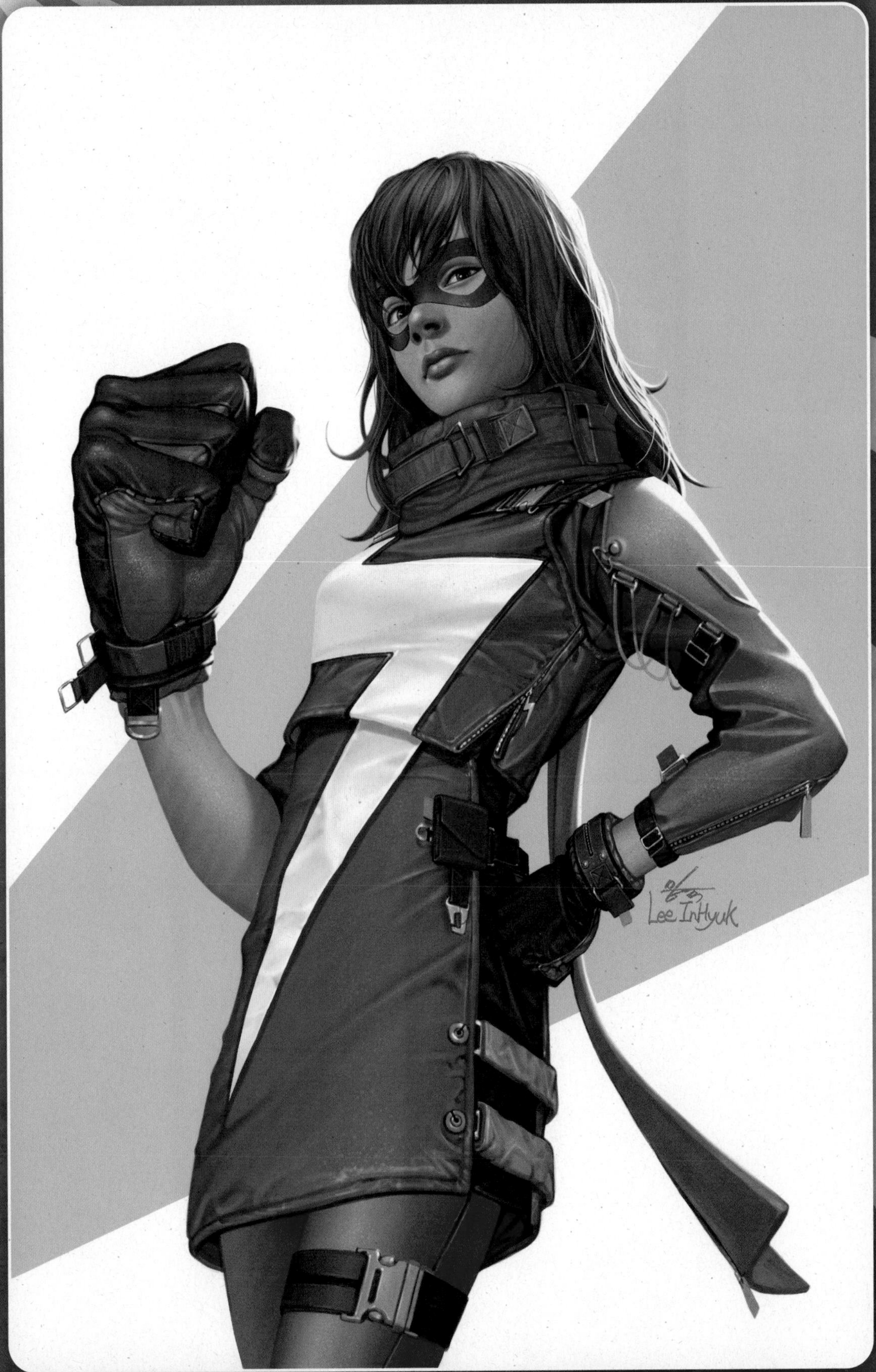

Lee InHyuk

INHYUK LEE
#31 MARVEL ASIAN VOICES VARIANT

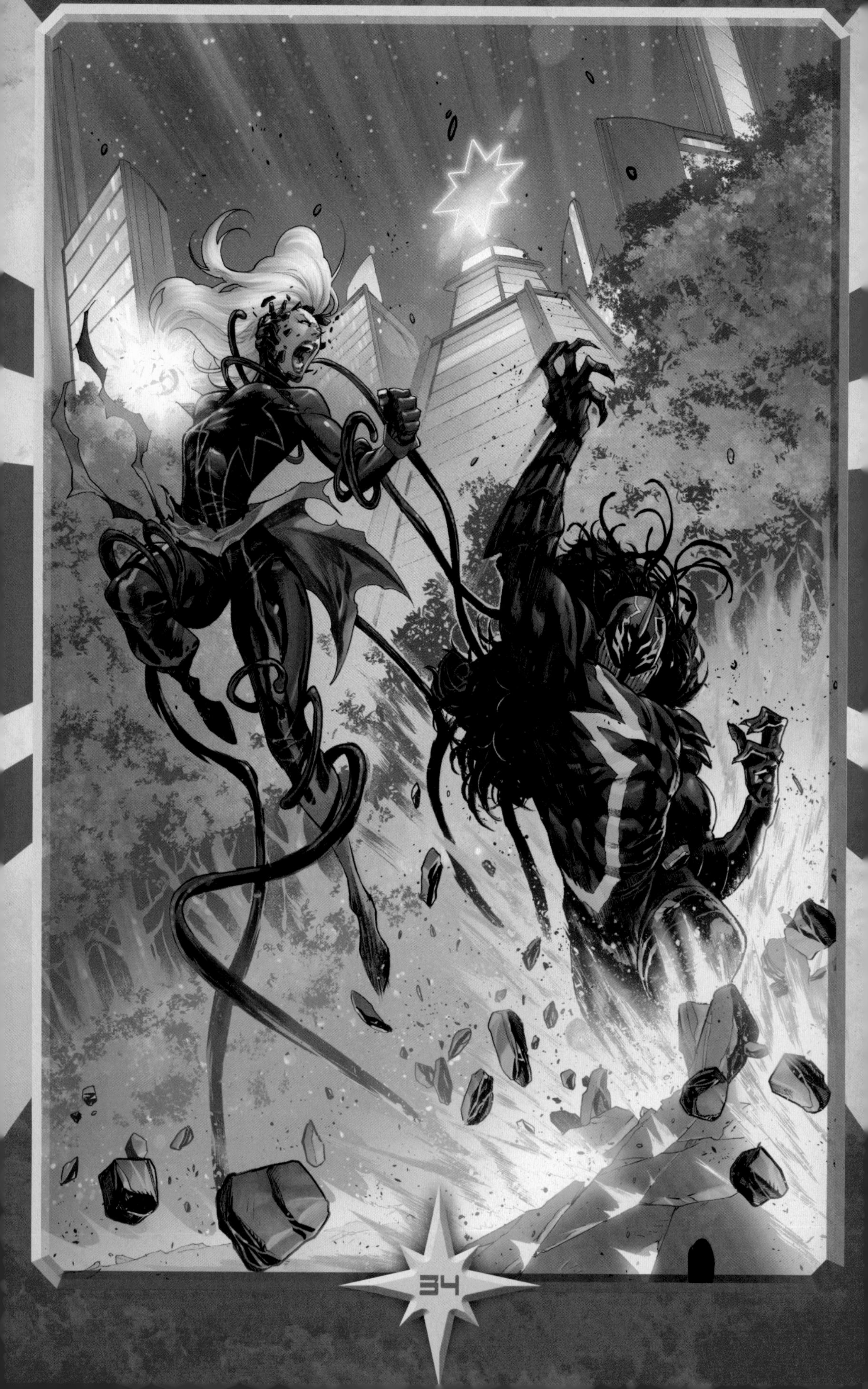

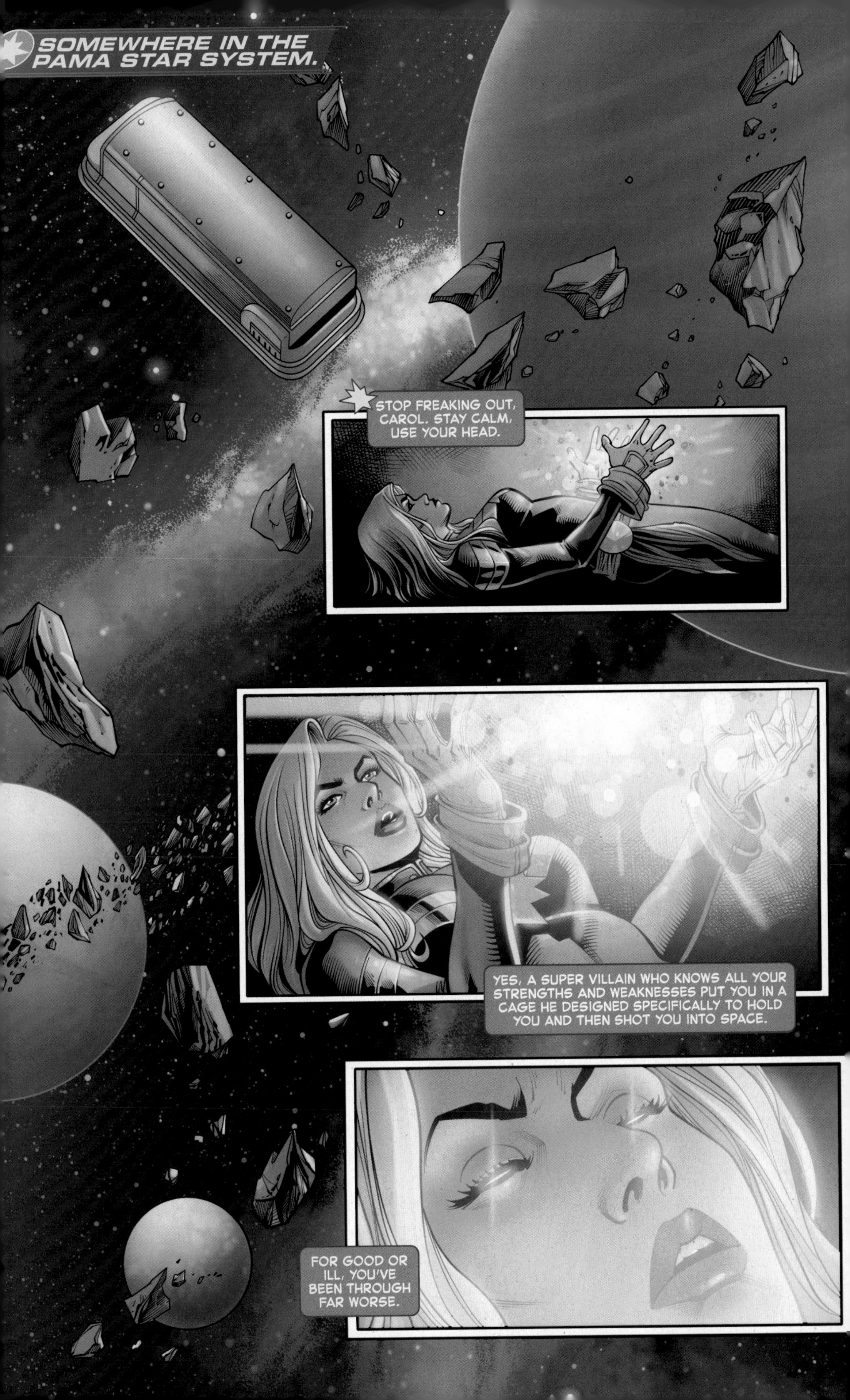

SOMEWHERE IN THE PAMA STAR SYSTEM.
STOP FREAKING OUT, CAROL. STAY CALM, USE YOUR HEAD.
YES, A SUPER VILLAIN WHO KNOWS ALL YOUR STRENGTHS AND WEAKNESSES PUT YOU IN A CAGE HE DESIGNED SPECIFICALLY TO HOLD YOU AND THEN SHOT YOU INTO SPACE.
FOR GOOD OR ILL, YOU'VE BEEN THROUGH FAR WORSE.

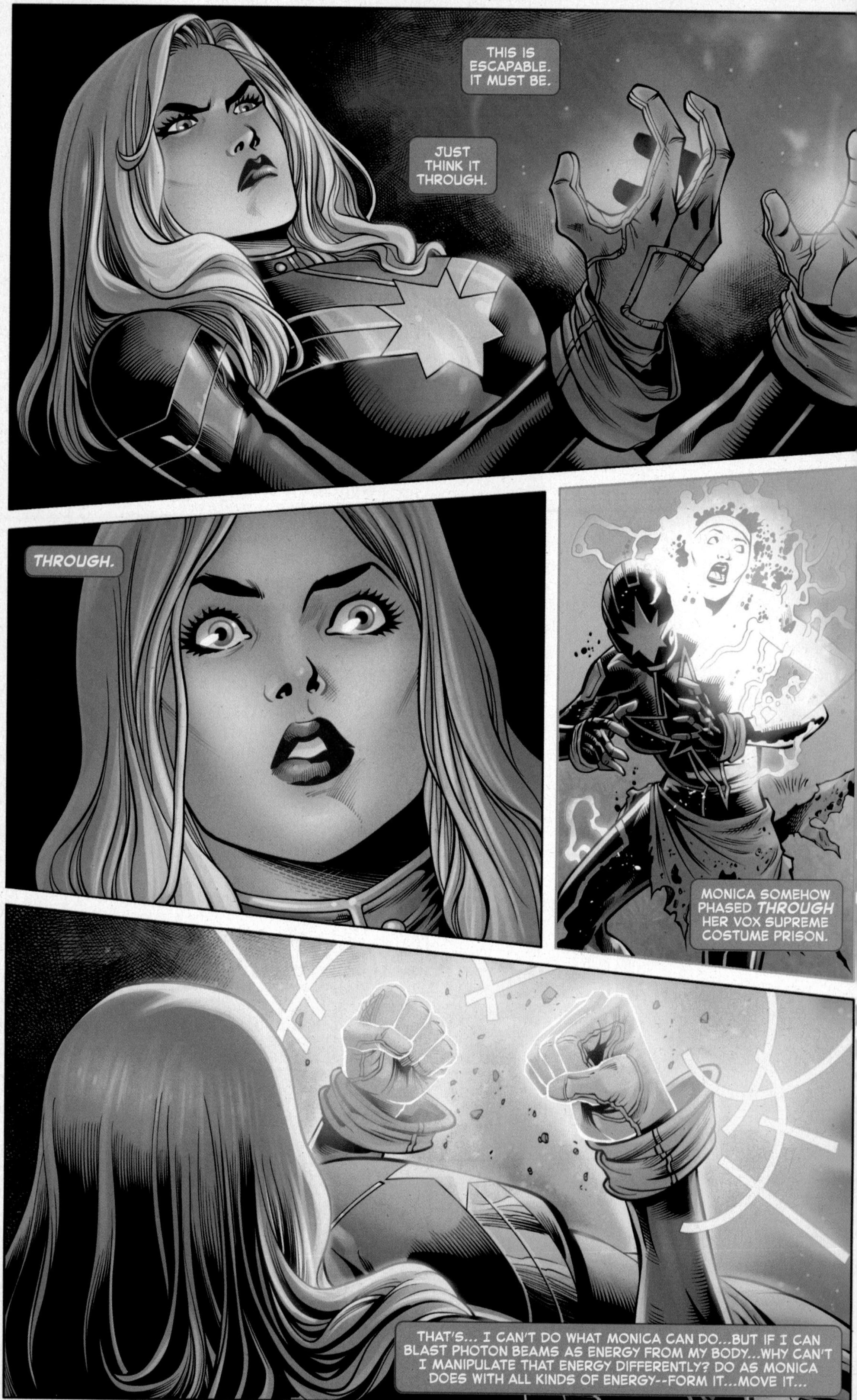
THIS IS ESCAPABLE. IT MUST BE.
JUST THINK IT THROUGH.
THROUGH.
MONICA SOMEHOW PHASED THROUGH HER VOX SUPREME COSTUME PRISON.
THAT'S... I CAN'T DO WHAT MONICA CAN DO...BUT IF I CAN BLAST PHOTON BEAMS AS ENERGY FROM MY BODY...WHY CAN'T I MANIPULATE THAT ENERGY DIFFERENTLY? DO AS MONICA DOES WITH ALL KINDS OF ENERGY--FORM IT...MOVE IT...

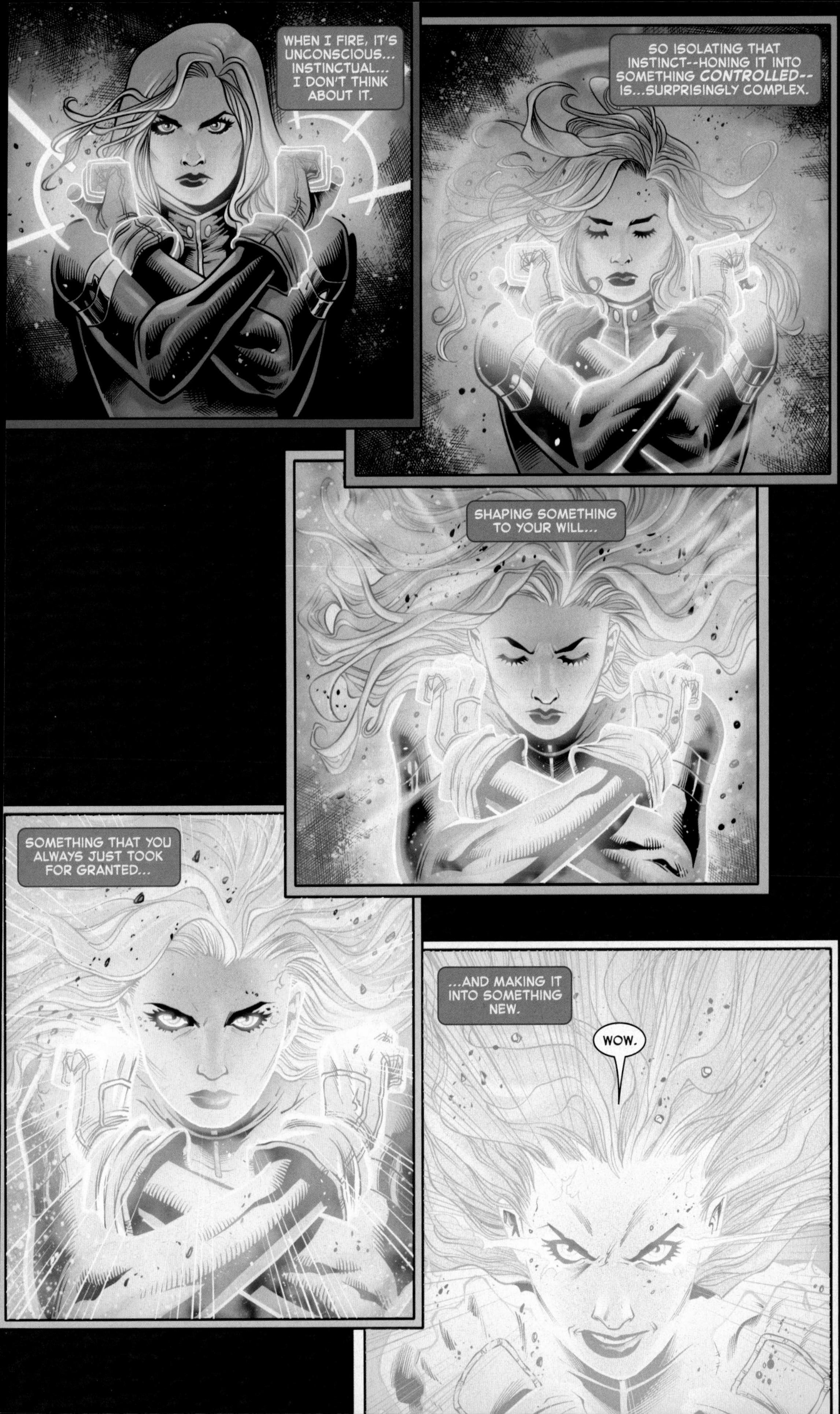
WHEN I FIRE, IT'S UNCONSCIOUS... INSTINCTUAL... I DON'T THINK ABOUT IT.
SO ISOLATING THAT INSTINCT--HONING IT INTO SOMETHING CONTROLLED--IS...SURPRISINGLY COMPLEX.
SHAPING SOMETHING TO YOUR WILL...
SOMETHING THAT YOU ALWAYS JUST TOOK FOR GRANTED...
...AND MAKING IT INTO SOMETHING NEW.
WOW.

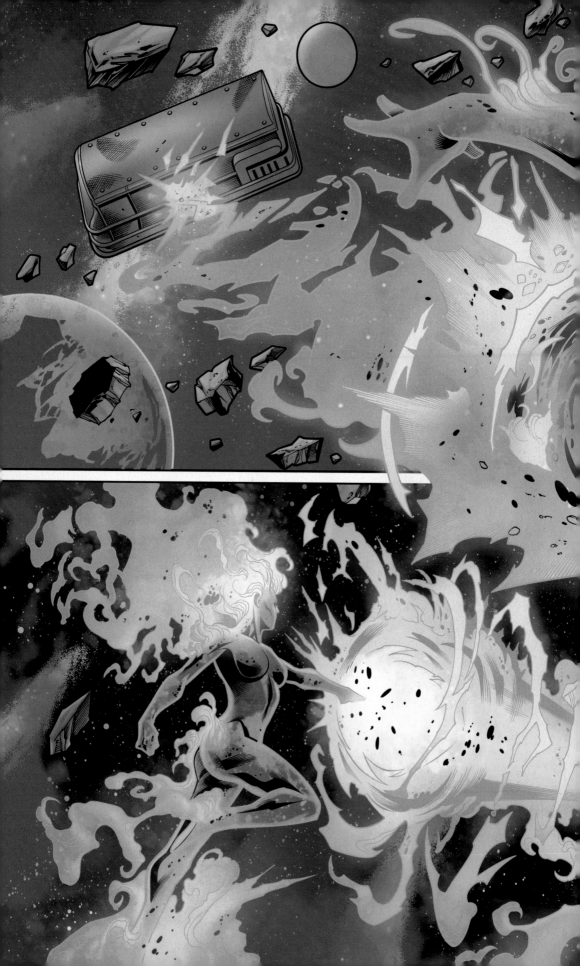

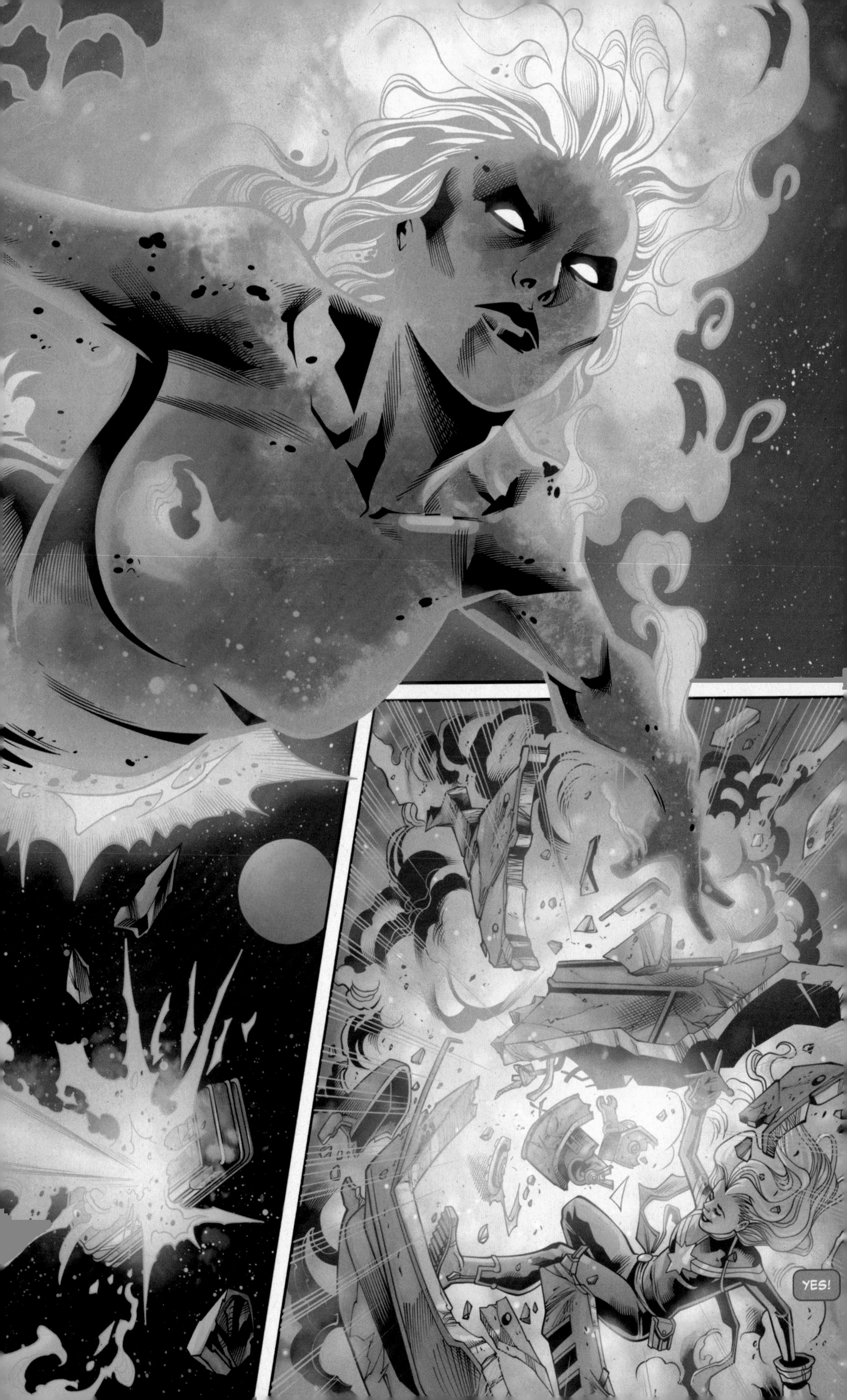
YES!

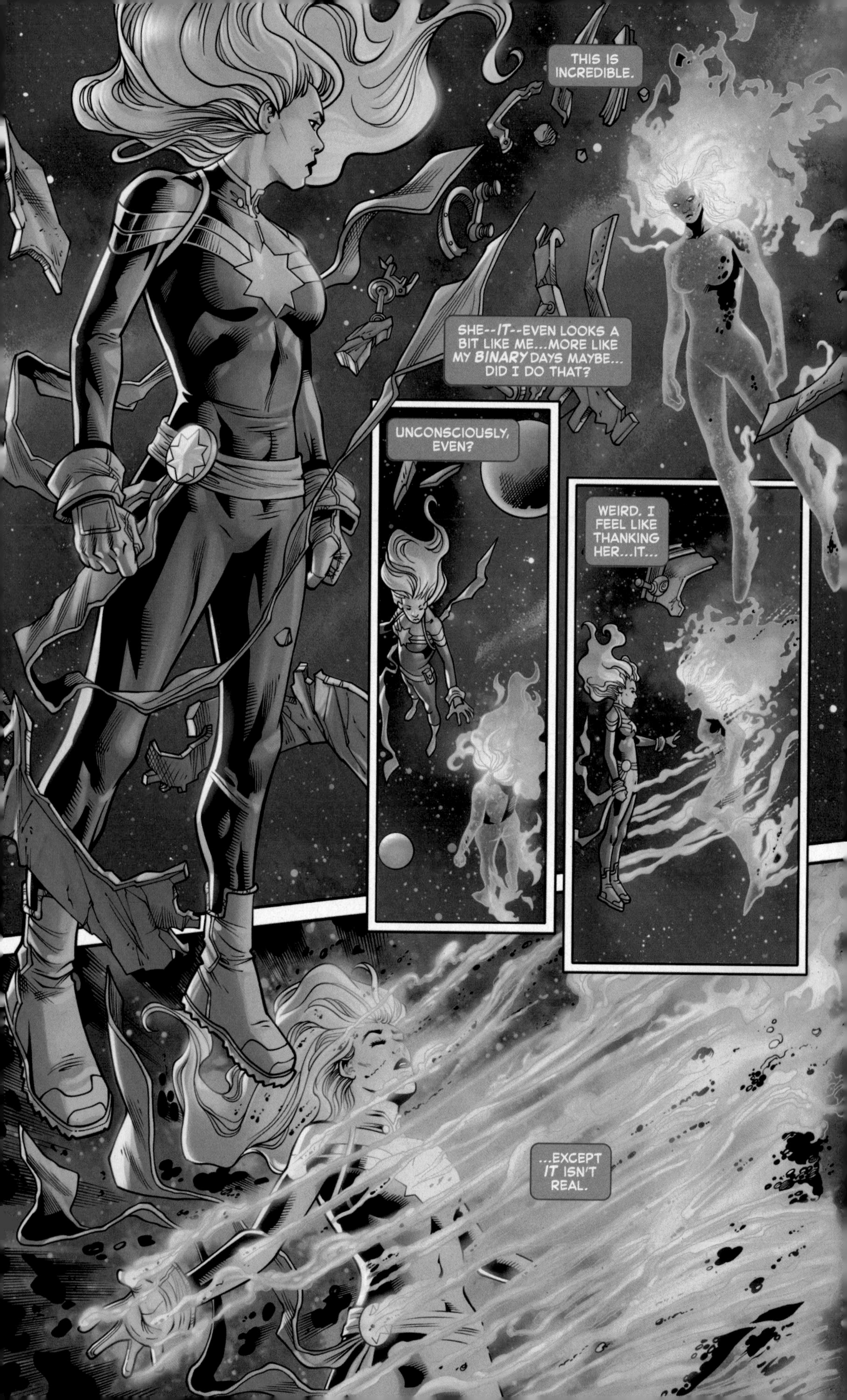
THIS IS INCREDIBLE.
SHE--IT--EVEN LOOKS A BIT LIKE ME...MORE LIKE MY BINARY DAYS MAYBE... DID I DO THAT?
UNCONSCIOUSLY, EVEN?
WEIRD. I FEEL LIKE THANKING HER...IT...
...EXCEPT IT ISN'T REAL.

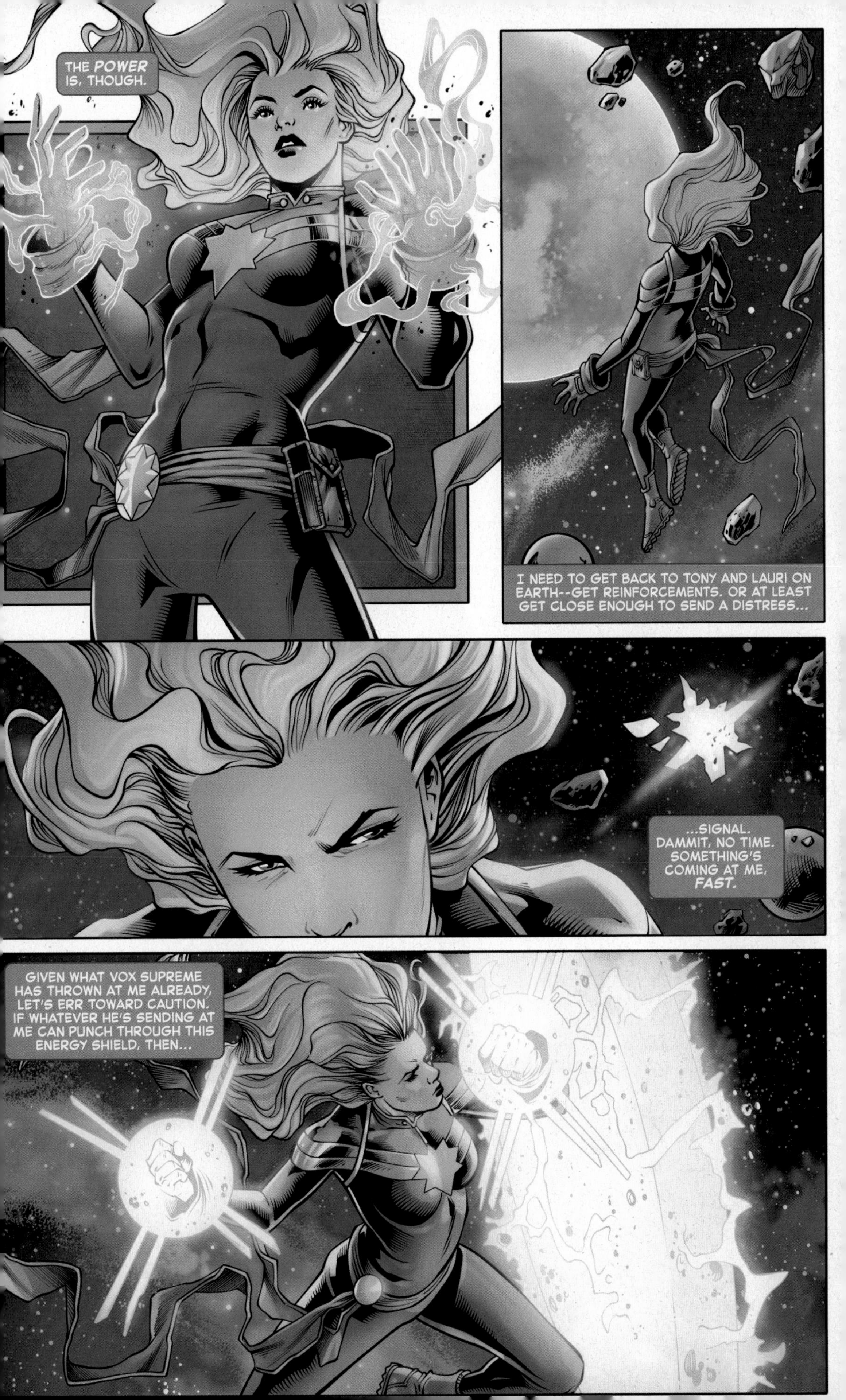
THE POWER IS, THOUGH.
I NEED TO GET BACK TO TONY AND LAURI ON EARTH--GET REINFORCEMENTS. OR AT LEAST GET CLOSE ENOUGH TO SEND A DISTRESS...
...SIGNAL. DAMMIT, NO TIME. SOMETHING'S COMING AT ME, FAST.
GIVEN WHAT VOX SUPREME HAS THROWN AT ME ALREADY, LET'S ERR TOWARD CAUTION. IF WHATEVER HE'S SENDING AT ME CAN PUNCH THROUGH THIS ENERGY SHIELD, THEN...

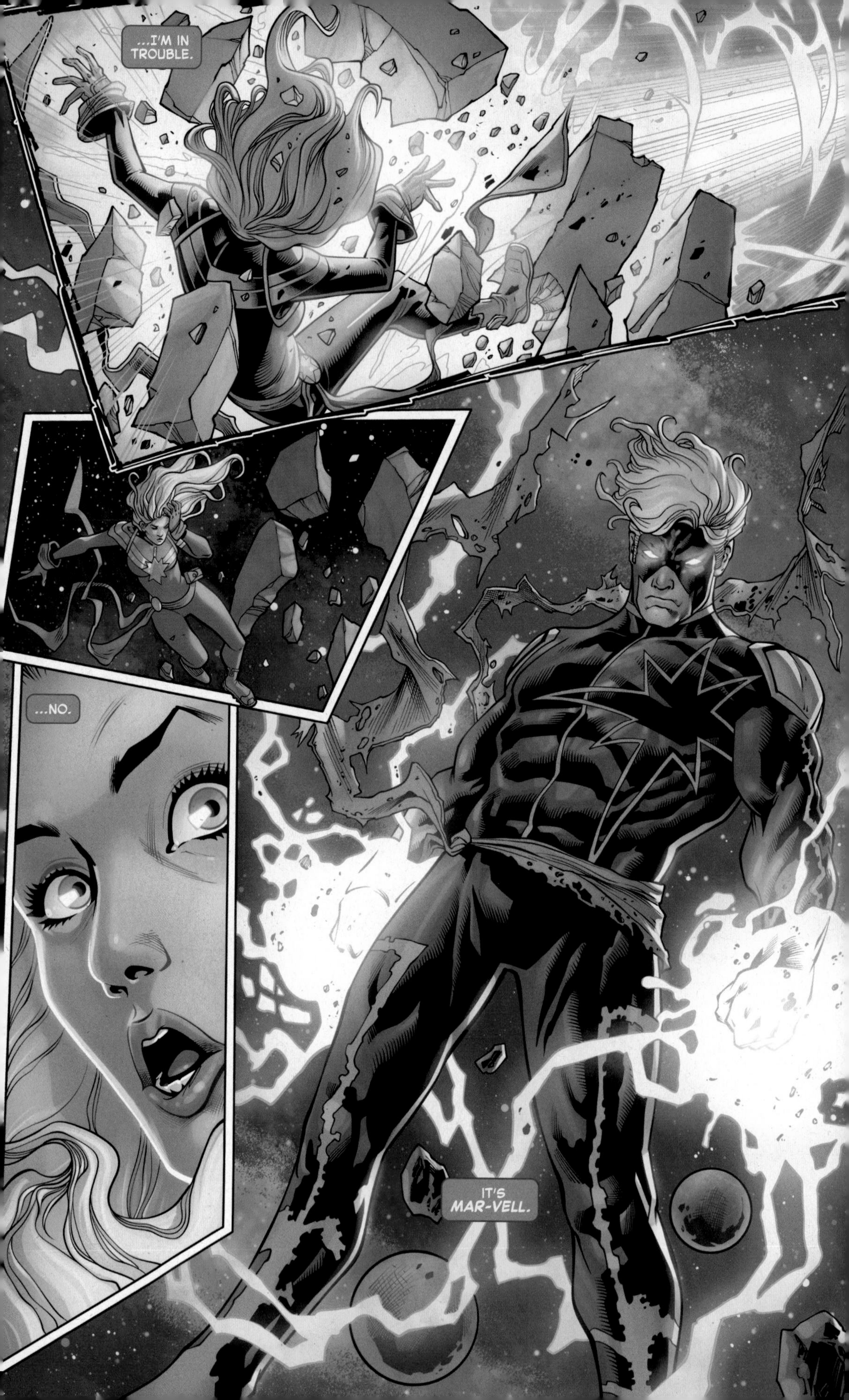
...I'M IN TROUBLE.
...NO.
IT'S MAR-VELL.

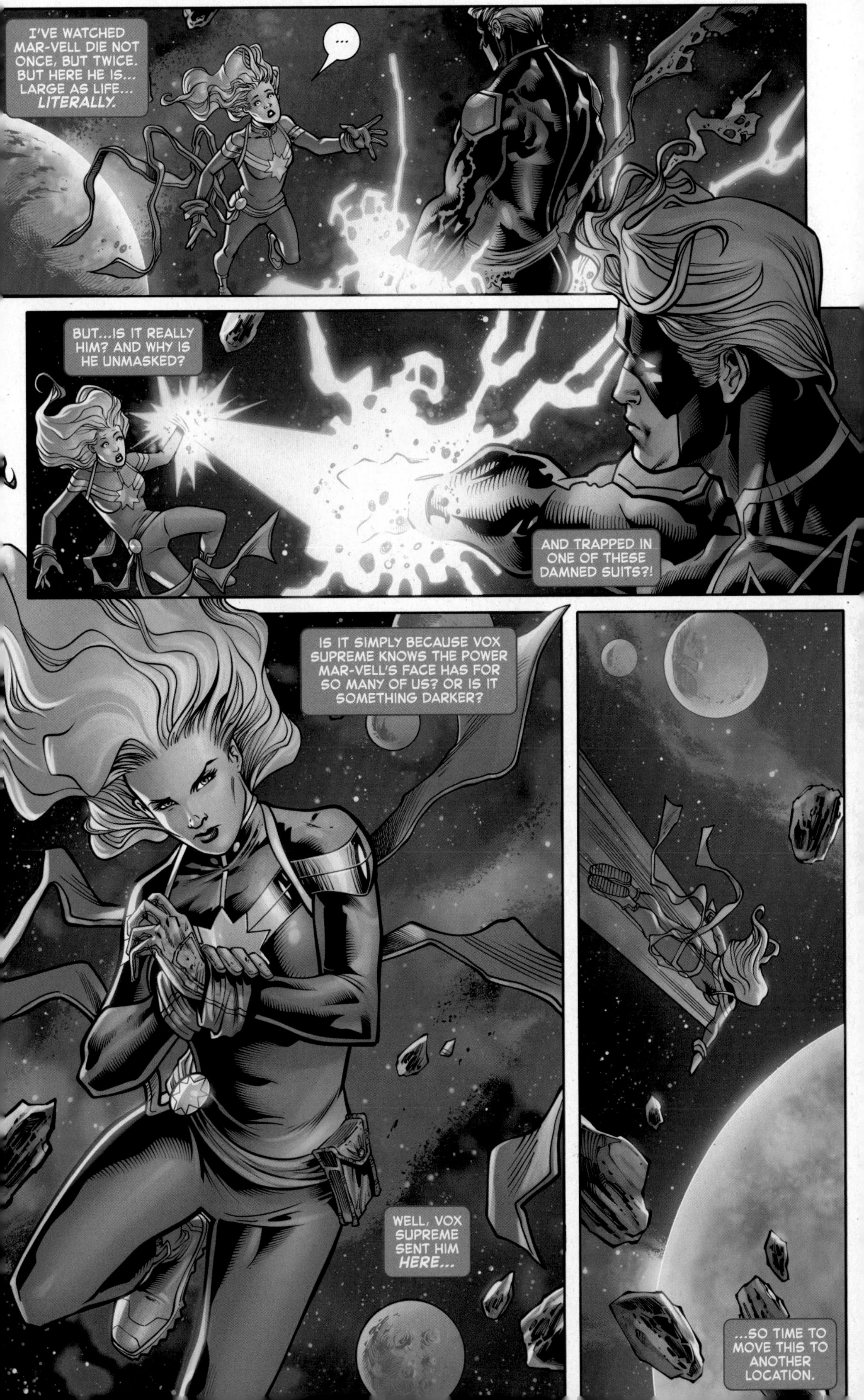

I'VE WATCHED MAR-VELL DIE NOT ONCE, BUT TWICE. BUT HERE HE IS... LARGE AS LIFE... *LITERALLY.*
...
BUT...IS IT REALLY HIM? AND WHY IS HE UNMASKED?
AND TRAPPED IN ONE OF THESE DAMNED SUITS?!
IS IT SIMPLY BECAUSE VOX SUPREME KNOWS THE POWER MAR-VELL'S FACE HAS FOR SO MANY OF US? OR IS IT SOMETHING DARKER?
WELL, VOX SUPREME SENT HIM *HERE...*
...SO TIME TO MOVE THIS TO ANOTHER LOCATION.

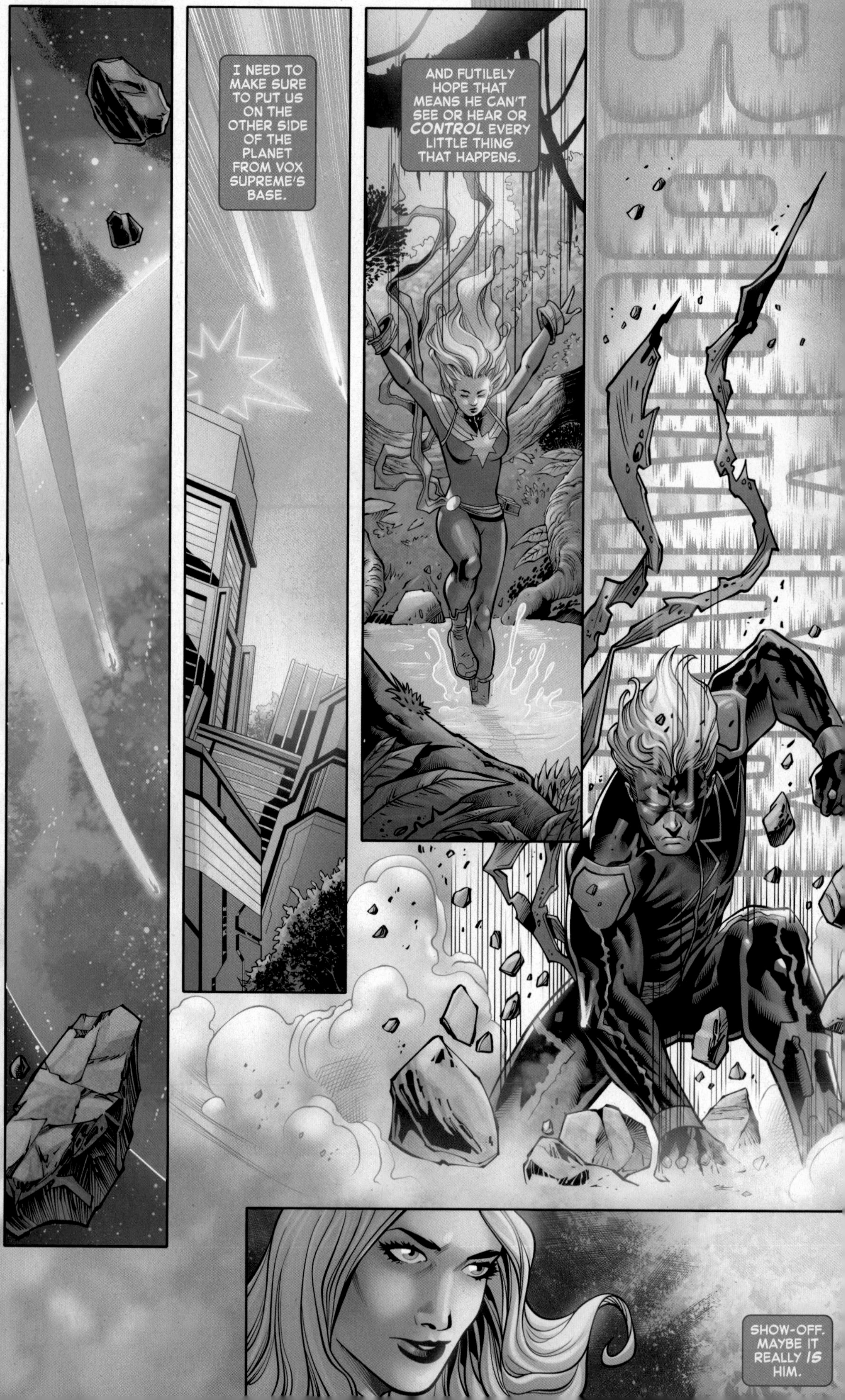
I NEED TO MAKE SURE TO PUT US ON THE OTHER SIDE OF THE PLANET FROM VOX SUPREME'S BASE.
AND FUTILELY HOPE THAT MEANS HE CAN'T SEE OR HEAR OR *CONTROL* EVERY LITTLE THING THAT HAPPENS.
SHOW-OFF. MAYBE IT REALLY *IS* HIM.

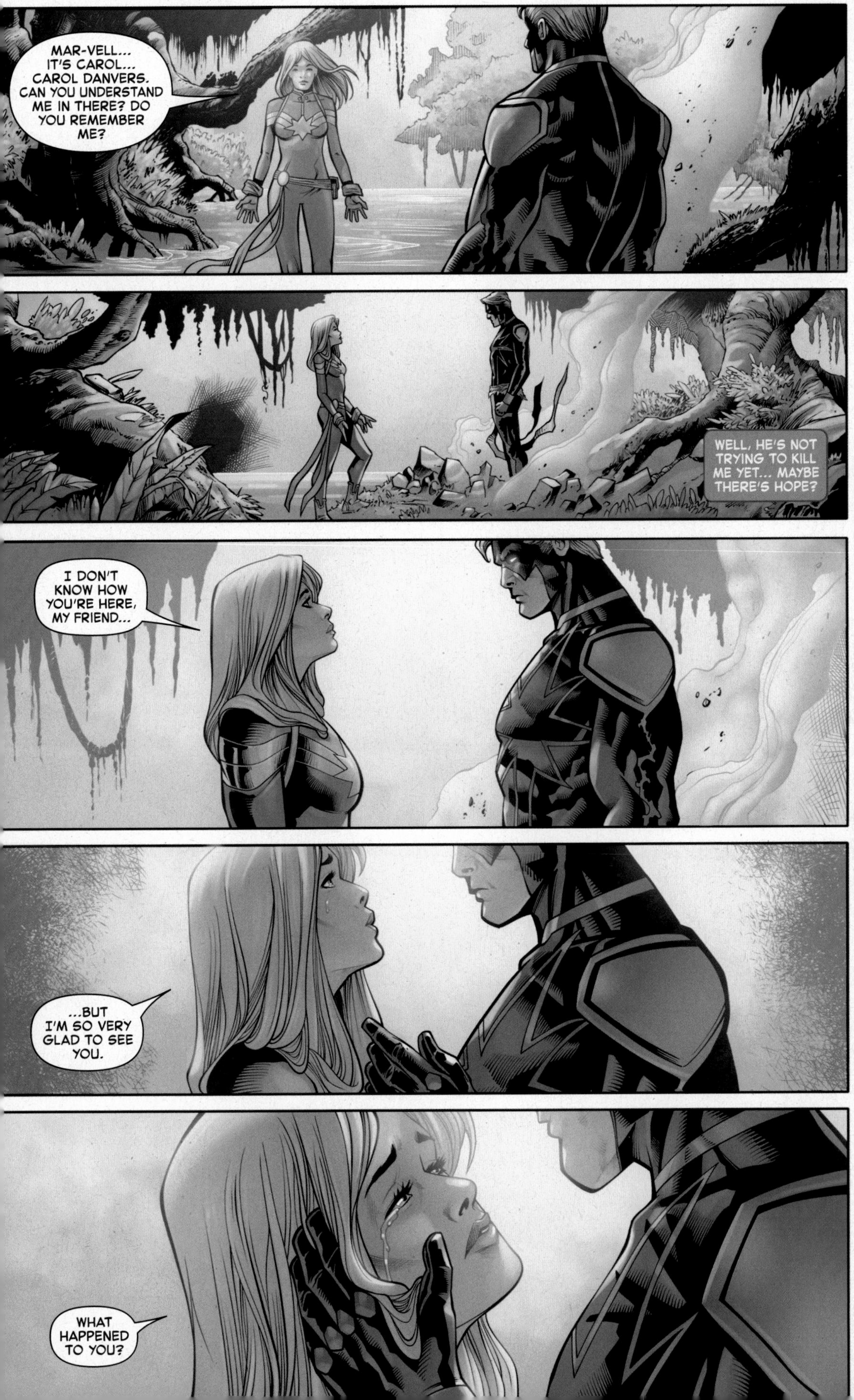

MAR-VELL... IT'S CAROL... CAROL DANVERS. CAN YOU UNDERSTAND ME IN THERE? DO YOU REMEMBER ME?
WELL, HE'S NOT TRYING TO KILL ME YET... MAYBE THERE'S HOPE?
I DON'T KNOW HOW YOU'RE HERE, MY FRIEND...
...BUT I'M SO VERY GLAD TO SEE YOU.
WHAT HAPPENED TO YOU?

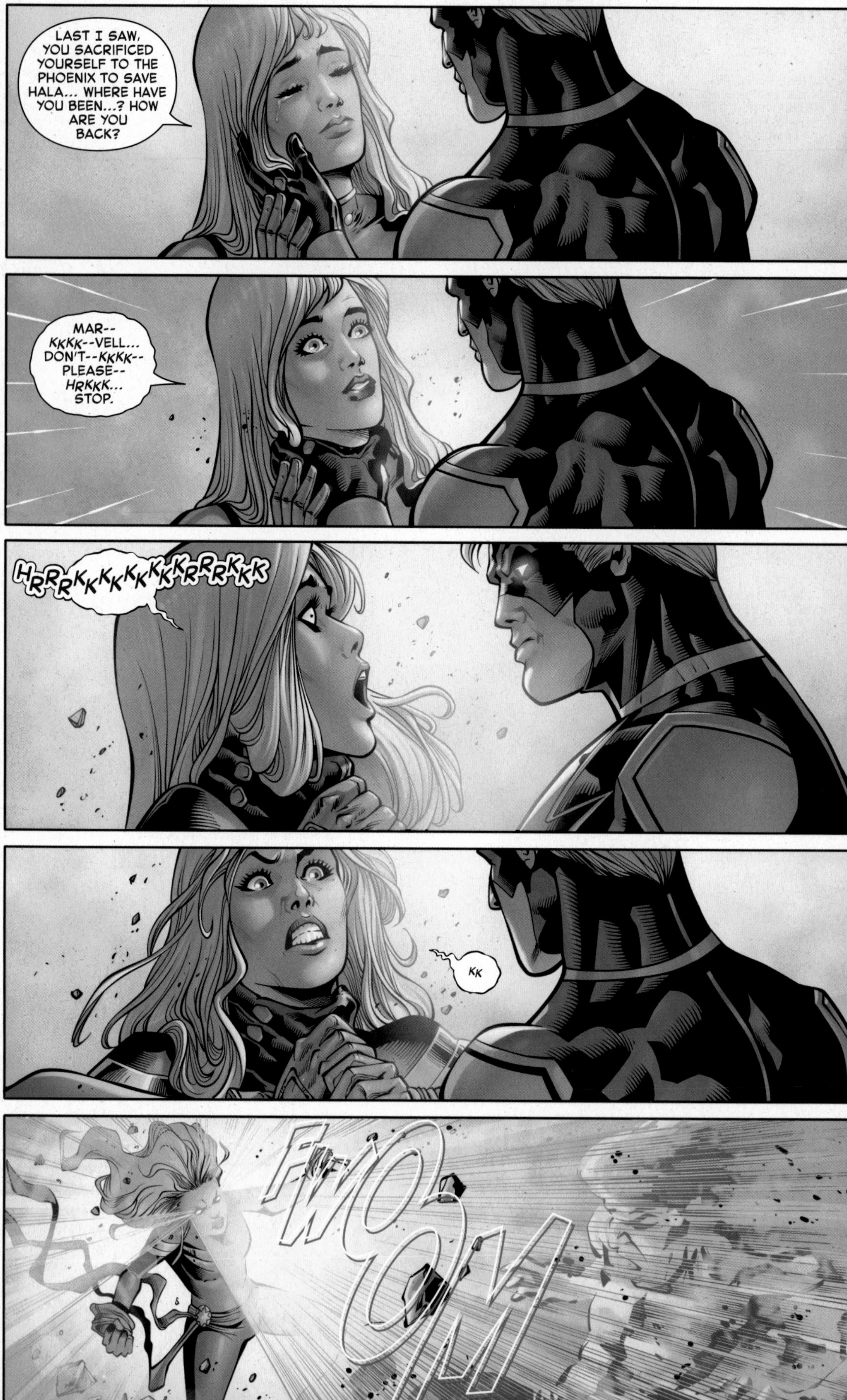
LAST I SAW, YOU SACRIFICED YOURSELF TO THE PHOENIX TO SAVE HALA... WHERE HAVE YOU BEEN...? HOW ARE YOU BACK?
MAR-- KKKK--VELL... DON'T--KKKK-- PLEASE-- HRKKK... STOP.
HRRRKKKKKKKKRRRKKK
KK
FWOOM

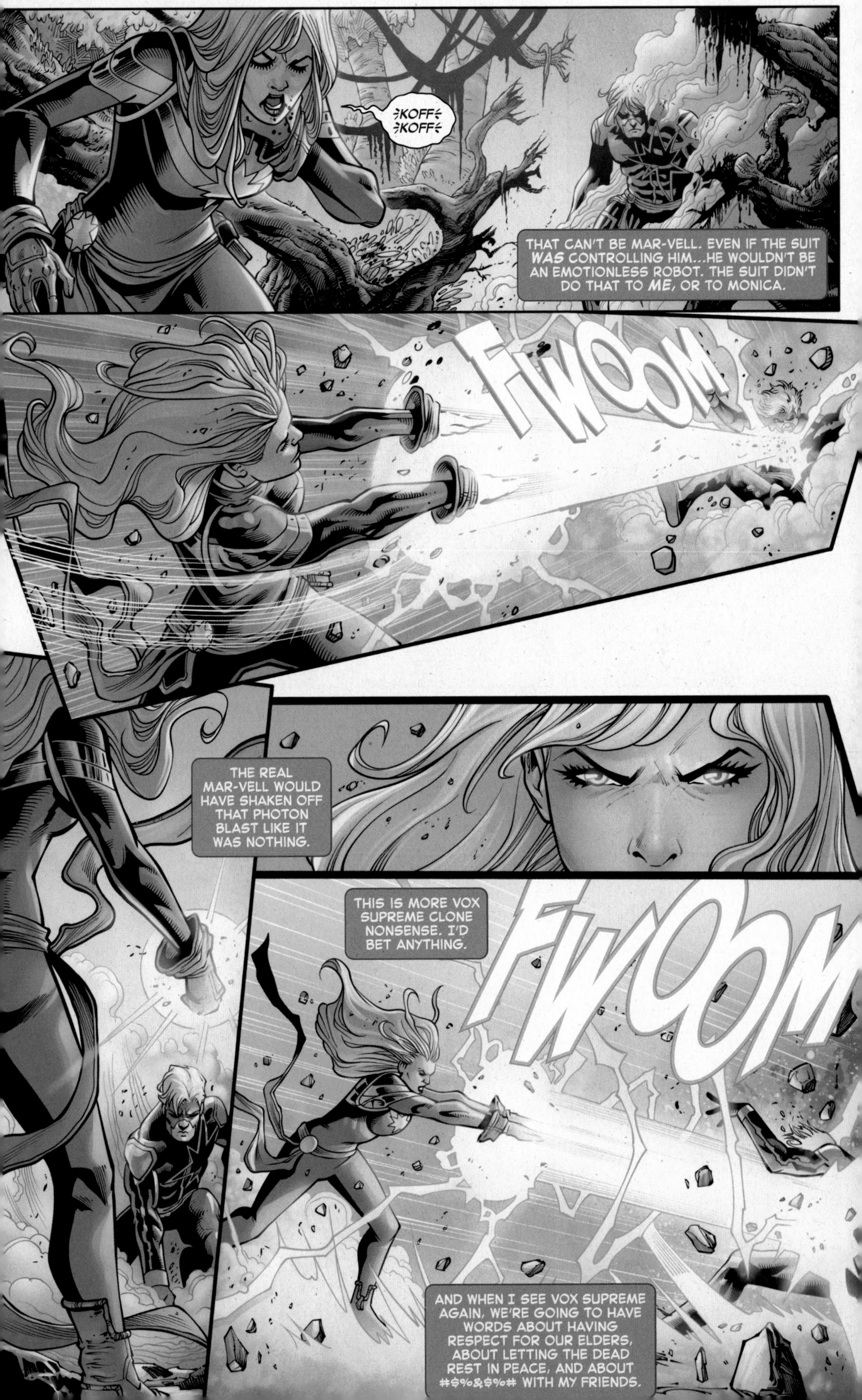

KOFF KOFF
THAT CAN'T BE MAR-VELL. EVEN IF THE SUIT WAS CONTROLLING HIM...HE WOULDN'T BE AN EMOTIONLESS ROBOT. THE SUIT DIDN'T DO THAT TO ME, OR TO MONICA.
FWOOM
THE REAL MAR-VELL WOULD HAVE SHAKEN OFF THAT PHOTON BLAST LIKE IT WAS NOTHING.
THIS IS MORE VOX SUPREME CLONE NONSENSE. I'D BET ANYTHING.
FWOOM
AND WHEN I SEE VOX SUPREME AGAIN, WE'RE GOING TO HAVE WORDS ABOUT HAVING RESPECT FOR OUR ELDERS, ABOUT LETTING THE DEAD REST IN PEACE, AND ABOUT #$%&$%# WITH MY FRIENDS.

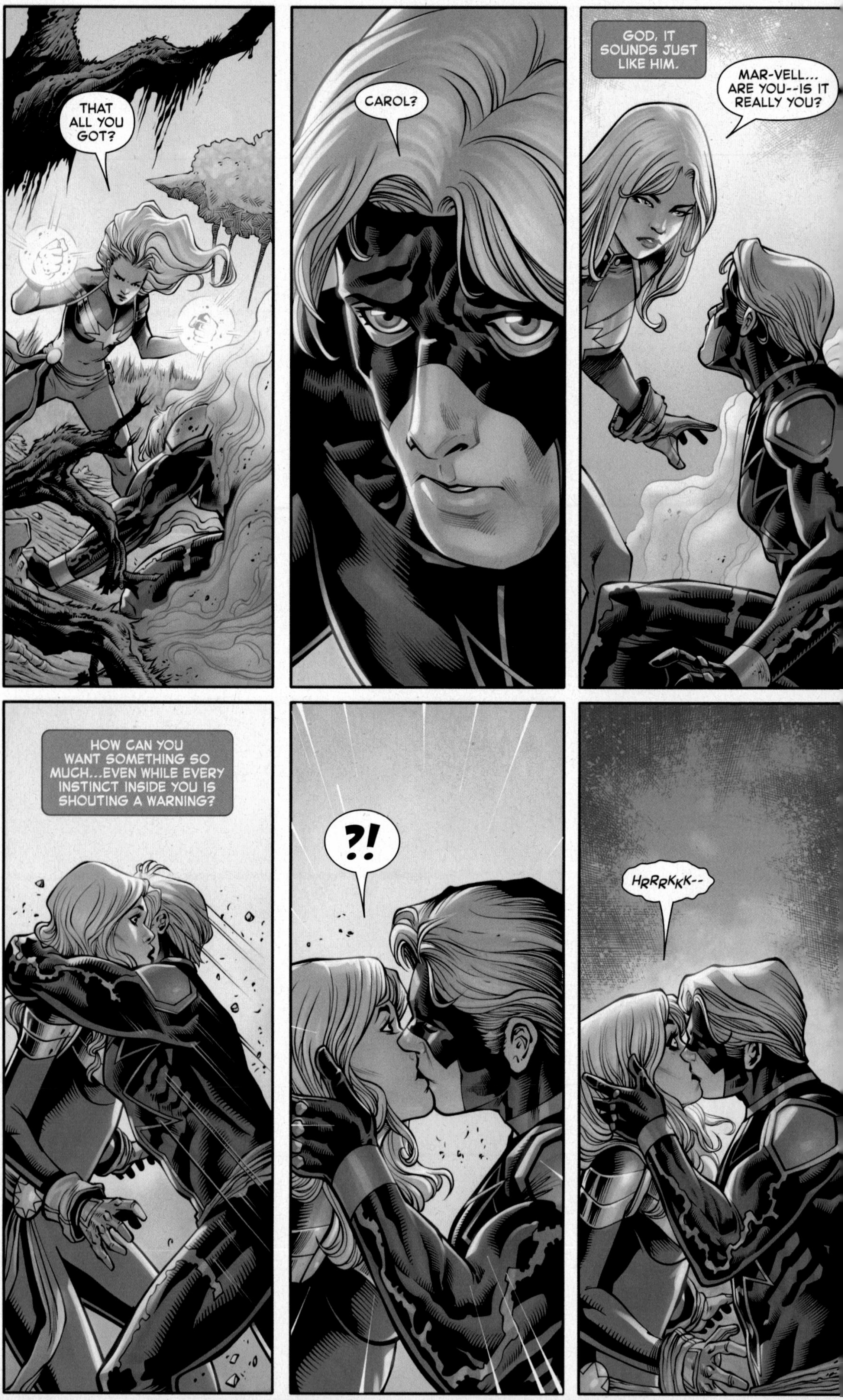
THAT ALL YOU GOT?
CAROL?
GOD, IT SOUNDS JUST LIKE HIM.
MAR-VELL... ARE YOU--IS IT REALLY YOU?
HOW CAN YOU WANT SOMETHING SO MUCH...EVEN WHILE EVERY INSTINCT INSIDE YOU IS SHOUTING A WARNING?
?!
HRRRKKK--

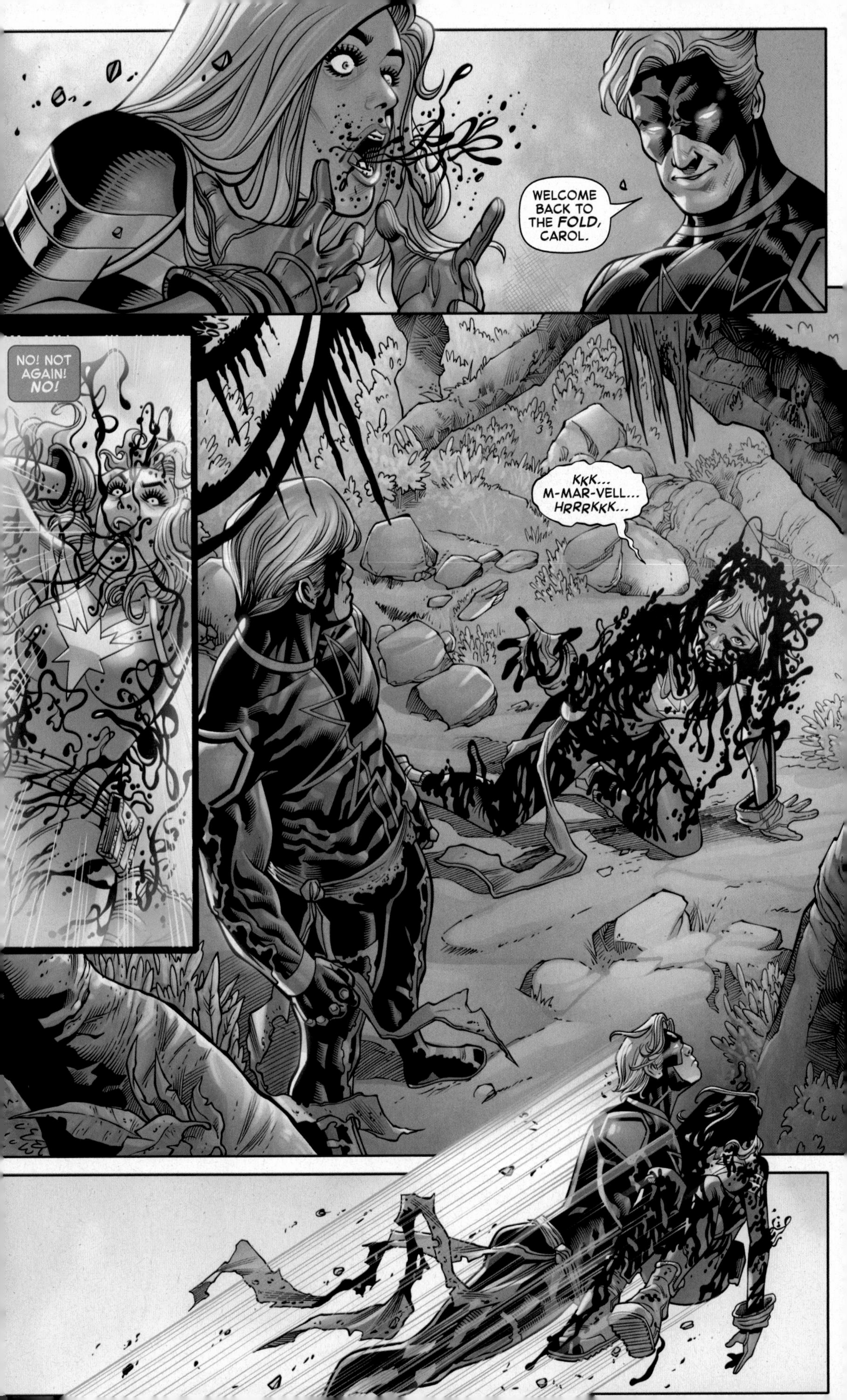
WELCOME BACK TO THE *FOLD*, CAROL.
NO! NOT AGAIN! *NO!*
KKK... M-MAR-VELL... HRRRKKK...

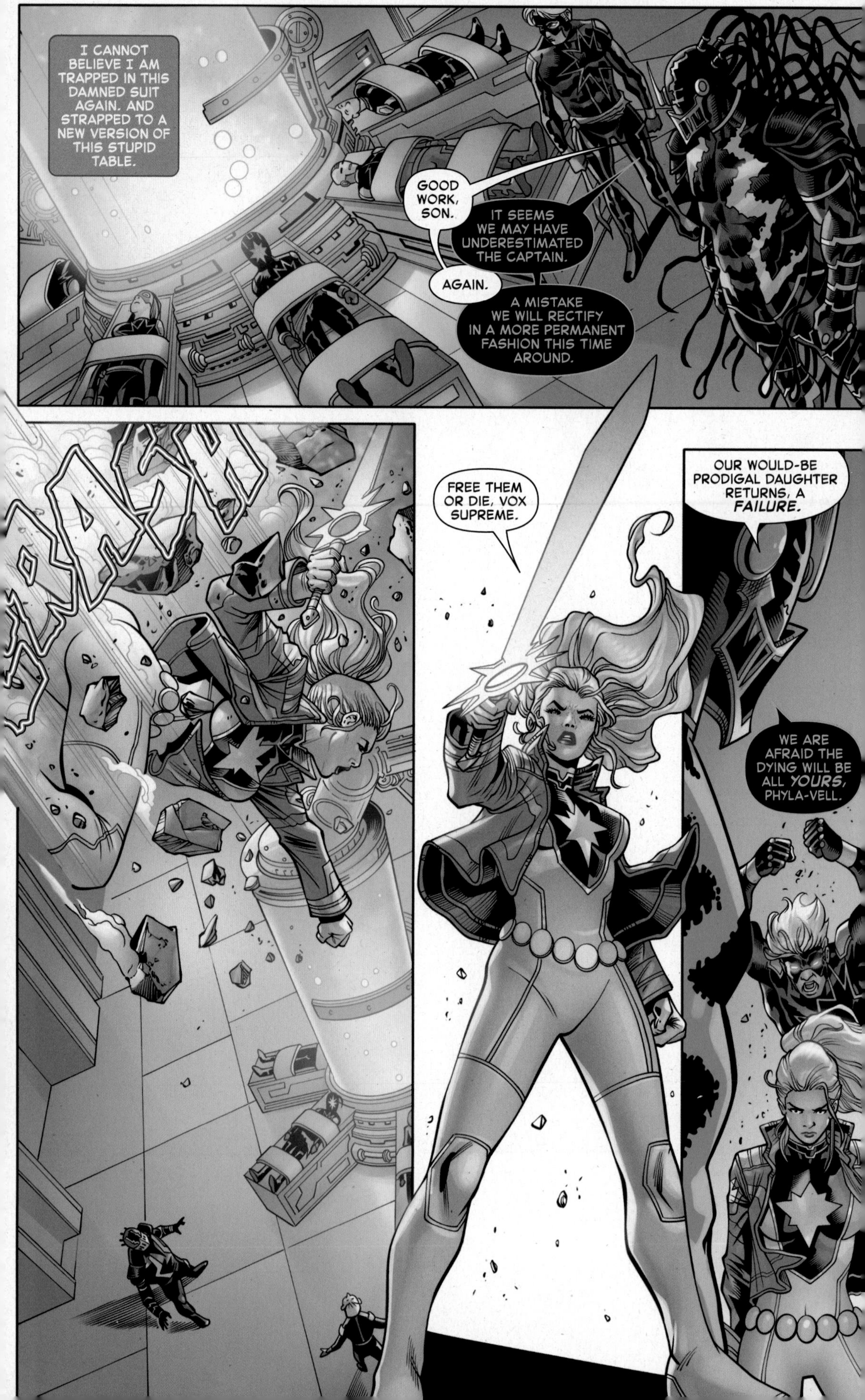
I CANNOT BELIEVE I AM TRAPPED IN THIS DAMNED SUIT AGAIN. AND STRAPPED TO A NEW VERSION OF THIS STUPID TABLE.
GOOD WORK, SON.
IT SEEMS WE MAY HAVE UNDERESTIMATED THE CAPTAIN.
AGAIN.
A MISTAKE WE WILL RECTIFY IN A MORE PERMANENT FASHION THIS TIME AROUND.
FREE THEM OR DIE, VOX SUPREME.
OUR WOULD-BE PRODIGAL DAUGHTER RETURNS, A *FAILURE.*
WE ARE AFRAID THE DYING WILL BE ALL *YOURS,* PHYLA-VELL.

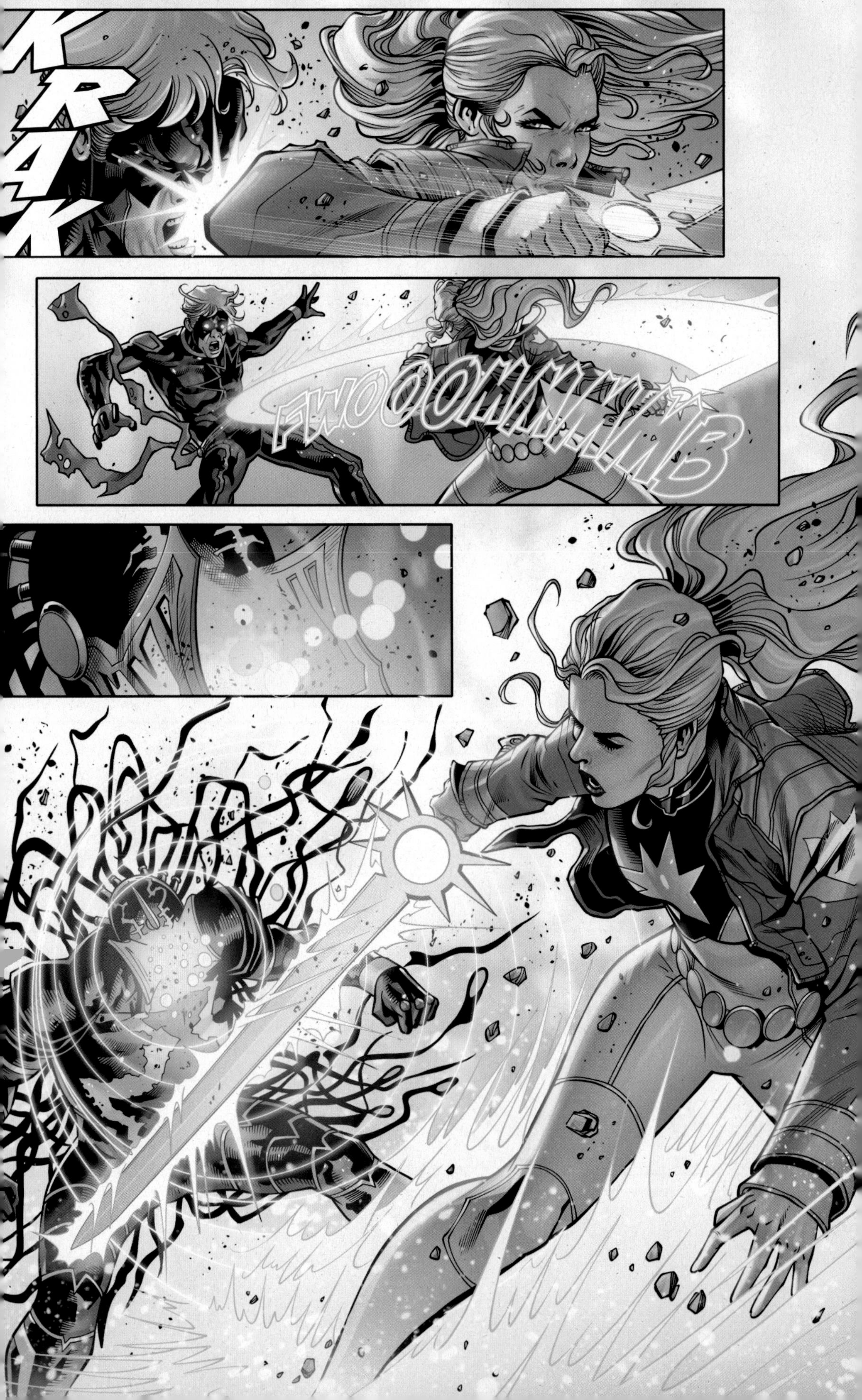
KRAK
FWOOOOMMMMMB

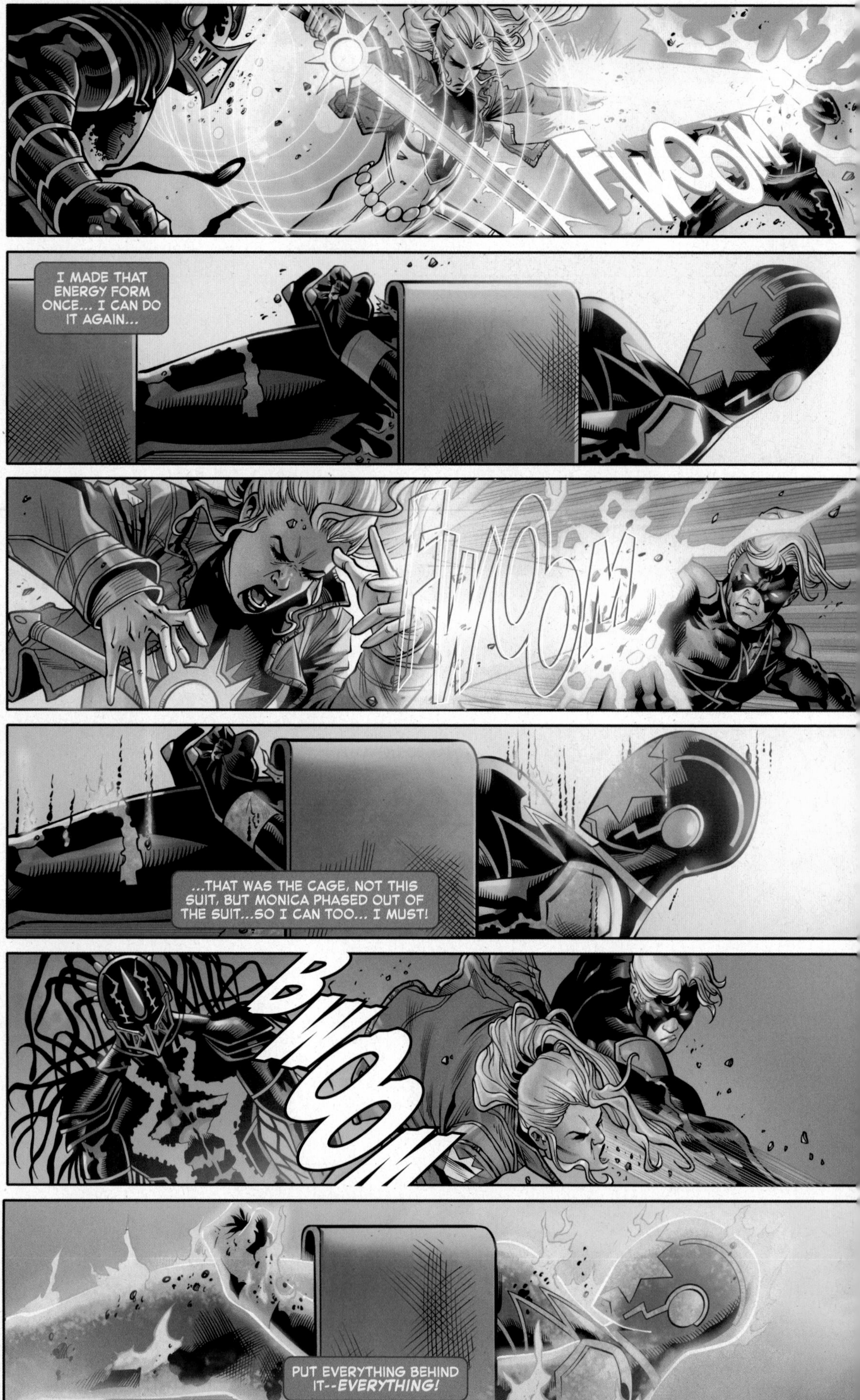
FWOOM
I MADE THAT ENERGY FORM ONCE... I CAN DO IT AGAIN...
FWOOM
...THAT WAS THE CAGE, NOT THIS SUIT, BUT MONICA PHASED OUT OF THE SUIT...SO I CAN TOO... I MUST!
BWOOM
PUT EVERYTHING BEHIND IT--*EVERYTHING!*

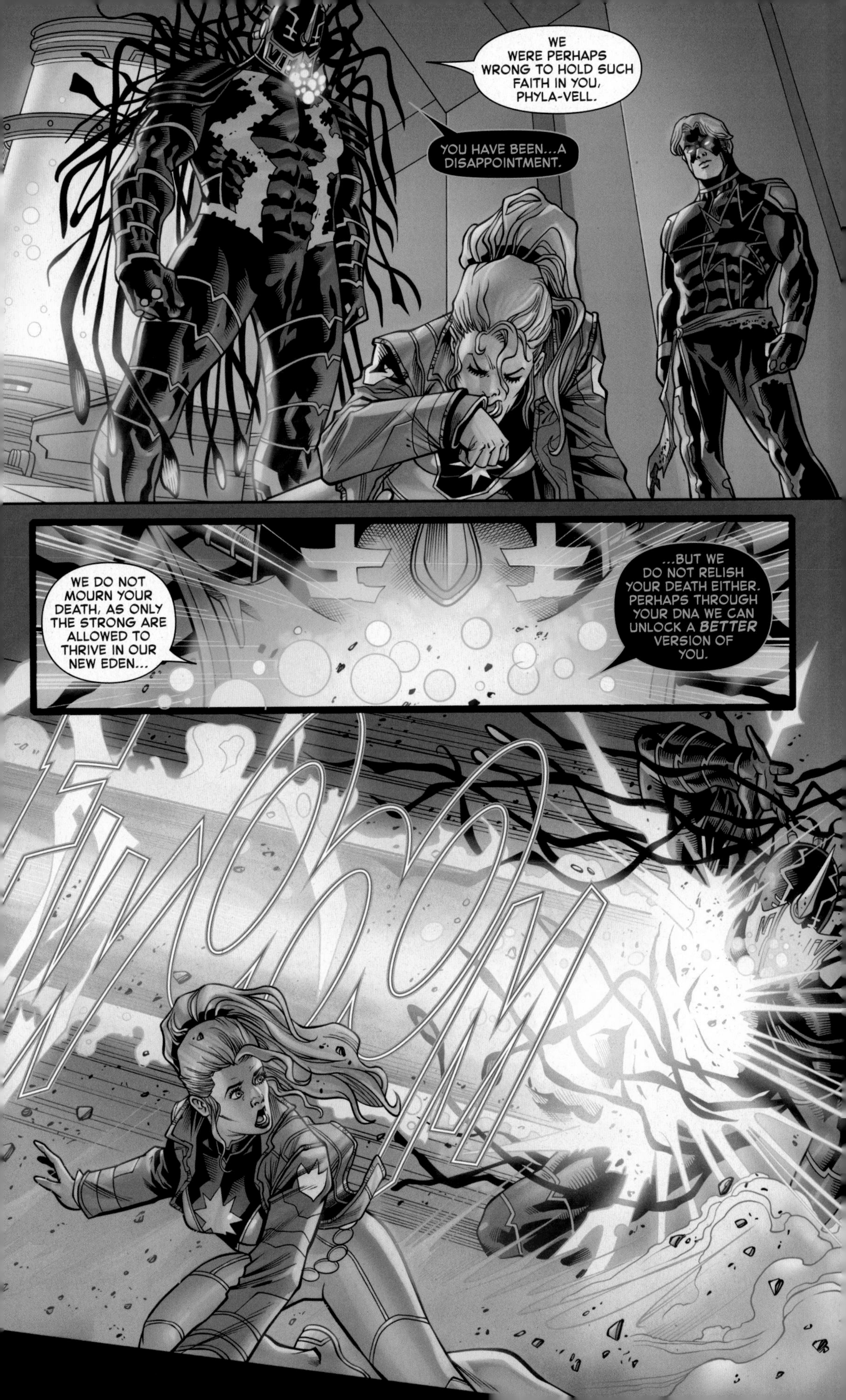
WE WERE PERHAPS WRONG TO HOLD SUCH FAITH IN YOU, PHYLA-VELL.
YOU HAVE BEEN...A DISAPPOINTMENT.
WE DO NOT MOURN YOUR DEATH, AS ONLY THE STRONG ARE ALLOWED TO THRIVE IN OUR NEW EDEN...
...BUT WE DO NOT RELISH YOUR DEATH EITHER. PERHAPS THROUGH YOUR DNA WE CAN UNLOCK A BETTER VERSION OF YOU.

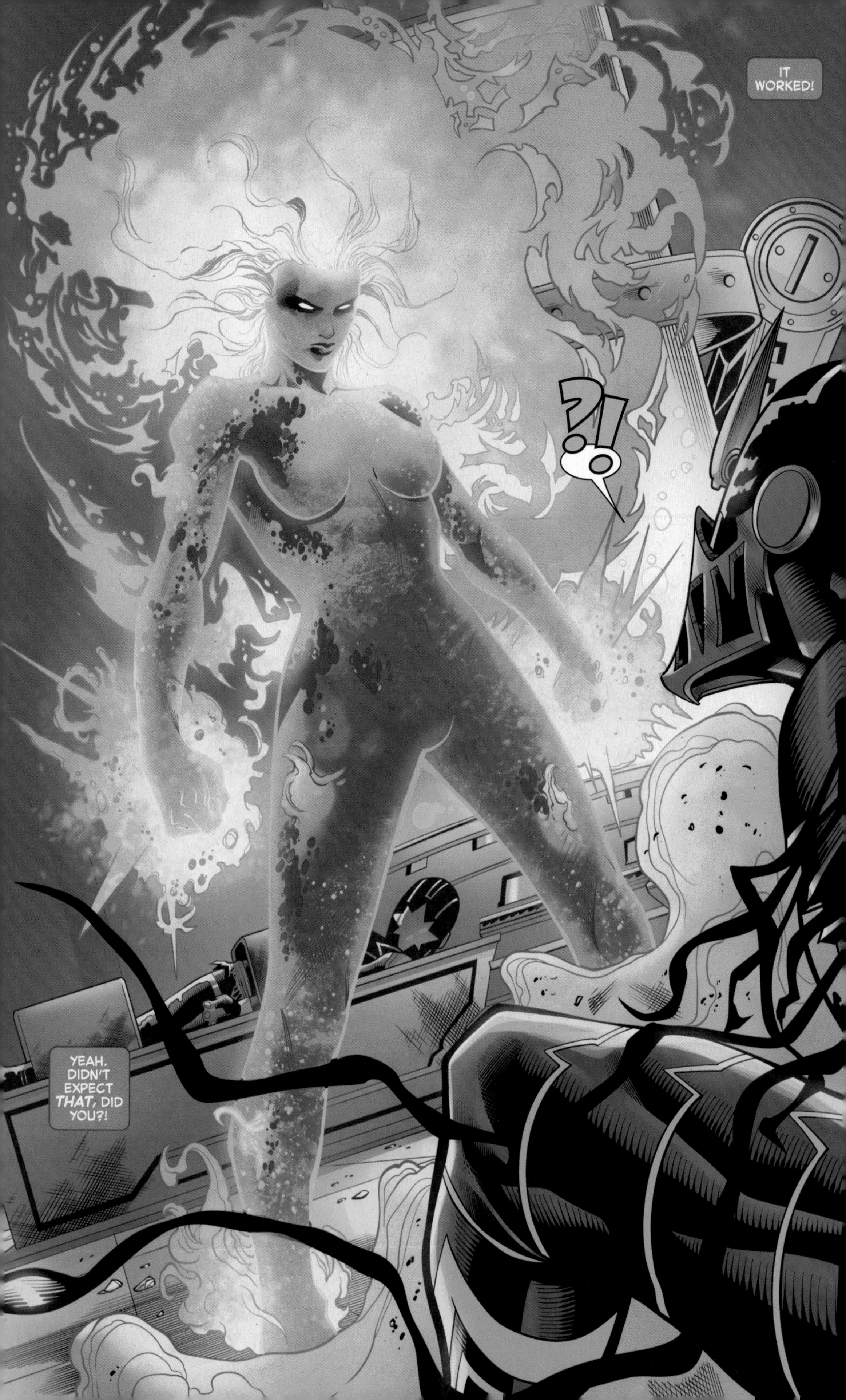
IT WORKED!
?!
YEAH. DIDN'T EXPECT THAT, DID YOU?!

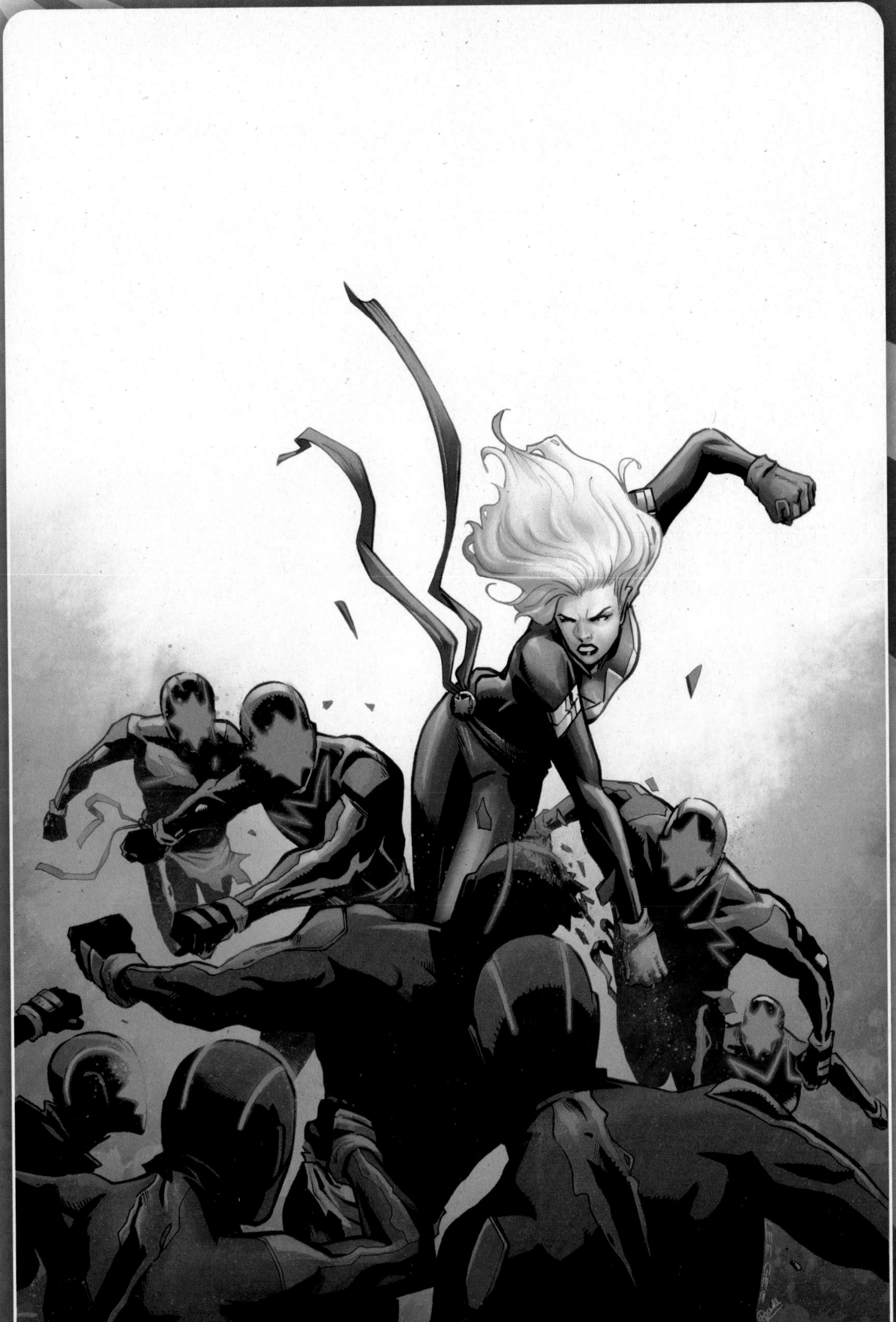

LEE GARBETT & RACHELLE ROSENBERG
#32 VARIANT

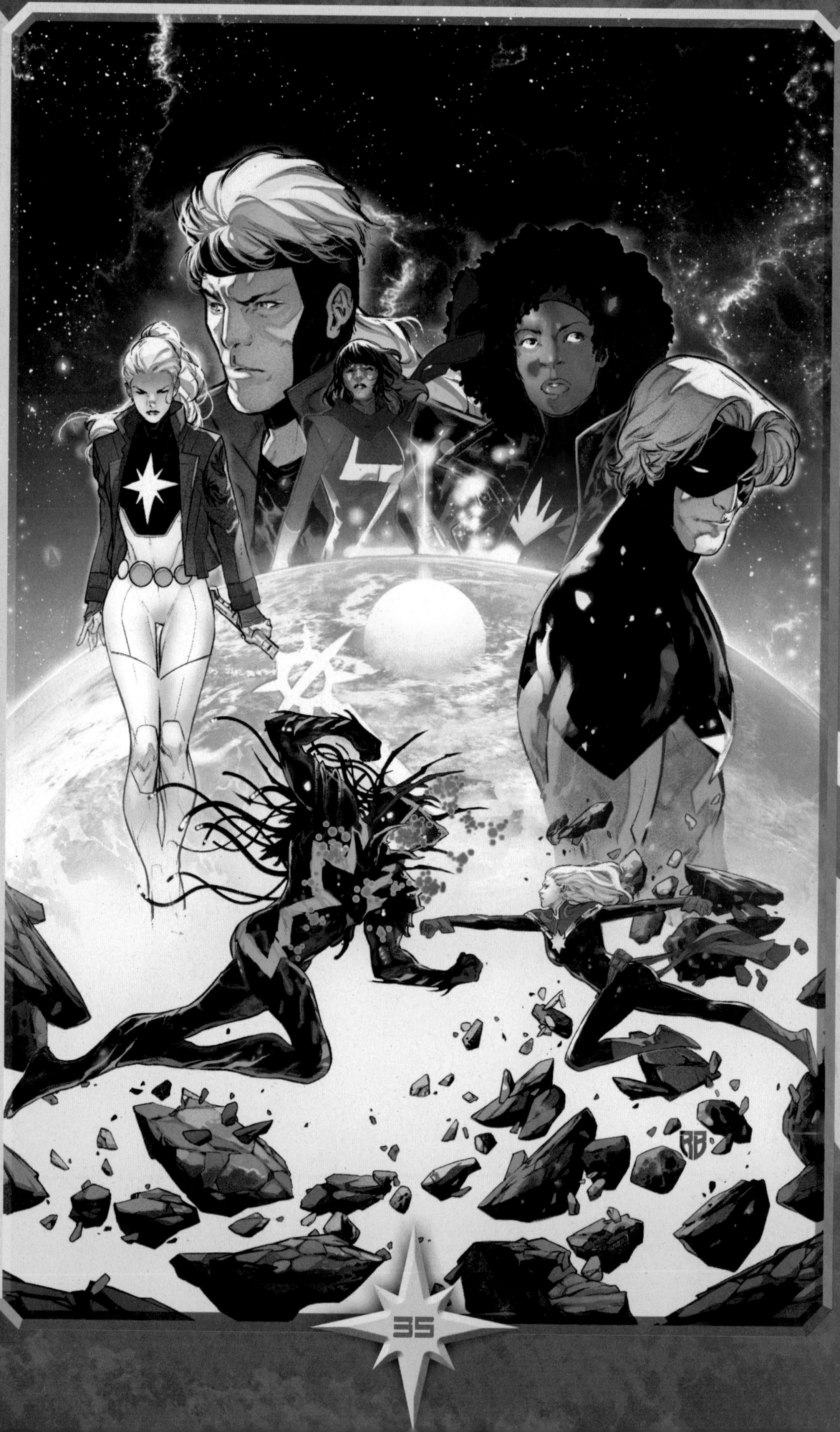
35

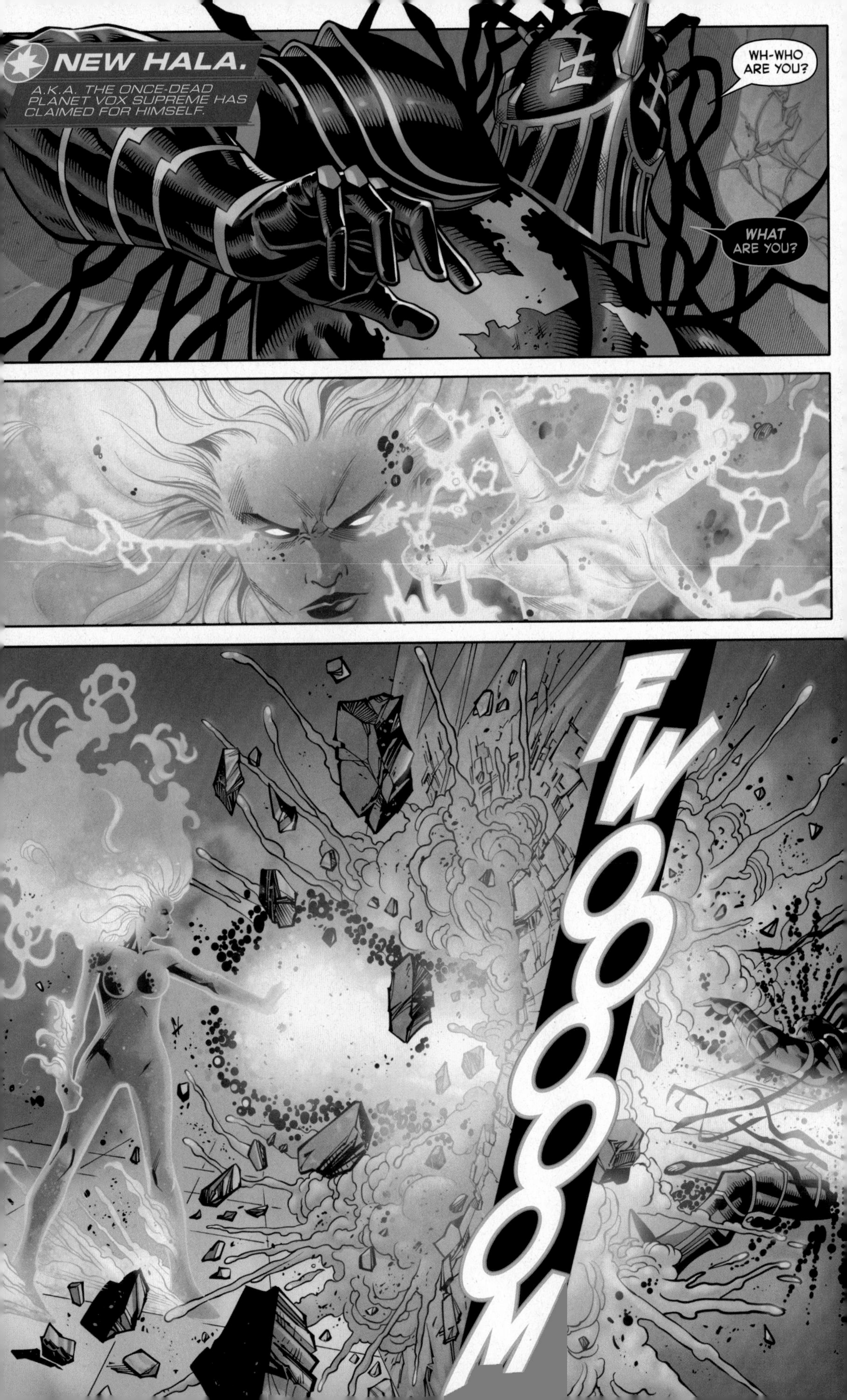
NEW HALA.
A.K.A. THE ONCE-DEAD PLANET VOX SUPREME HAS CLAIMED FOR HIMSELF.
WH-WHO ARE YOU?
WHAT ARE YOU?
FWOOOOOM

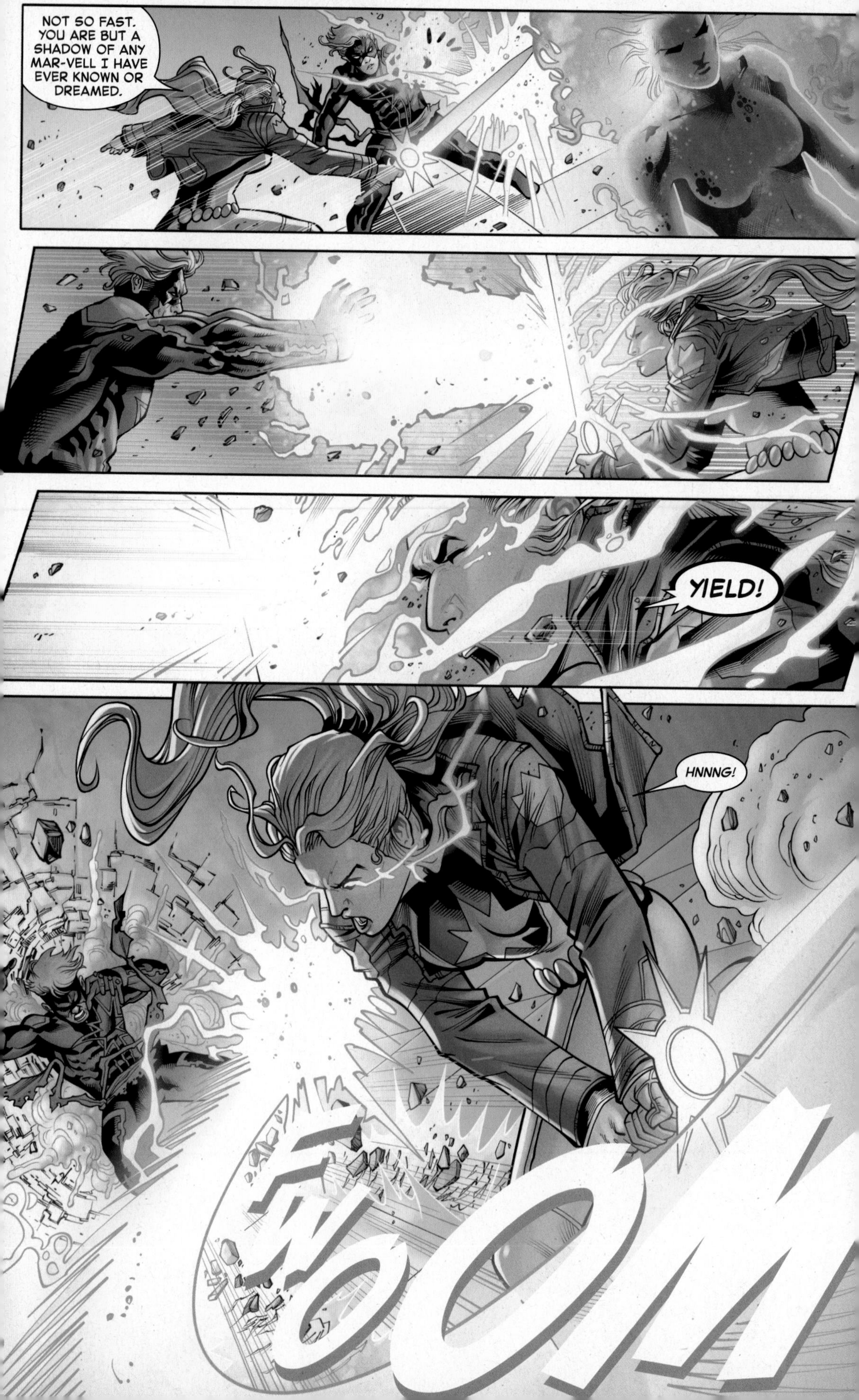
NOT SO FAST. YOU ARE BUT A SHADOW OF ANY MAR-VELL I HAVE EVER KNOWN OR DREAMED.
YIELD!
HNNNG!

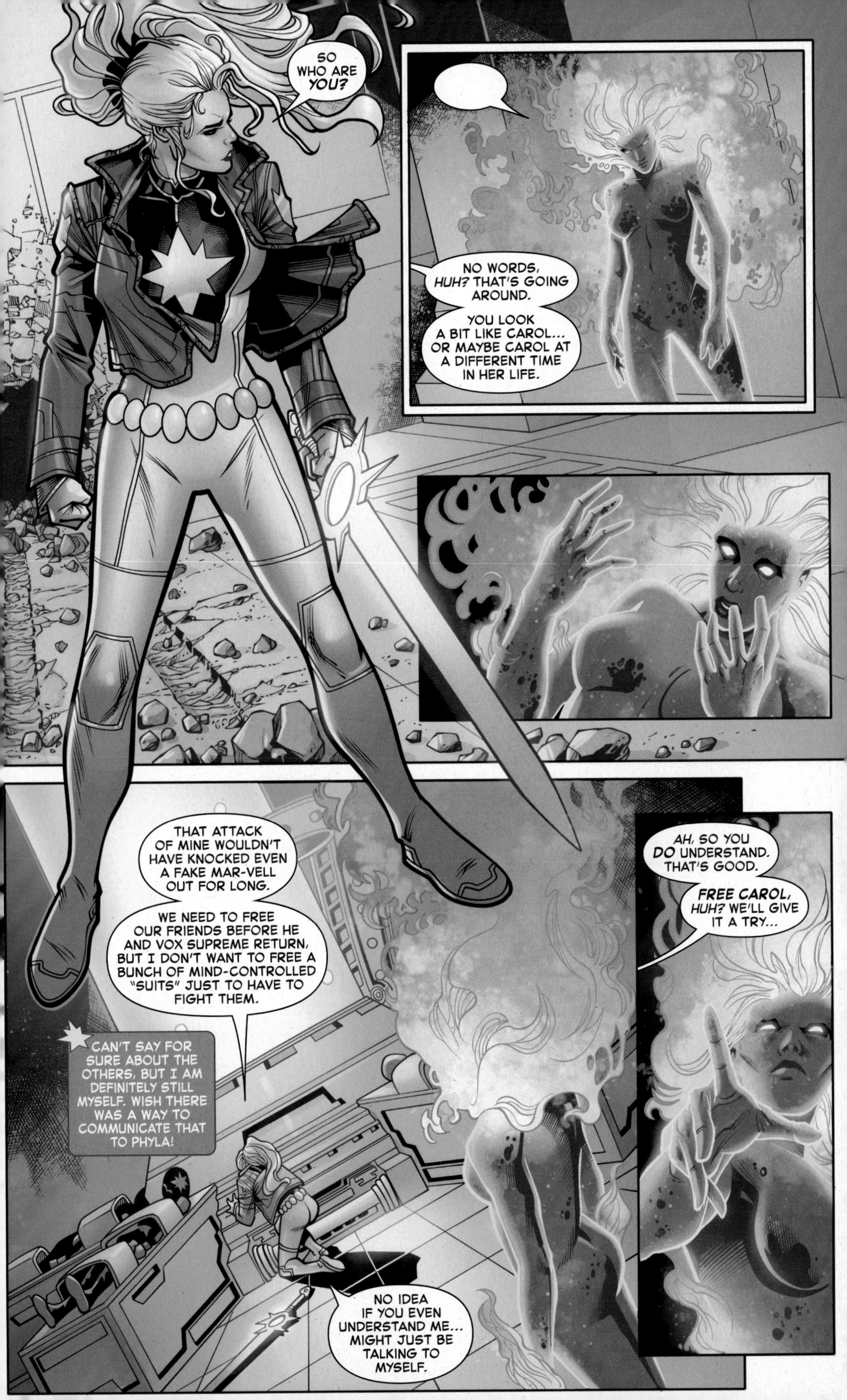
SO WHO ARE YOU?
NO WORDS, HUH? THAT'S GOING AROUND.
YOU LOOK A BIT LIKE CAROL... OR MAYBE CAROL AT A DIFFERENT TIME IN HER LIFE.
THAT ATTACK OF MINE WOULDN'T HAVE KNOCKED EVEN A FAKE MAR-VELL OUT FOR LONG.
WE NEED TO FREE OUR FRIENDS BEFORE HE AND VOX SUPREME RETURN, BUT I DON'T WANT TO FREE A BUNCH OF MIND-CONTROLLED "SUITS" JUST TO HAVE TO FIGHT THEM.
CAN'T SAY FOR SURE ABOUT THE OTHERS, BUT I AM DEFINITELY STILL MYSELF. WISH THERE WAS A WAY TO COMMUNICATE THAT TO PHYLA!
NO IDEA IF YOU EVEN UNDERSTAND ME... MIGHT JUST BE TALKING TO MYSELF.
AH, SO YOU DO UNDERSTAND. THAT'S GOOD.
FREE CAROL, HUH? WE'LL GIVE IT A TRY...

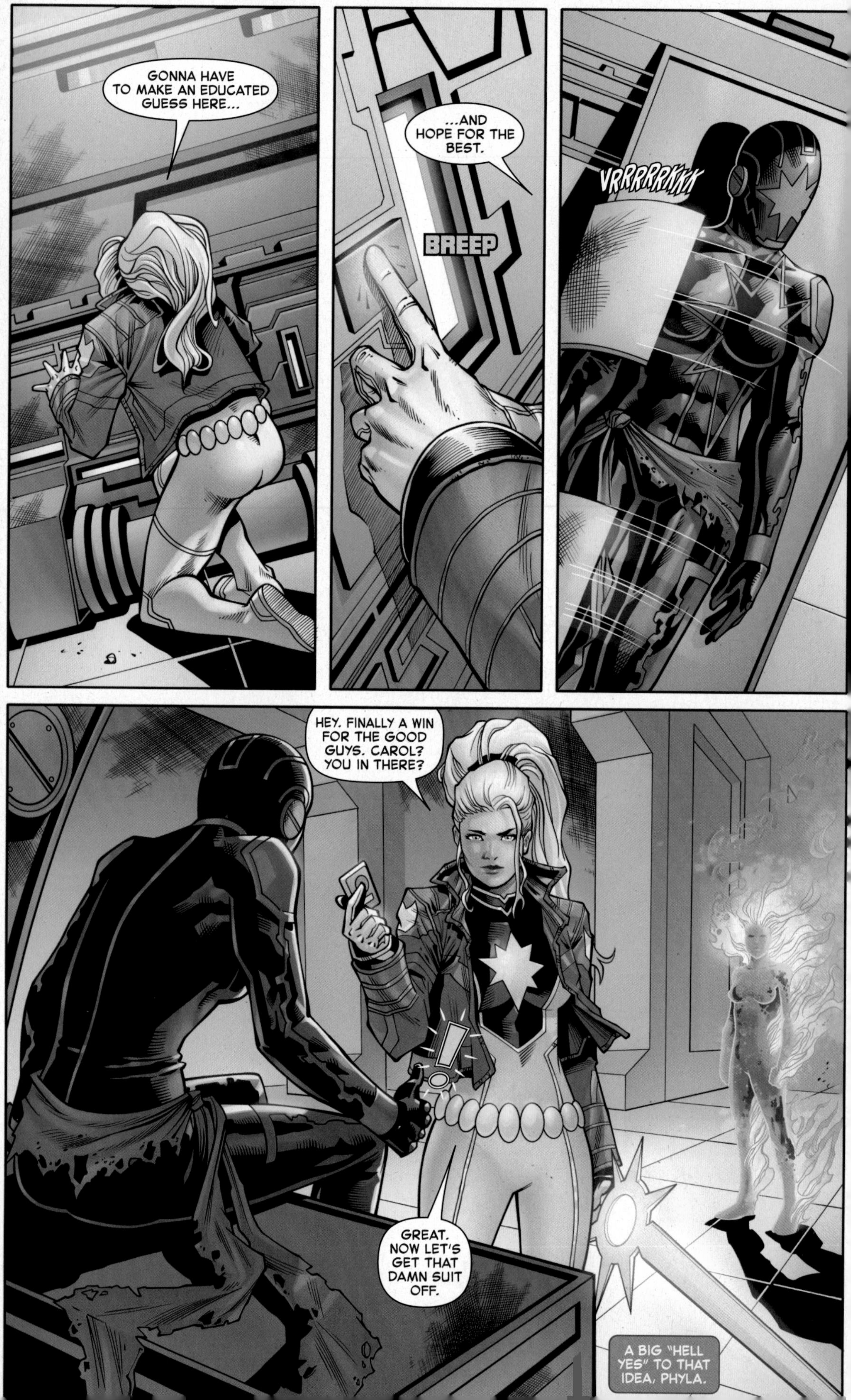
GONNA HAVE TO MAKE AN EDUCATED GUESS HERE...
...AND HOPE FOR THE BEST.
BREEP
VRRRRRKKK
HEY. FINALLY A WIN FOR THE GOOD GUYS. CAROL? YOU IN THERE?
GREAT. NOW LET'S GET THAT DAMN SUIT OFF.
A BIG "HELL YES" TO THAT IDEA, PHYLA.

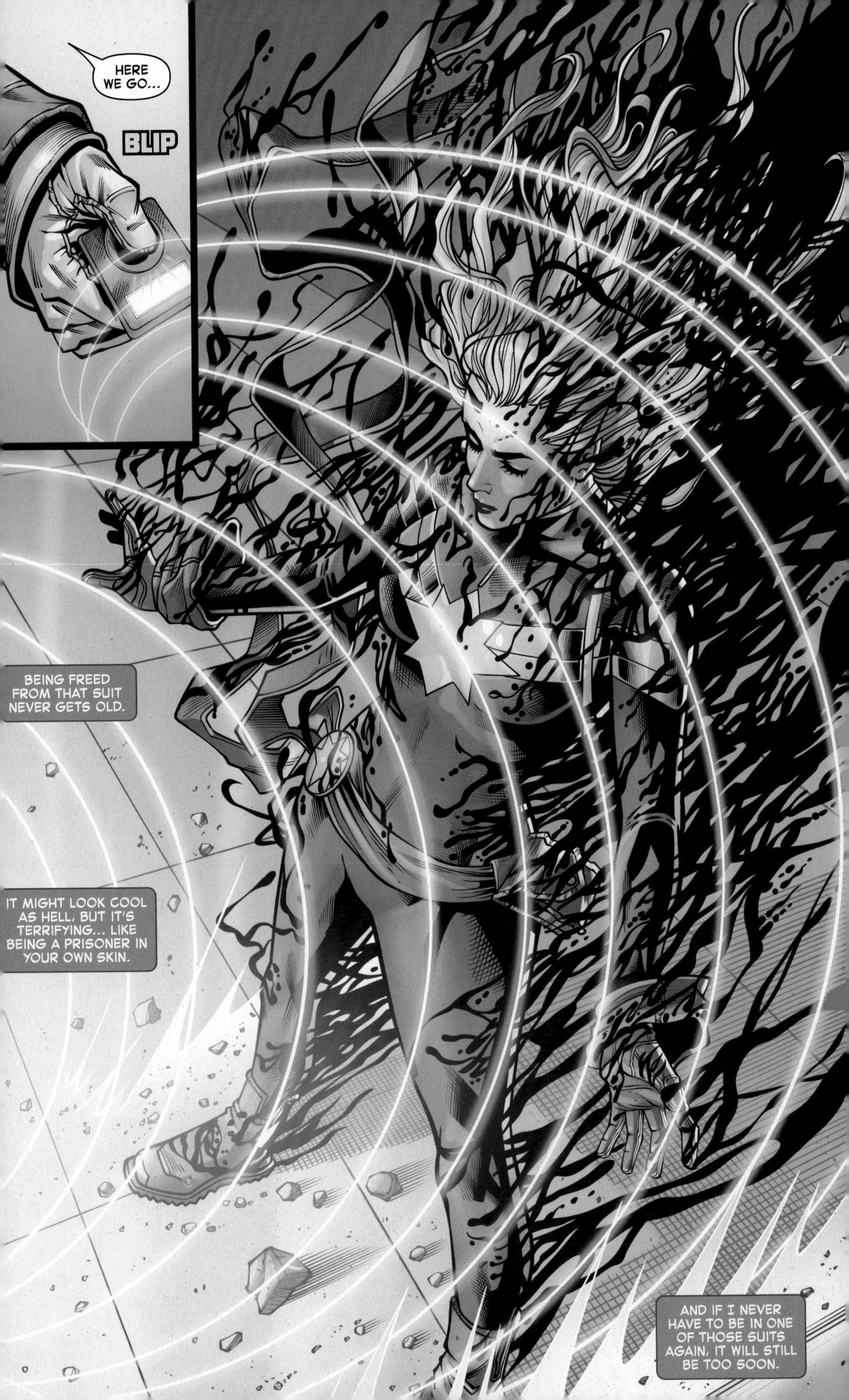
HERE WE GO...
BLIP
BEING FREED FROM THAT SUIT NEVER GETS OLD.
IT MIGHT LOOK COOL AS HELL, BUT IT'S TERRIFYING... LIKE BEING A PRISONER IN YOUR OWN SKIN.
AND IF I NEVER HAVE TO BE IN ONE OF THOSE SUITS AGAIN, IT WILL STILL BE TOO SOON.

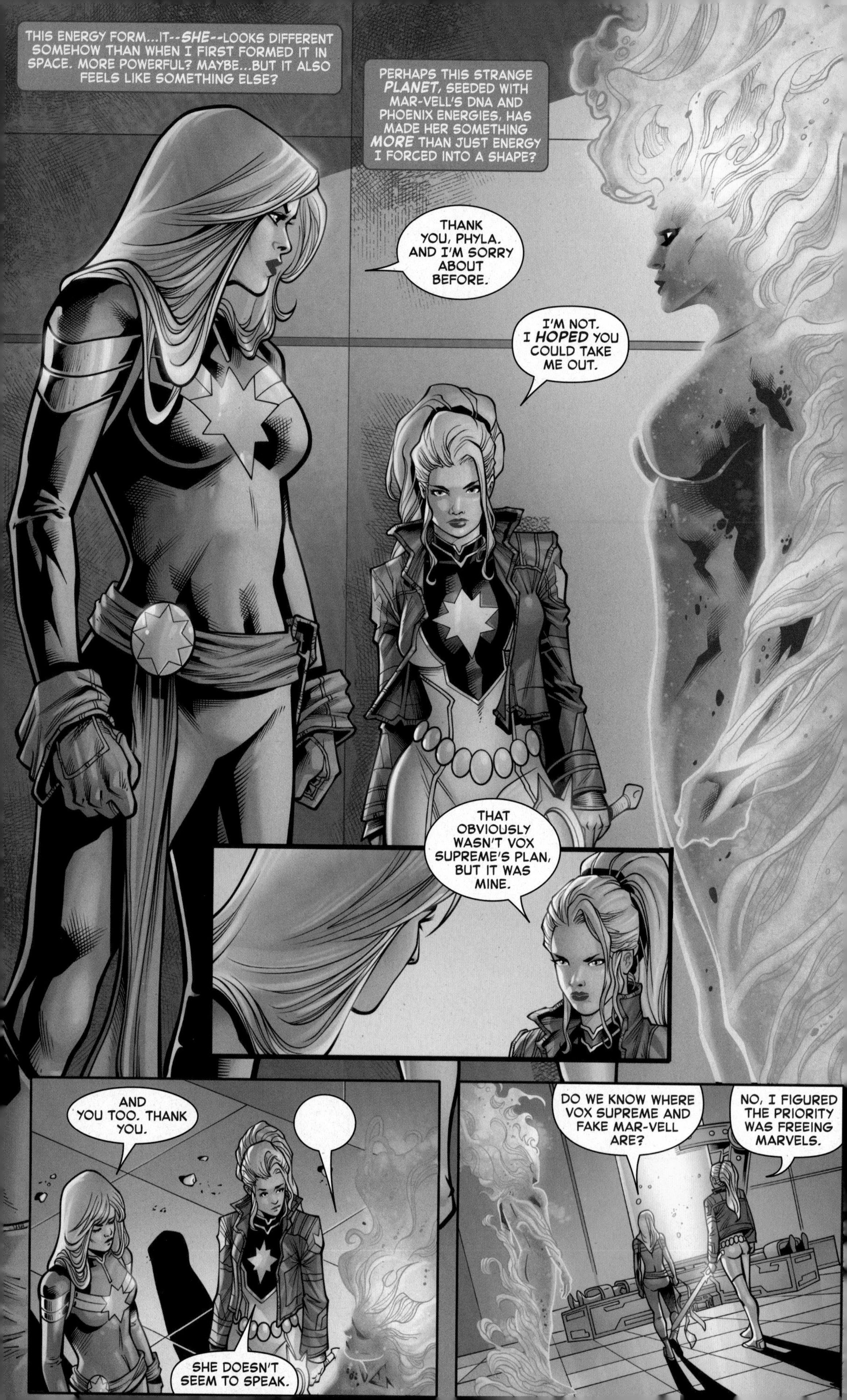
THIS ENERGY FORM...IT--SHE--LOOKS DIFFERENT SOMEHOW THAN WHEN I FIRST FORMED IT IN SPACE. MORE POWERFUL? MAYBE...BUT IT ALSO FEELS LIKE SOMETHING ELSE?
PERHAPS THIS STRANGE PLANET, SEEDED WITH MAR-VELL'S DNA AND PHOENIX ENERGIES, HAS MADE HER SOMETHING MORE THAN JUST ENERGY I FORCED INTO A SHAPE?
THANK YOU, PHYLA. AND I'M SORRY ABOUT BEFORE.
I'M NOT. I HOPED YOU COULD TAKE ME OUT.
THAT OBVIOUSLY WASN'T VOX SUPREME'S PLAN, BUT IT WAS MINE.
AND YOU TOO. THANK YOU.
SHE DOESN'T SEEM TO SPEAK.
DO WE KNOW WHERE VOX SUPREME AND FAKE MAR-VELL ARE?
NO, I FIGURED THE PRIORITY WAS FREEING MARVELS.

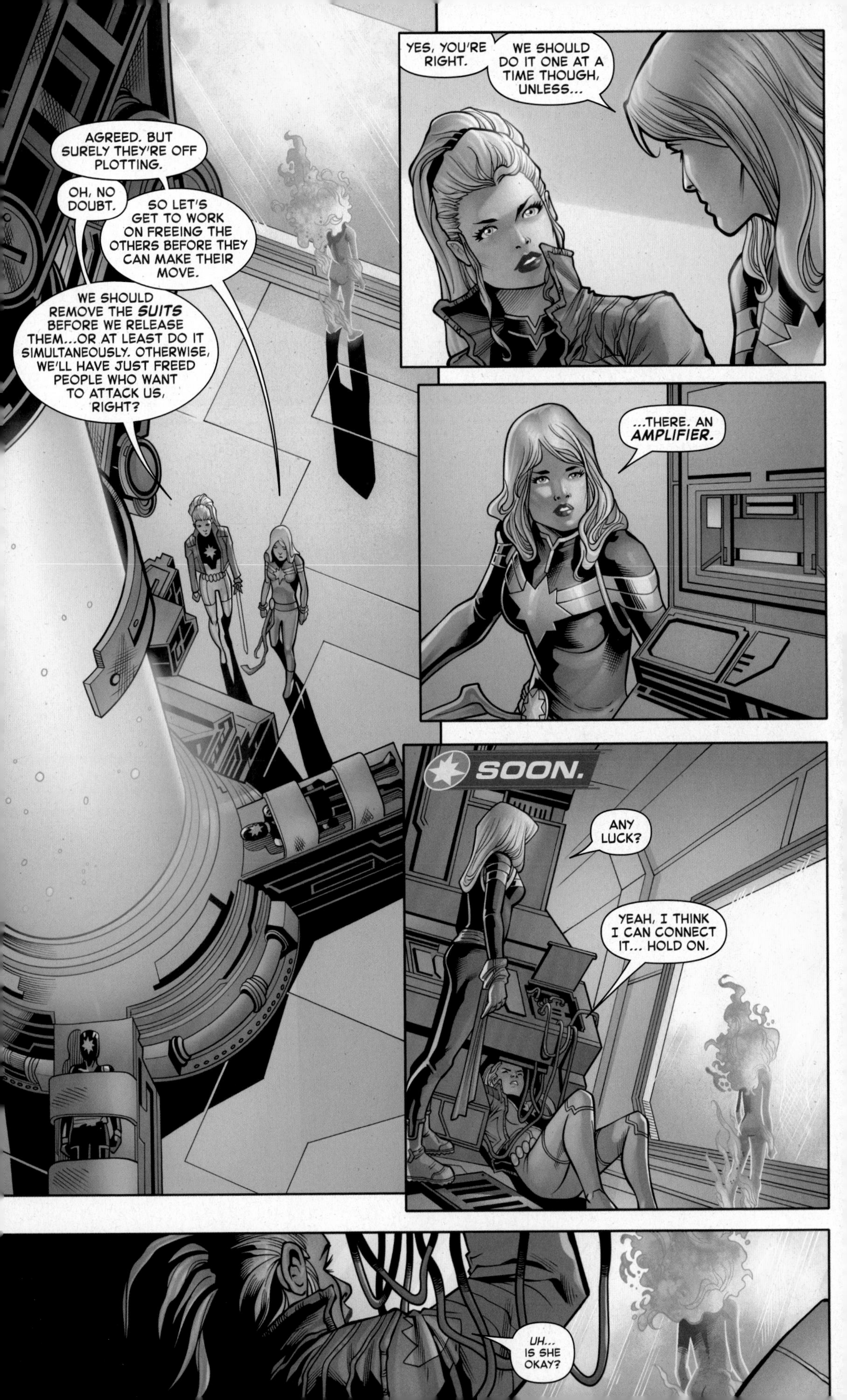
AGREED. BUT SURELY THEY'RE OFF PLOTTING.
OH, NO DOUBT.
SO LET'S GET TO WORK ON FREEING THE OTHERS BEFORE THEY CAN MAKE THEIR MOVE.
WE SHOULD REMOVE THE SUITS BEFORE WE RELEASE THEM...OR AT LEAST DO IT SIMULTANEOUSLY. OTHERWISE, WE'LL HAVE JUST FREED PEOPLE WHO WANT TO ATTACK US, RIGHT?
YES, YOU'RE RIGHT.
WE SHOULD DO IT ONE AT A TIME THOUGH, UNLESS...
...THERE. AN AMPLIFIER.
SOON.
ANY LUCK?
YEAH, I THINK I CAN CONNECT IT... HOLD ON.
UH... IS SHE OKAY?

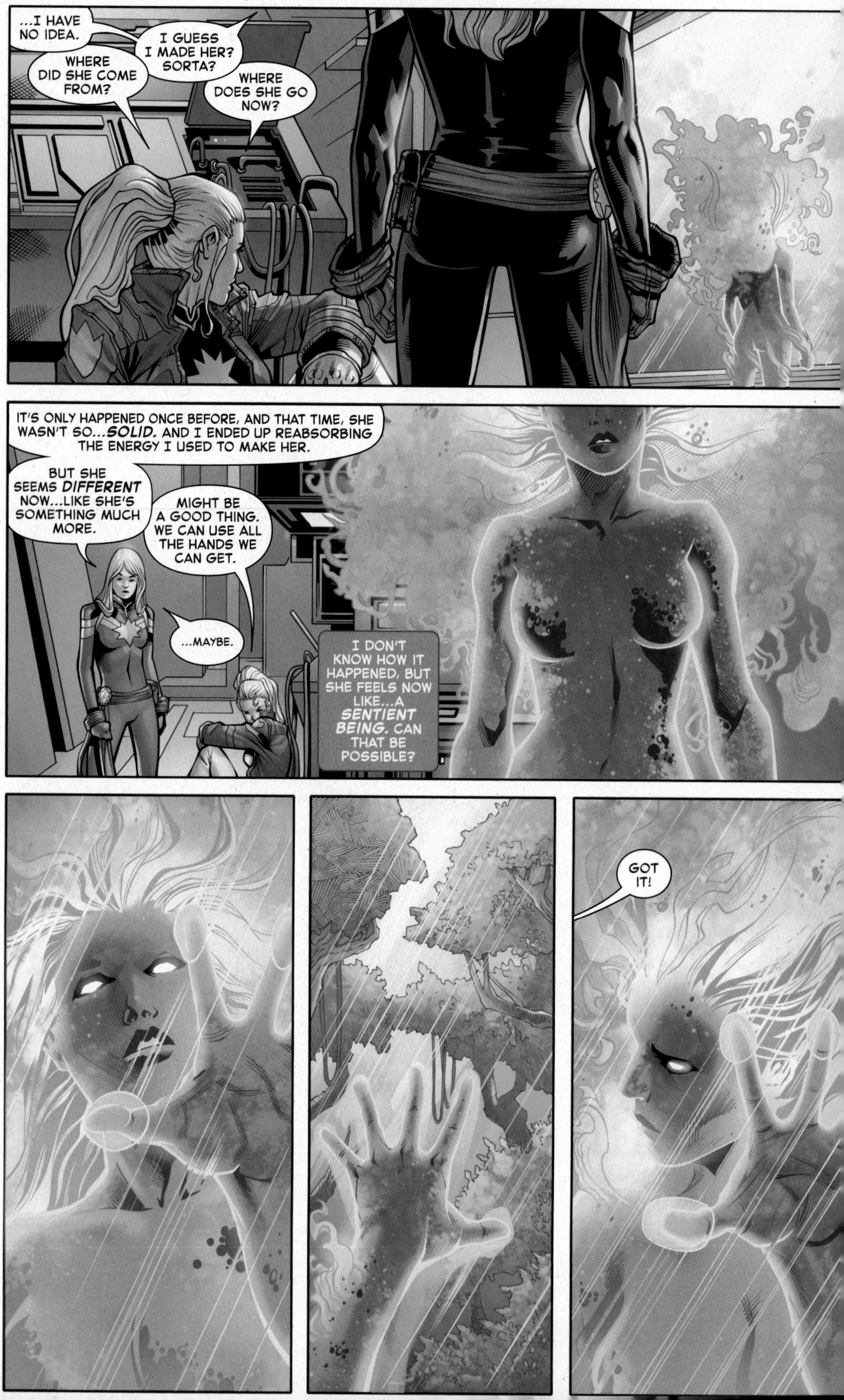
...I HAVE NO IDEA.
WHERE DID SHE COME FROM?
I GUESS I MADE HER? SORTA?
WHERE DOES SHE GO NOW?
IT'S ONLY HAPPENED ONCE BEFORE, AND THAT TIME, SHE WASN'T SO...SOLID. AND I ENDED UP REABSORBING THE ENERGY I USED TO MAKE HER.
BUT SHE SEEMS DIFFERENT NOW...LIKE SHE'S SOMETHING MUCH MORE.
MIGHT BE A GOOD THING. WE CAN USE ALL THE HANDS WE CAN GET.
...MAYBE.
I DON'T KNOW HOW IT HAPPENED, BUT SHE FEELS NOW LIKE...A SENTIENT BEING. CAN THAT BE POSSIBLE?
GOT IT!

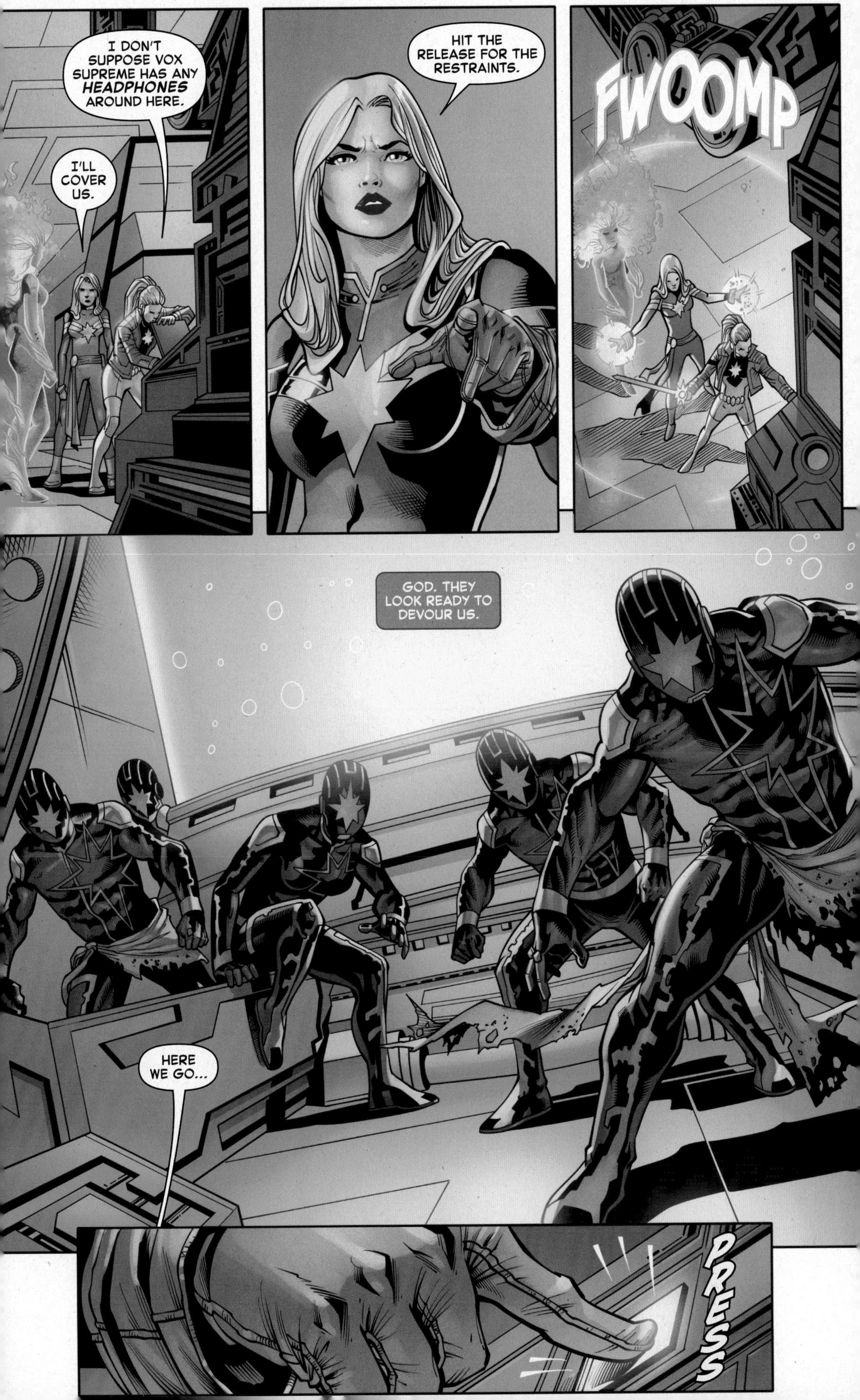

I DON'T SUPPOSE VOX SUPREME HAS ANY *HEADPHONES* AROUND HERE.
I'LL COVER US.
HIT THE RELEASE FOR THE RESTRAINTS.
FWOOMP
GOD. THEY LOOK READY TO DEVOUR US.
HERE WE GO...
PRESS

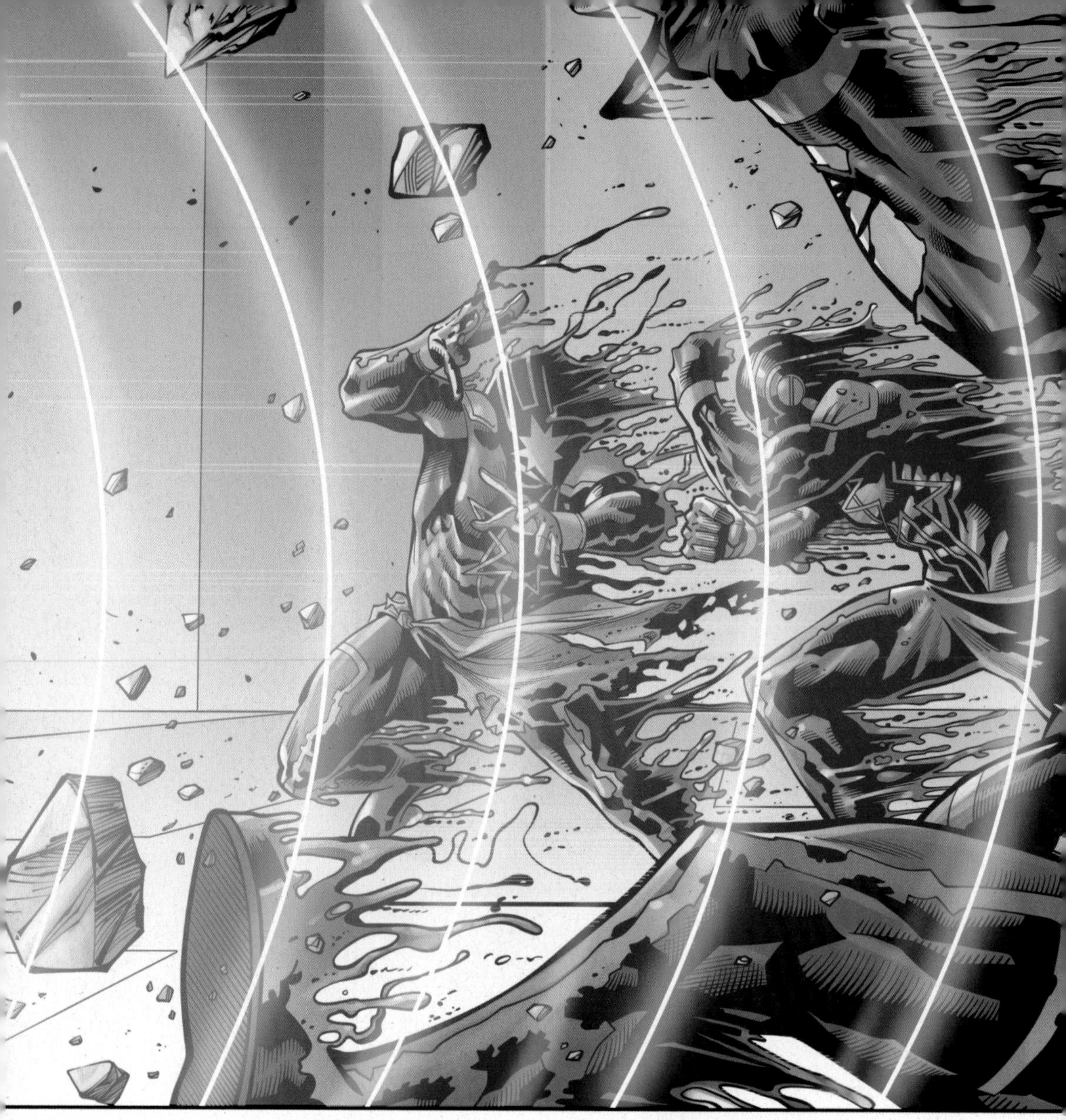

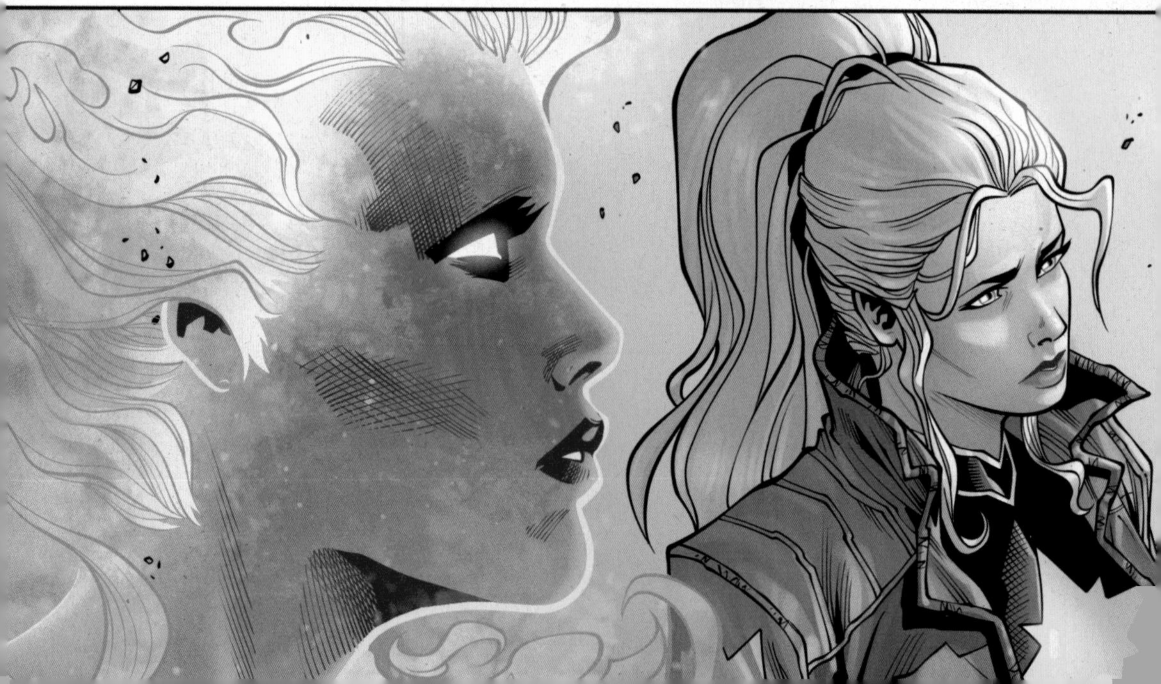

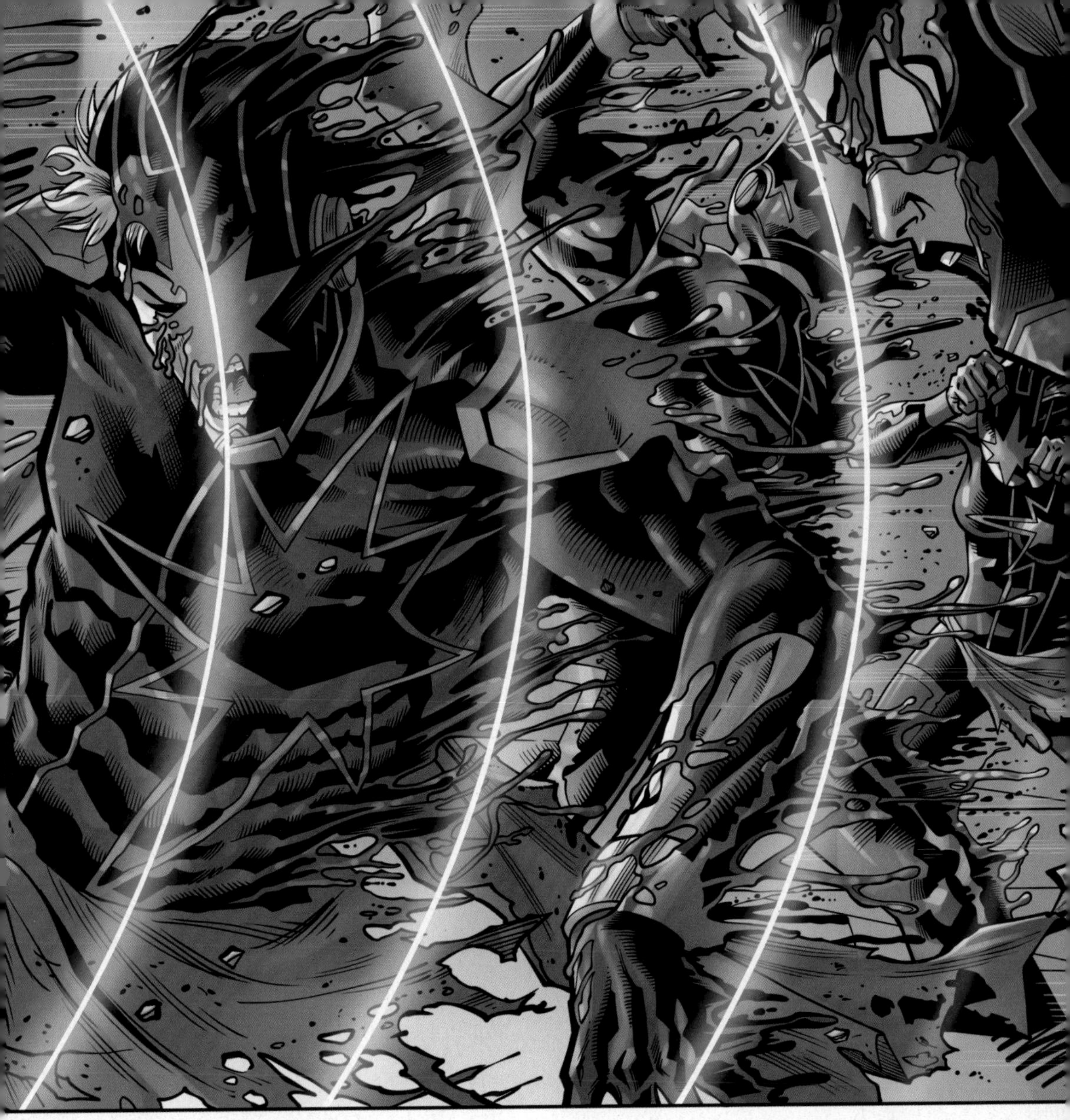

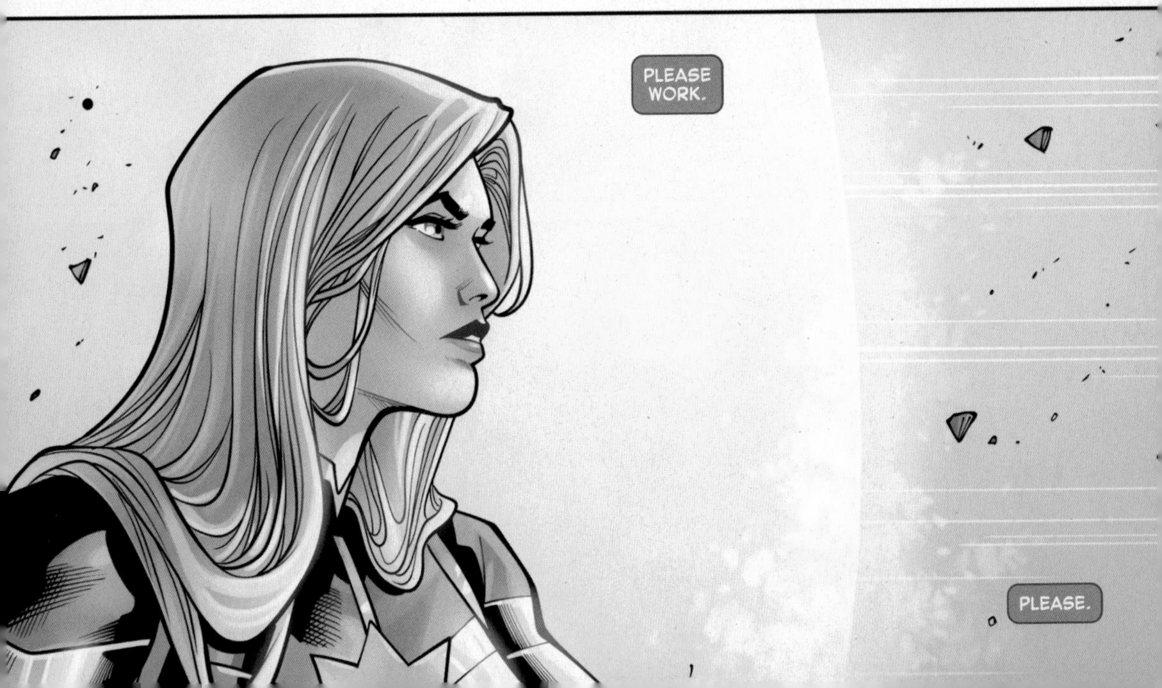
PLEASE WORK.
PLEASE.

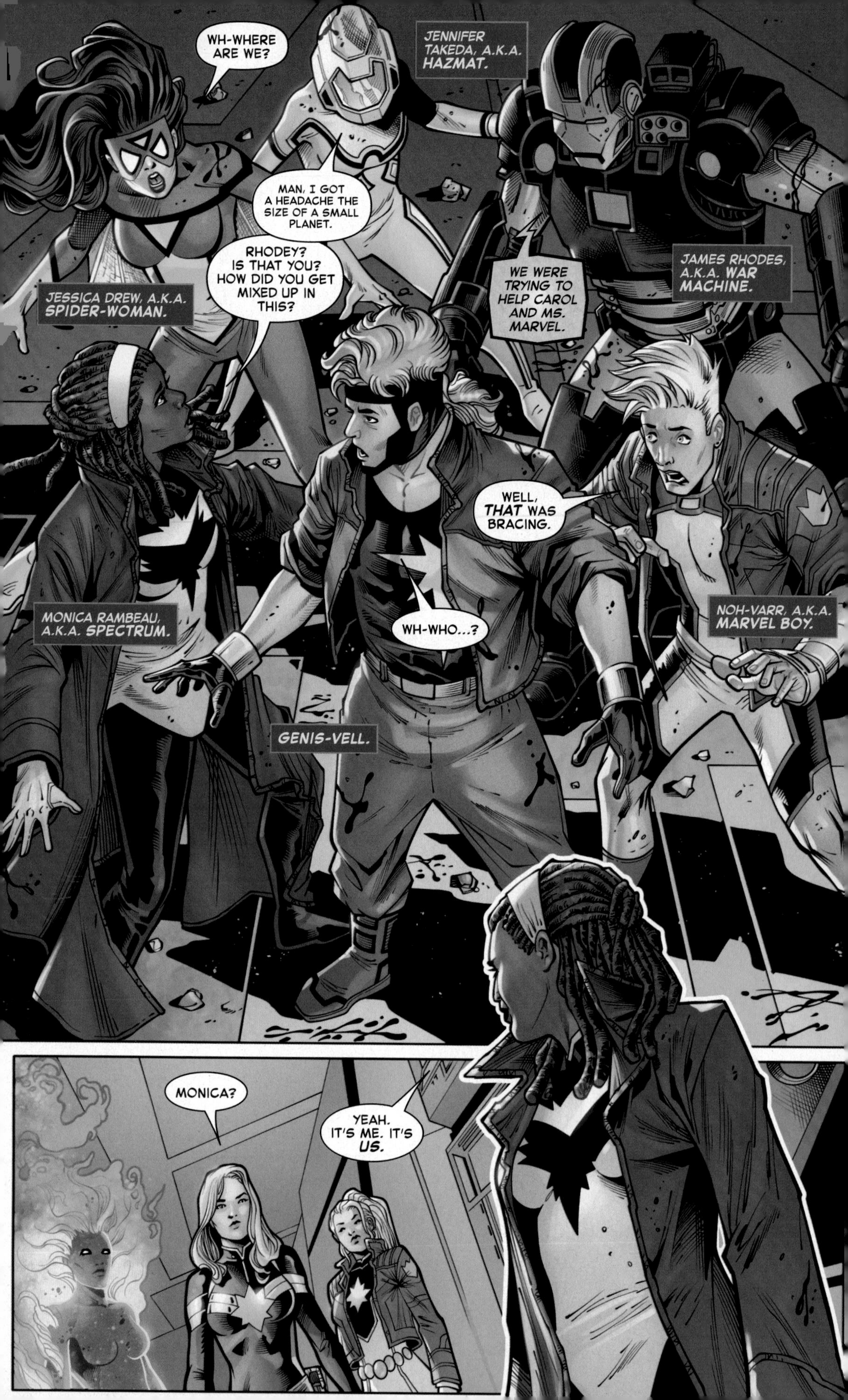

WH-WHERE ARE WE?
JENNIFER TAKEDA, A.K.A. HAZMAT.
MAN, I GOT A HEADACHE THE SIZE OF A SMALL PLANET.
JAMES RHODES, A.K.A. WAR MACHINE.
RHODEY? IS THAT YOU? HOW DID YOU GET MIXED UP IN THIS?
WE WERE TRYING TO HELP CAROL AND MS. MARVEL.
JESSICA DREW, A.K.A. SPIDER-WOMAN.
WELL, THAT WAS BRACING.
MONICA RAMBEAU, A.K.A. SPECTRUM.
WH-WHO...?
NOH-VARR, A.K.A. MARVEL BOY.
GENIS-VELL.
MONICA?
YEAH. IT'S ME. IT'S US.

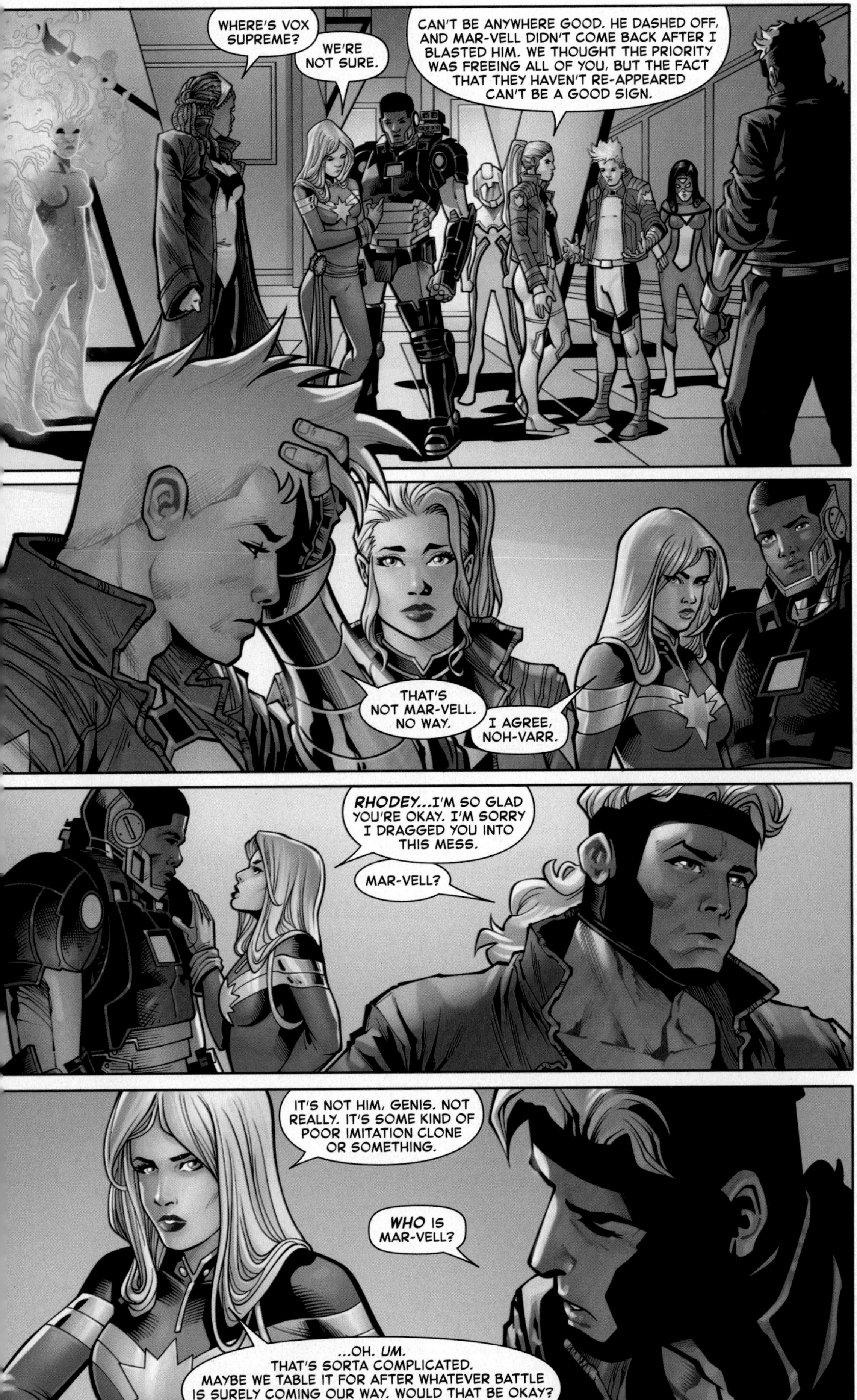
WHERE'S VOX SUPREME?
WE'RE NOT SURE.
CAN'T BE ANYWHERE GOOD. HE DASHED OFF, AND MAR-VELL DIDN'T COME BACK AFTER I BLASTED HIM. WE THOUGHT THE PRIORITY WAS FREEING ALL OF YOU, BUT THE FACT THAT THEY HAVEN'T RE-APPEARED CAN'T BE A GOOD SIGN.
THAT'S NOT MAR-VELL. NO WAY.
I AGREE, NOH-VARR.
RHODEY...I'M SO GLAD YOU'RE OKAY. I'M SORRY I DRAGGED YOU INTO THIS MESS.
MAR-VELL?
IT'S NOT HIM, GENIS. NOT REALLY. IT'S SOME KIND OF POOR IMITATION CLONE OR SOMETHING.
WHO IS MAR-VELL?
...OH. UM. THAT'S SORTA COMPLICATED. MAYBE WE TABLE IT FOR AFTER WHATEVER BATTLE IS SURELY COMING OUR WAY. WOULD THAT BE OKAY?

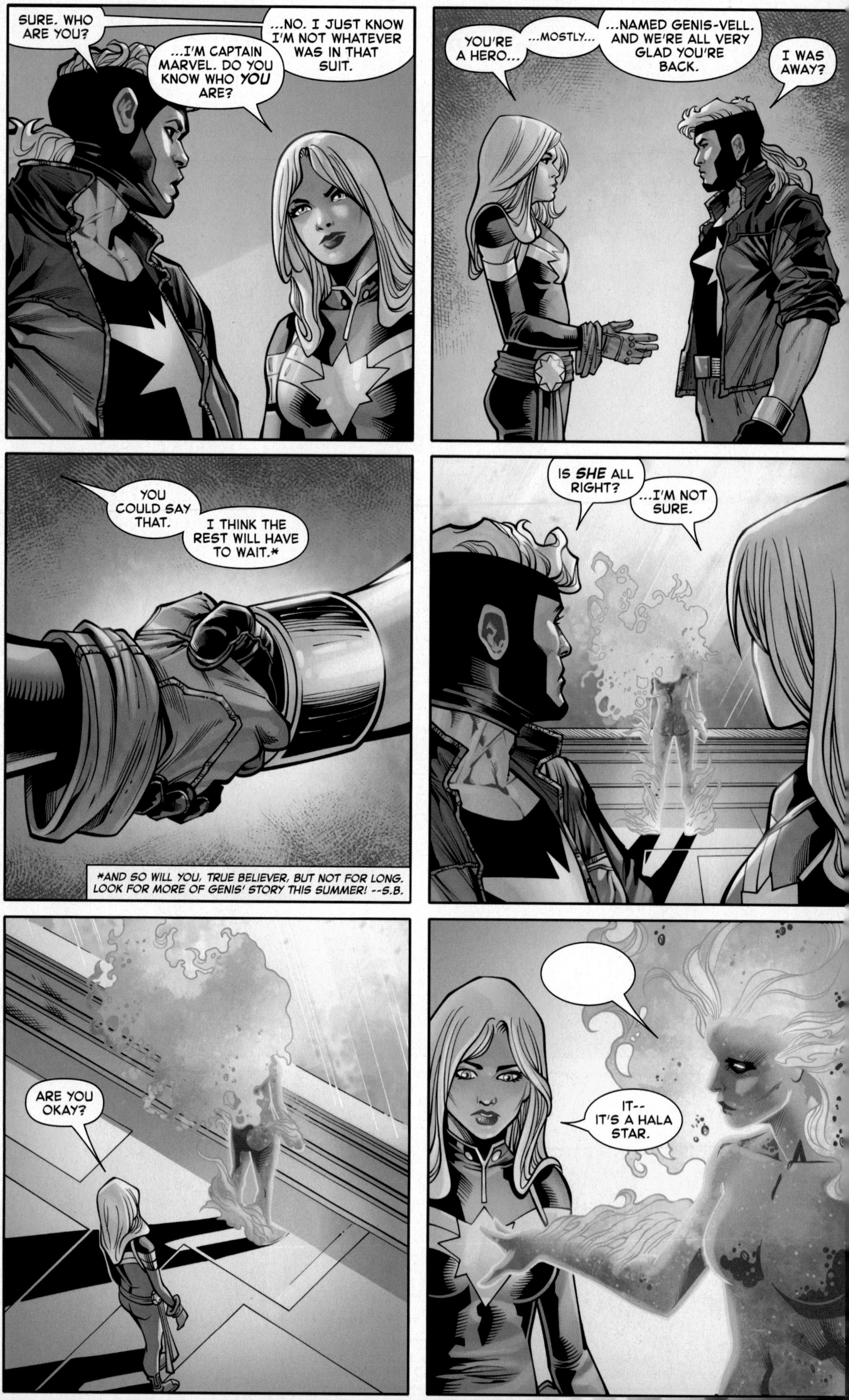
SURE. WHO ARE YOU?
...I'M CAPTAIN MARVEL. DO YOU KNOW WHO YOU ARE?
...NO. I JUST KNOW I'M NOT WHATEVER WAS IN THAT SUIT.
YOU'RE A HERO...
...MOSTLY...
...NAMED GENIS-VELL. AND WE'RE ALL VERY GLAD YOU'RE BACK.
I WAS AWAY?
YOU COULD SAY THAT.
I THINK THE REST WILL HAVE TO WAIT.*
*AND SO WILL YOU, TRUE BELIEVER, BUT NOT FOR LONG. LOOK FOR MORE OF GENIS' STORY THIS SUMMER! --S.B.
IS SHE ALL RIGHT?
...I'M NOT SURE.
ARE YOU OKAY?
IT-- IT'S A HALA STAR.

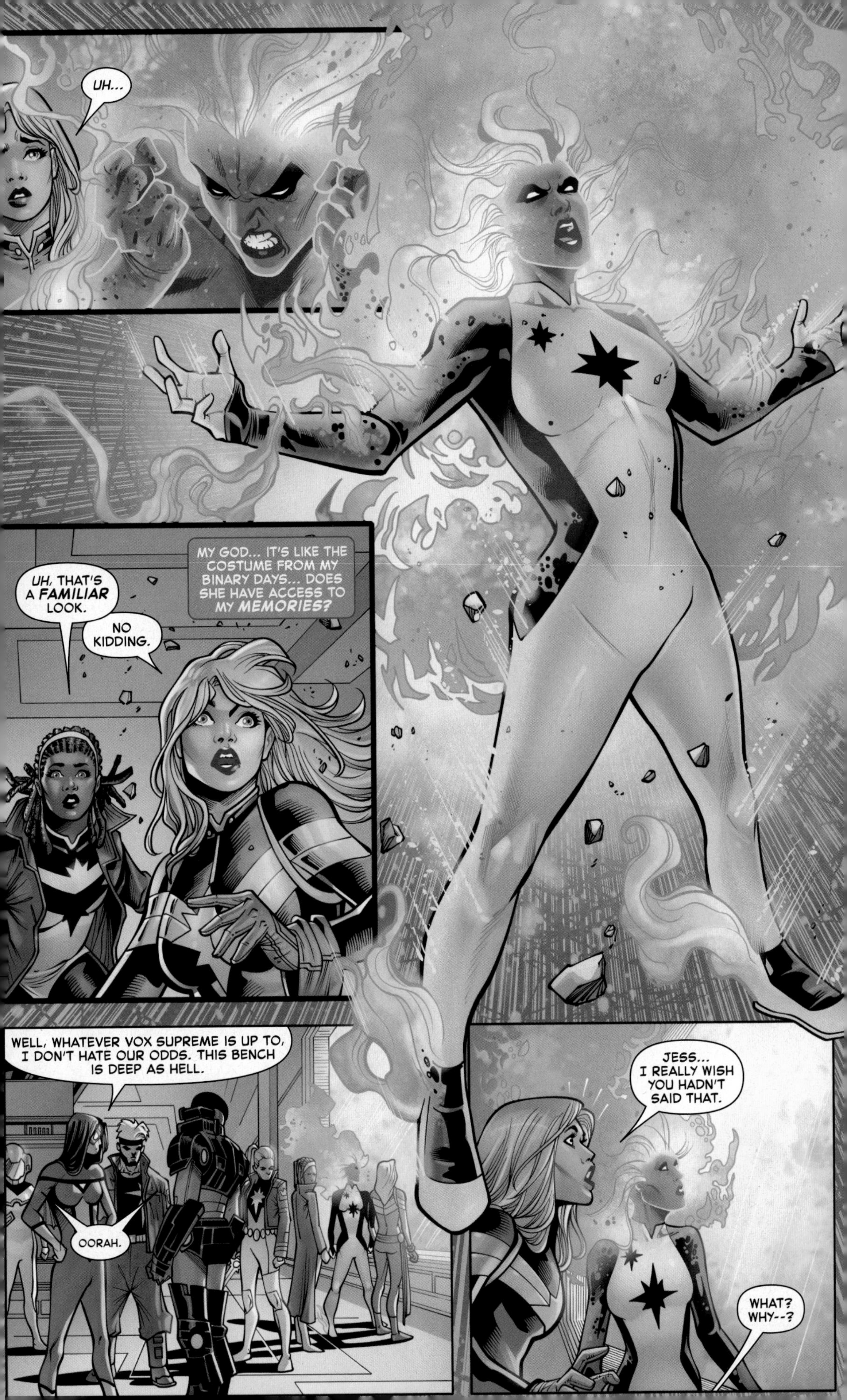
UH...
MY GOD... IT'S LIKE THE COSTUME FROM MY BINARY DAYS... DOES SHE HAVE ACCESS TO MY MEMORIES?
UH, THAT'S A FAMILIAR LOOK.
NO KIDDING.
WELL, WHATEVER VOX SUPREME IS UP TO, I DON'T HATE OUR ODDS. THIS BENCH IS DEEP AS HELL.
OORAH.
JESS... I REALLY WISH YOU HADN'T SAID THAT.
WHAT? WHY--?

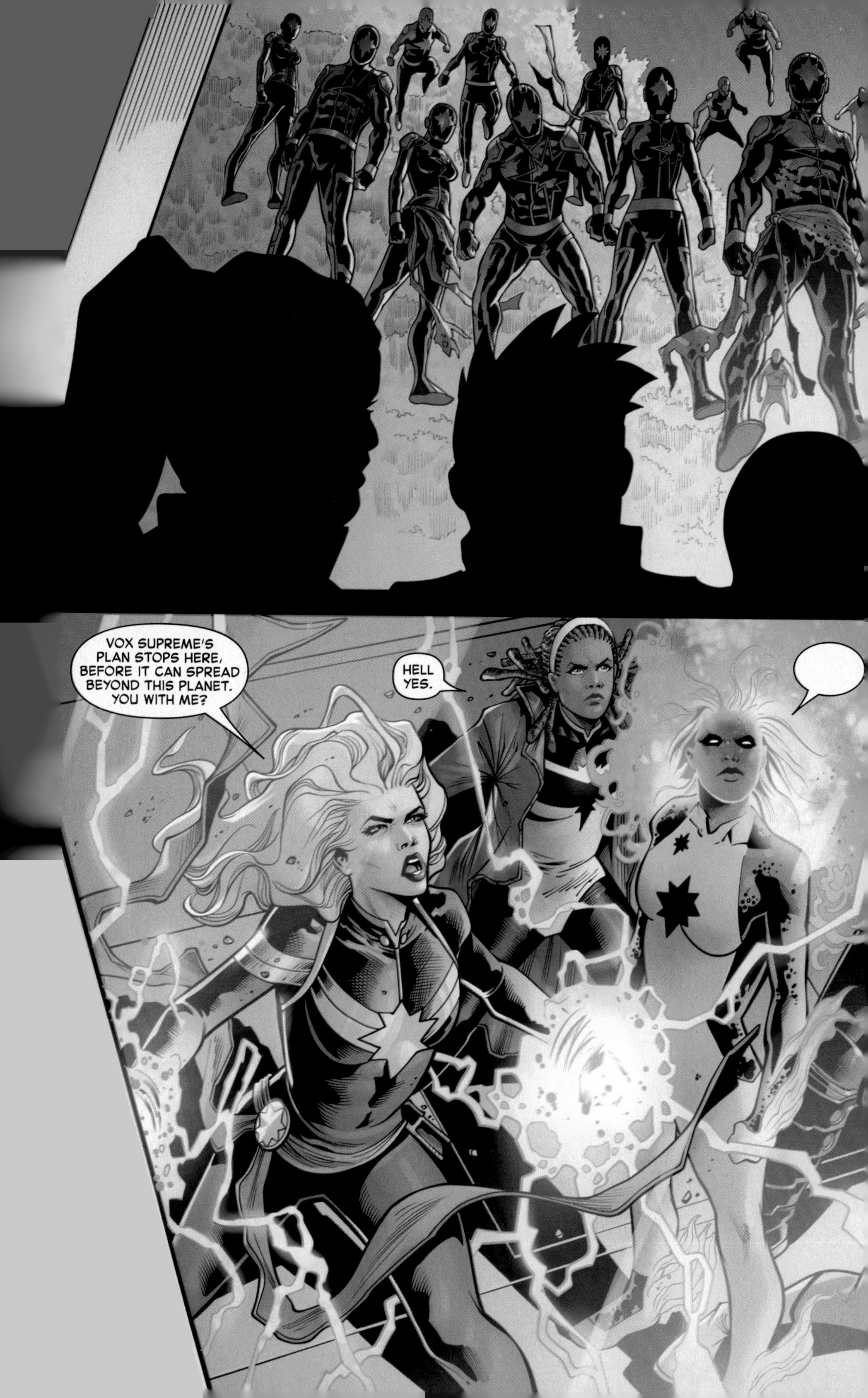
VOX SUPREME'S PLAN STOPS HERE, BEFORE IT CAN SPREAD BEYOND THIS PLANET. YOU WITH ME?
HELL YES.

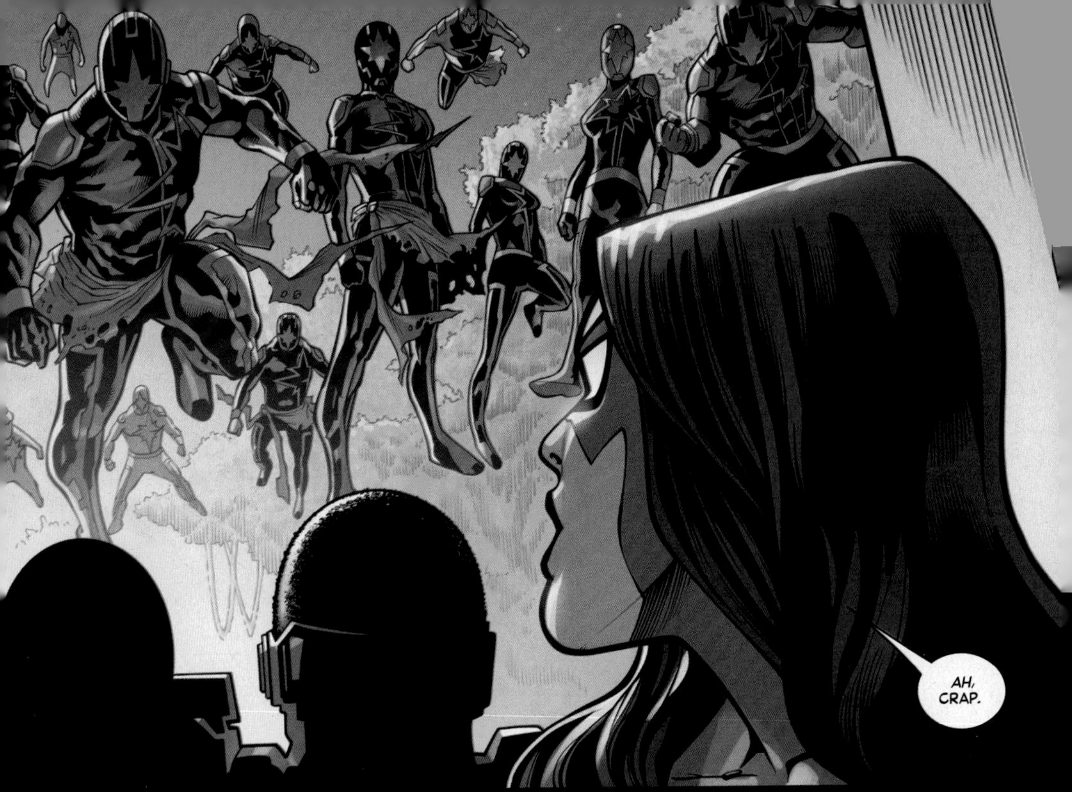
AH, CRAP.

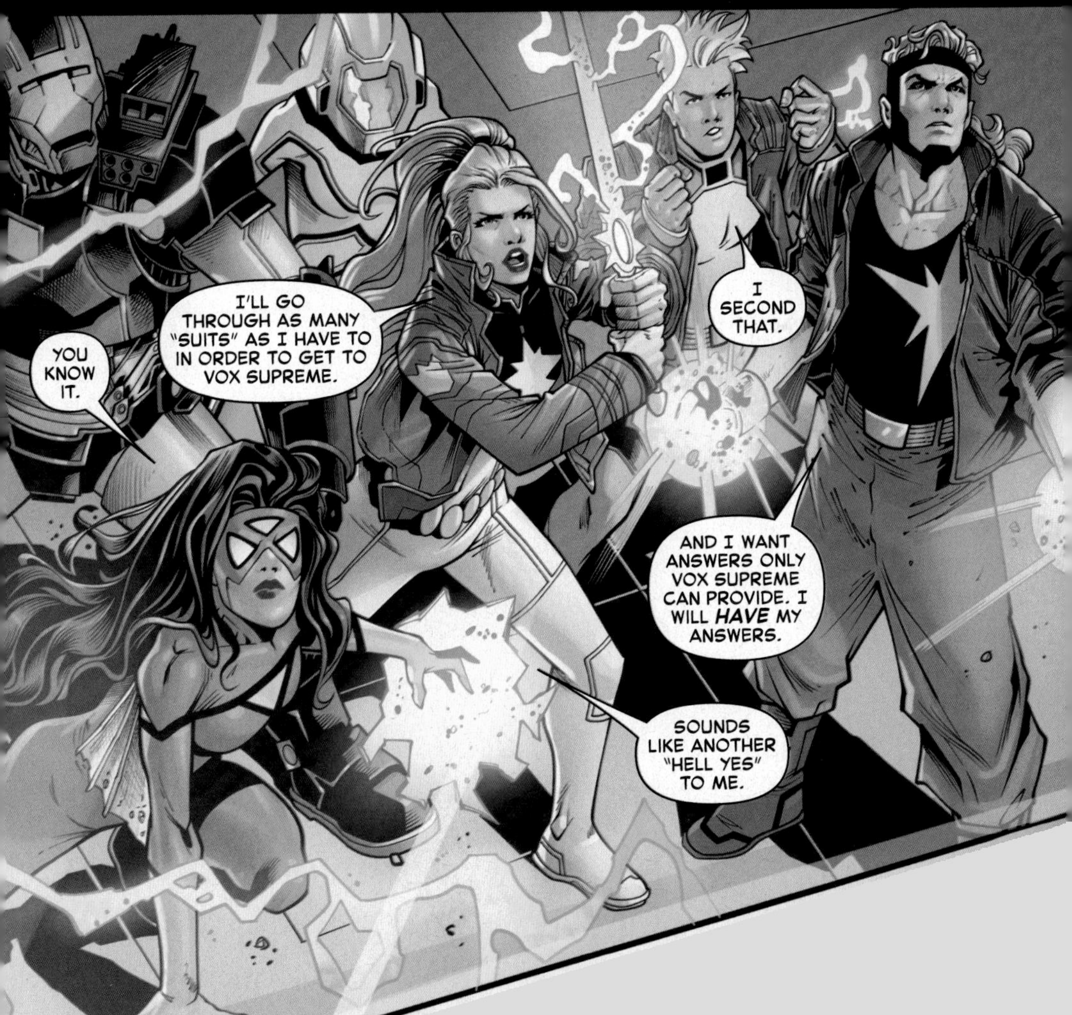
I'LL GO THROUGH AS MANY "SUITS" AS I HAVE TO IN ORDER TO GET TO VOX SUPREME.
YOU KNOW IT.
I SECOND THAT.
AND I WANT ANSWERS ONLY VOX SUPREME CAN PROVIDE. I WILL *HAVE* MY ANSWERS.
SOUNDS LIKE ANOTHER "HELL YES" TO ME.

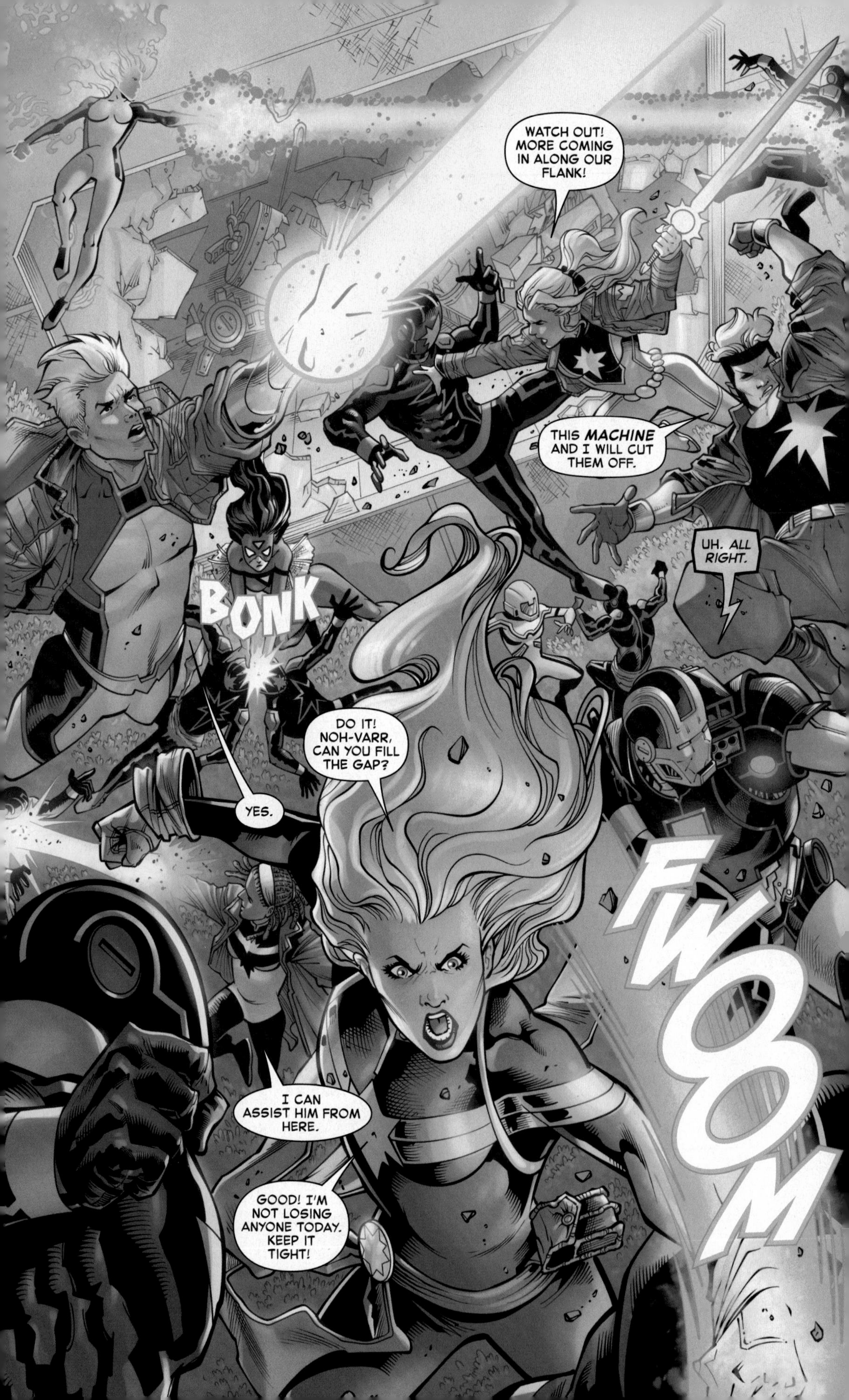
WATCH OUT! MORE COMING IN ALONG OUR FLANK!
THIS MACHINE AND I WILL CUT THEM OFF.
UH. ALL RIGHT.
BONK
DO IT! NOH-VARR, CAN YOU FILL THE GAP?
YES.
I CAN ASSIST HIM FROM HERE.
GOOD! I'M NOT LOSING ANYONE TODAY. KEEP IT TIGHT!
FWOOM

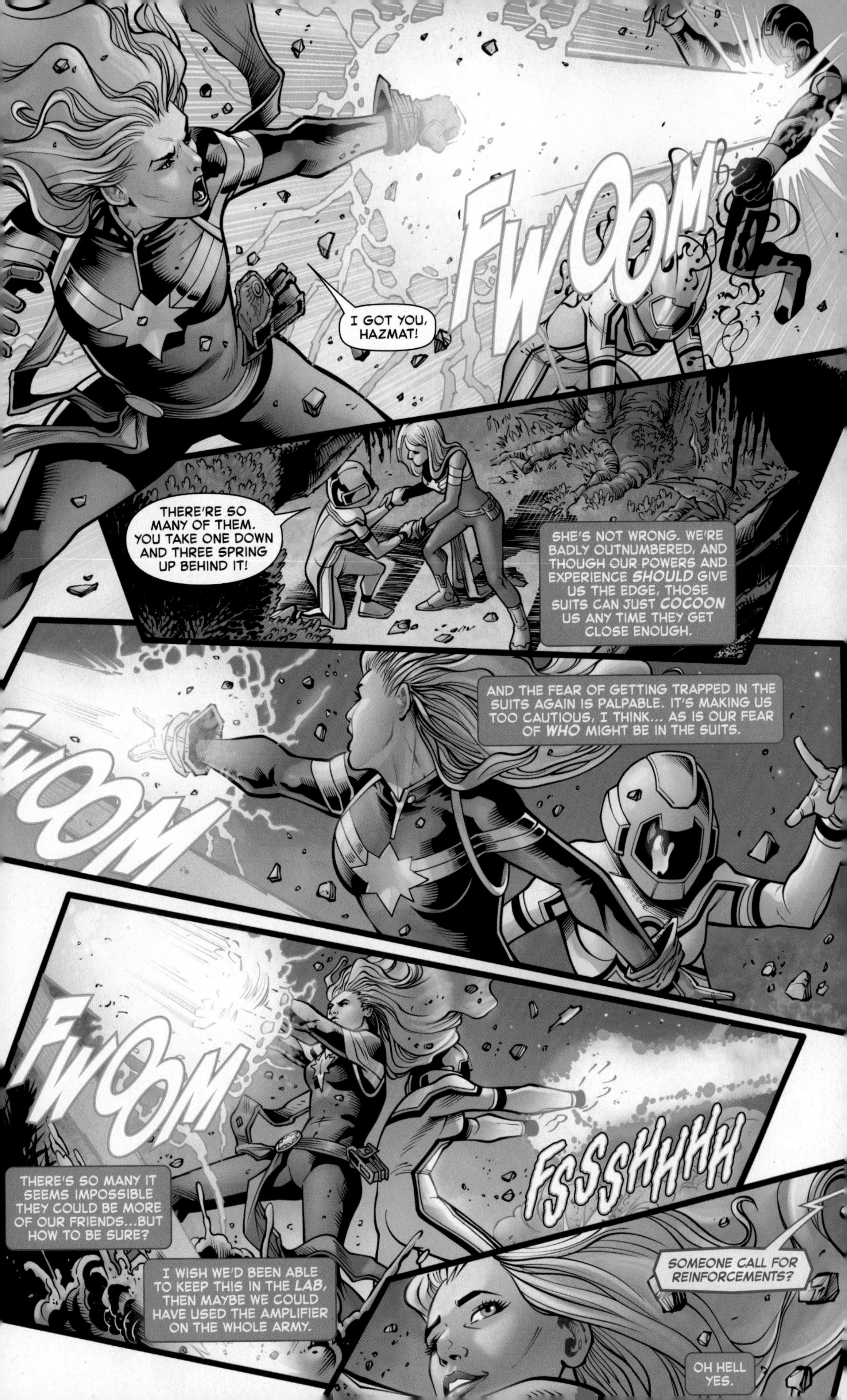
I GOT YOU, HAZMAT!
FWOOM
THERE'RE SO MANY OF THEM. YOU TAKE ONE DOWN AND THREE SPRING UP BEHIND IT!
SHE'S NOT WRONG. WE'RE BADLY OUTNUMBERED, AND THOUGH OUR POWERS AND EXPERIENCE SHOULD GIVE US THE EDGE, THOSE SUITS CAN JUST COCOON US ANY TIME THEY GET CLOSE ENOUGH.
AND THE FEAR OF GETTING TRAPPED IN THE SUITS AGAIN IS PALPABLE. IT'S MAKING US TOO CAUTIOUS, I THINK... AS IS OUR FEAR OF WHO MIGHT BE IN THE SUITS.
FWOOM
FWOOM
FSSSHHHH
THERE'S SO MANY IT SEEMS IMPOSSIBLE THEY COULD BE MORE OF OUR FRIENDS...BUT HOW TO BE SURE?
I WISH WE'D BEEN ABLE TO KEEP THIS IN THE LAB, THEN MAYBE WE COULD HAVE USED THE AMPLIFIER ON THE WHOLE ARMY.
SOMEONE CALL FOR REINFORCEMENTS?
OH HELL YES.

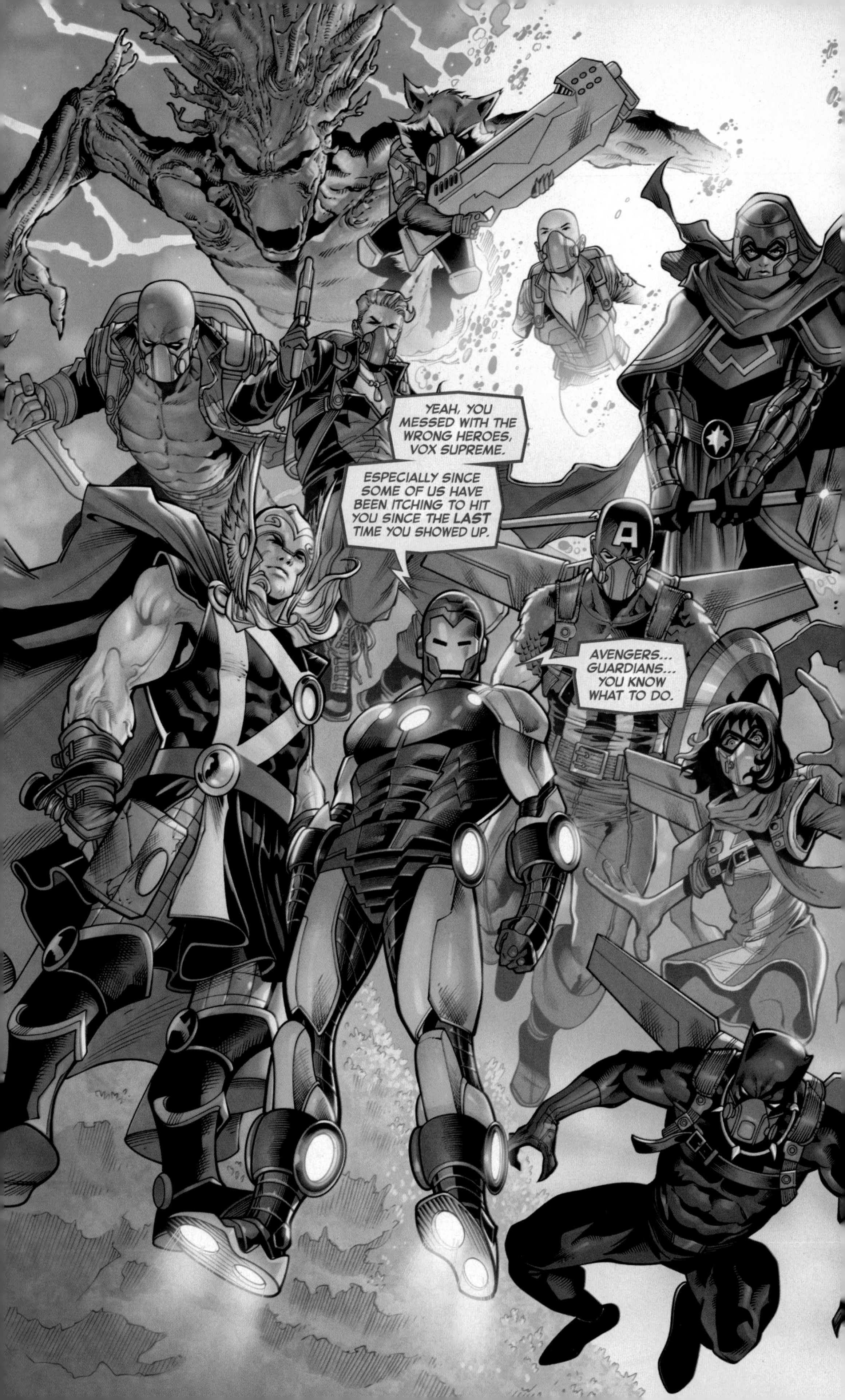
YEAH, YOU MESSED WITH THE WRONG HEROES, VOX SUPREME.
ESPECIALLY SINCE SOME OF US HAVE BEEN ITCHING TO HIT YOU SINCE THE **LAST** TIME YOU SHOWED UP.
AVENGERS... GUARDIANS... YOU KNOW WHAT TO DO.

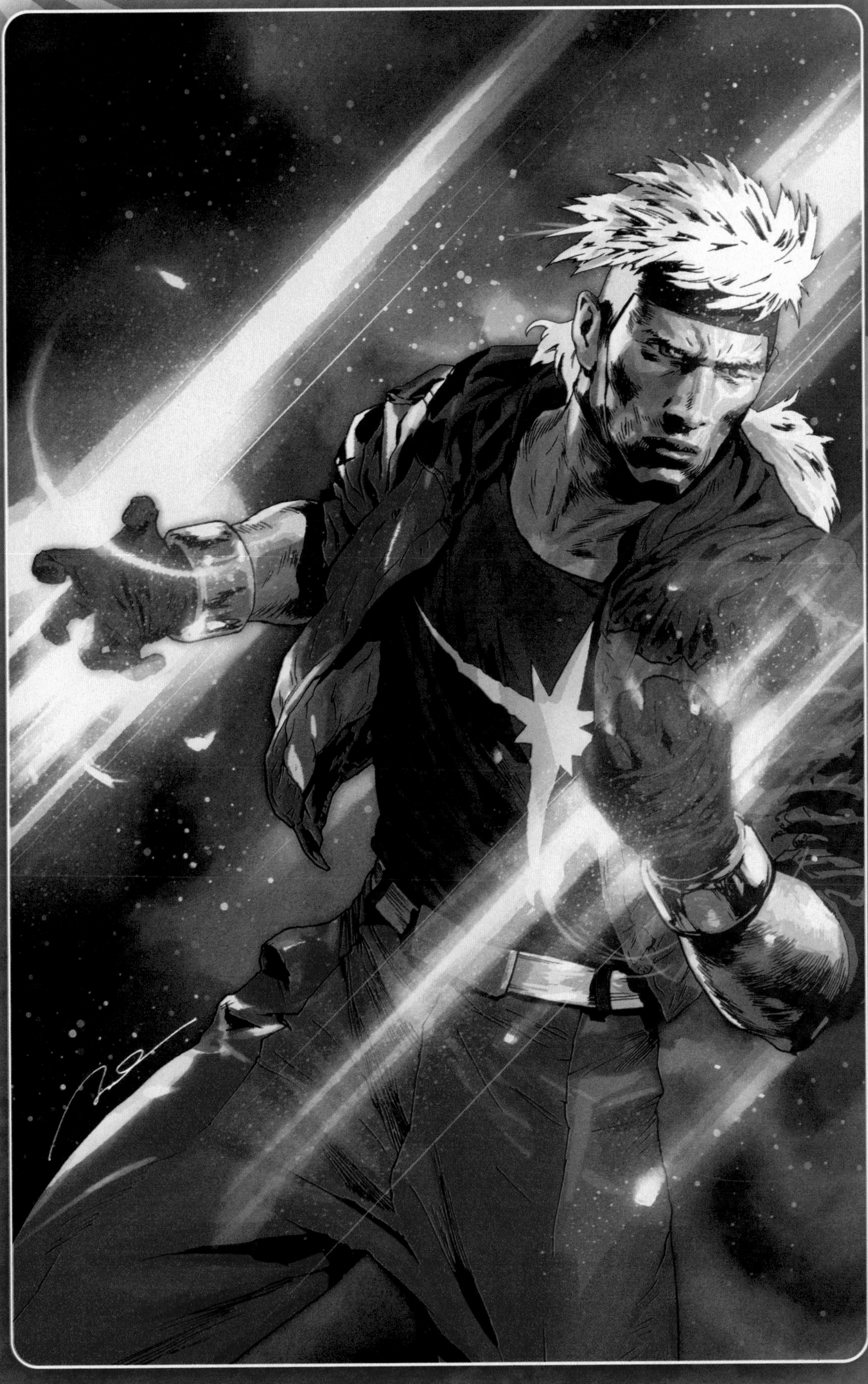

GERALD PAREL
#33 TEASER VARIANT

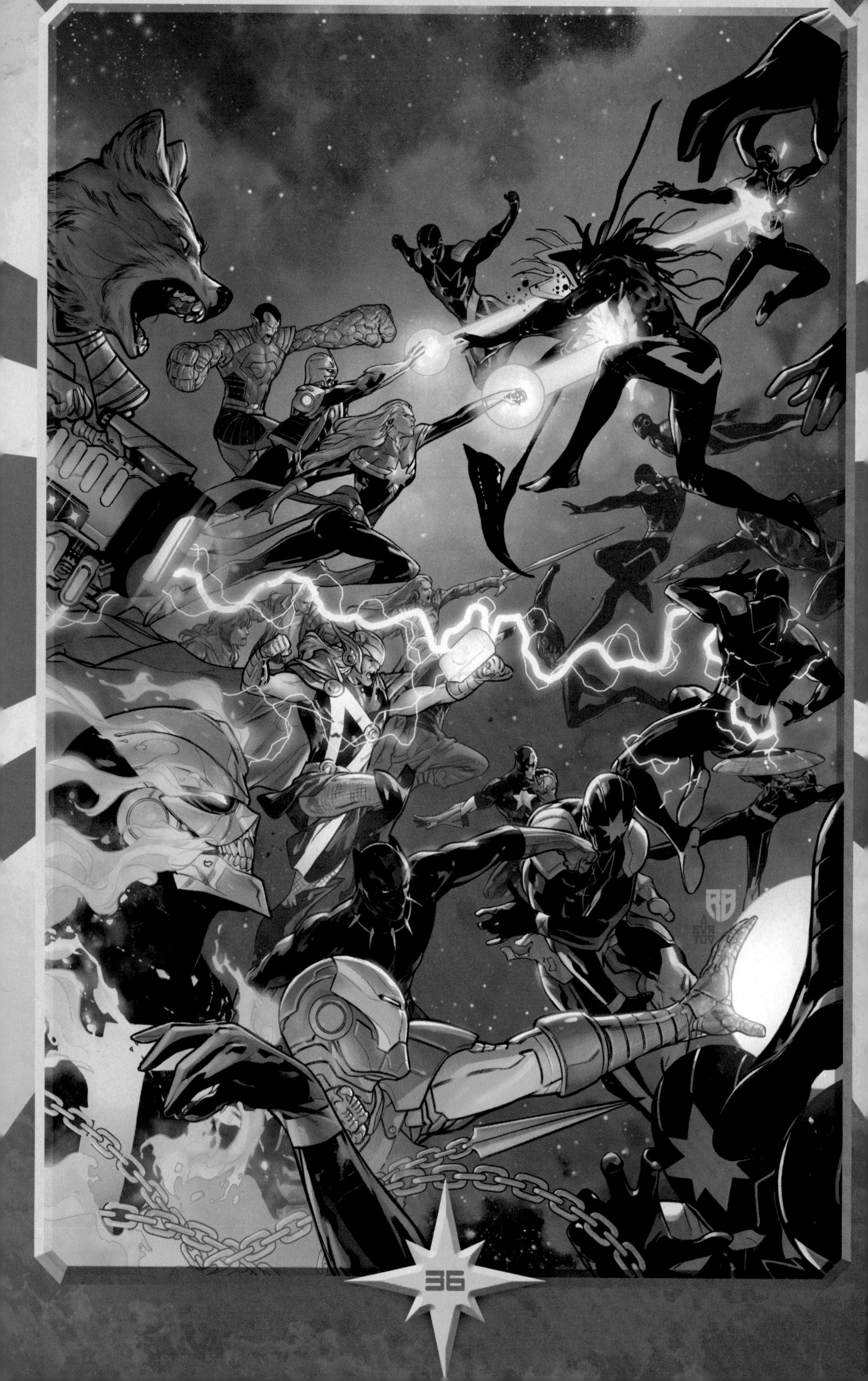

36

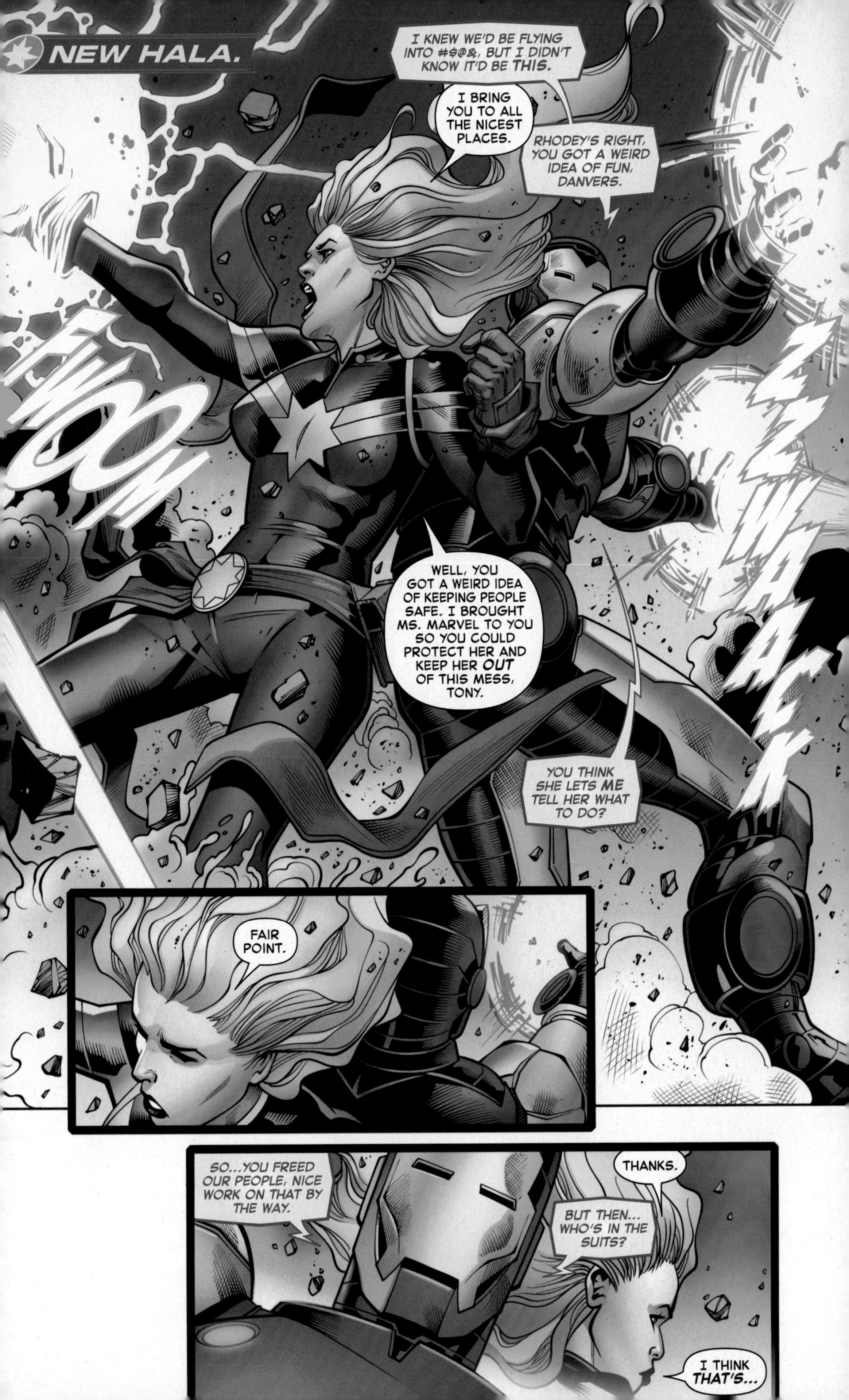
NEW HALA.
I KNEW WE'D BE FLYING INTO #$@&, BUT I DIDN'T KNOW IT'D BE THIS.
I BRING YOU TO ALL THE NICEST PLACES.
RHODEY'S RIGHT, YOU GOT A WEIRD IDEA OF FUN, DANVERS.
FWOOM
ZZWHACK
WELL, YOU GOT A WEIRD IDEA OF KEEPING PEOPLE SAFE. I BROUGHT MS. MARVEL TO YOU SO YOU COULD PROTECT HER AND KEEP HER OUT OF THIS MESS, TONY.
YOU THINK SHE LETS ME TELL HER WHAT TO DO?
FAIR POINT.
SO...YOU FREED OUR PEOPLE, NICE WORK ON THAT BY THE WAY.
THANKS.
BUT THEN... WHO'S IN THE SUITS?
I THINK THAT'S...

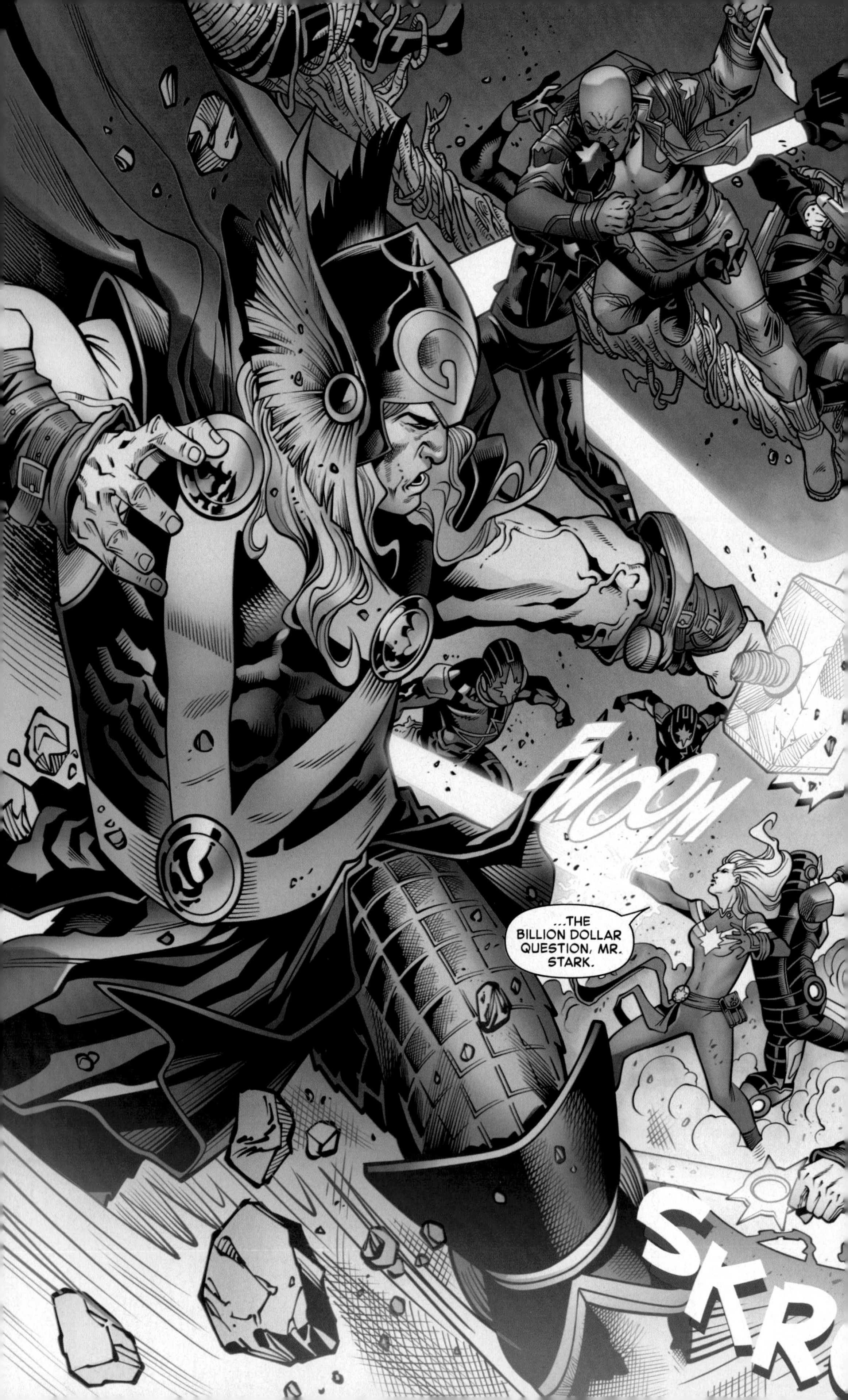
FWOOM
...THE BILLION DOLLAR QUESTION, MR. STARK.
SKR

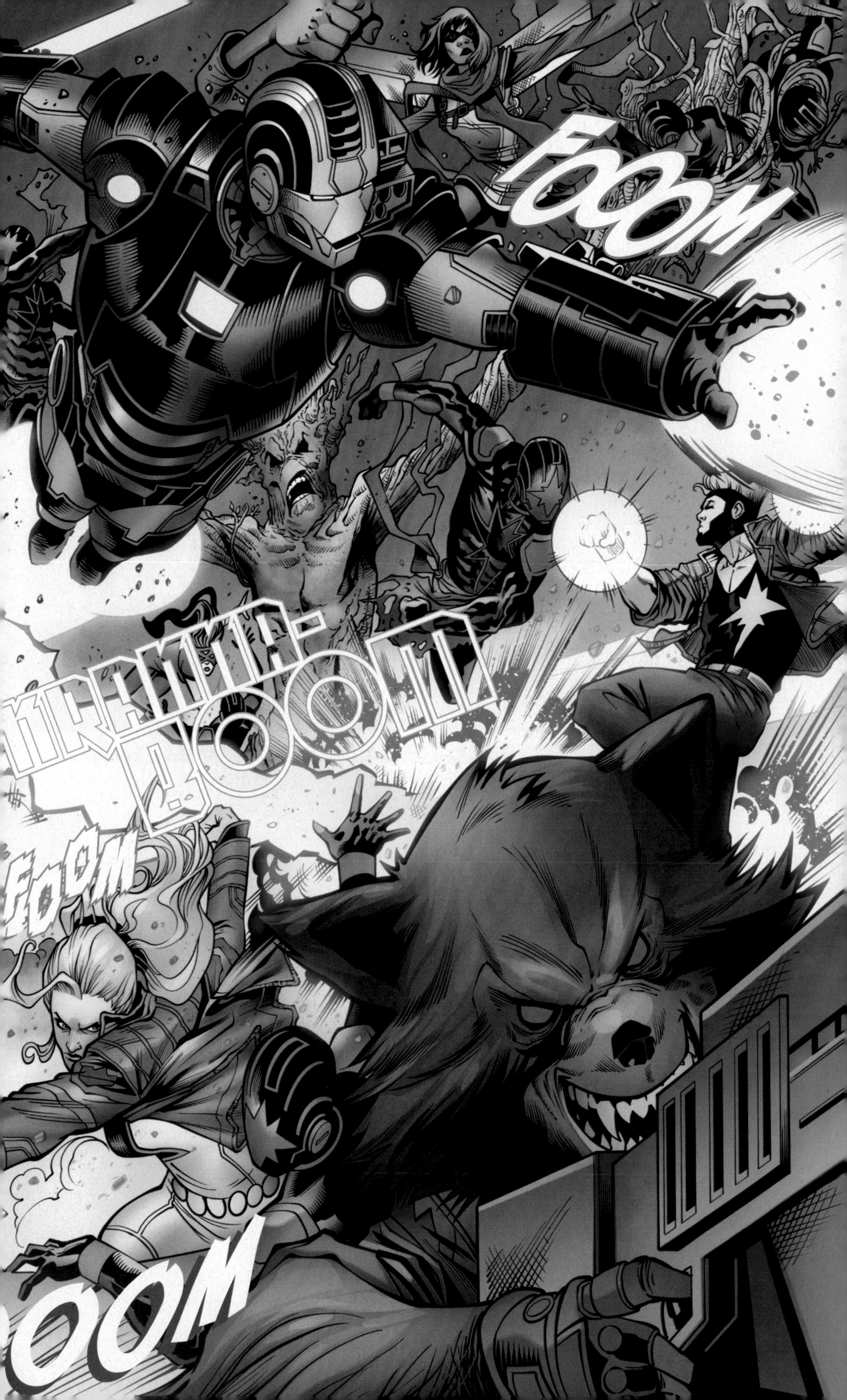
FOOM
KRAKKA-BOOM!
FOOM
OOM

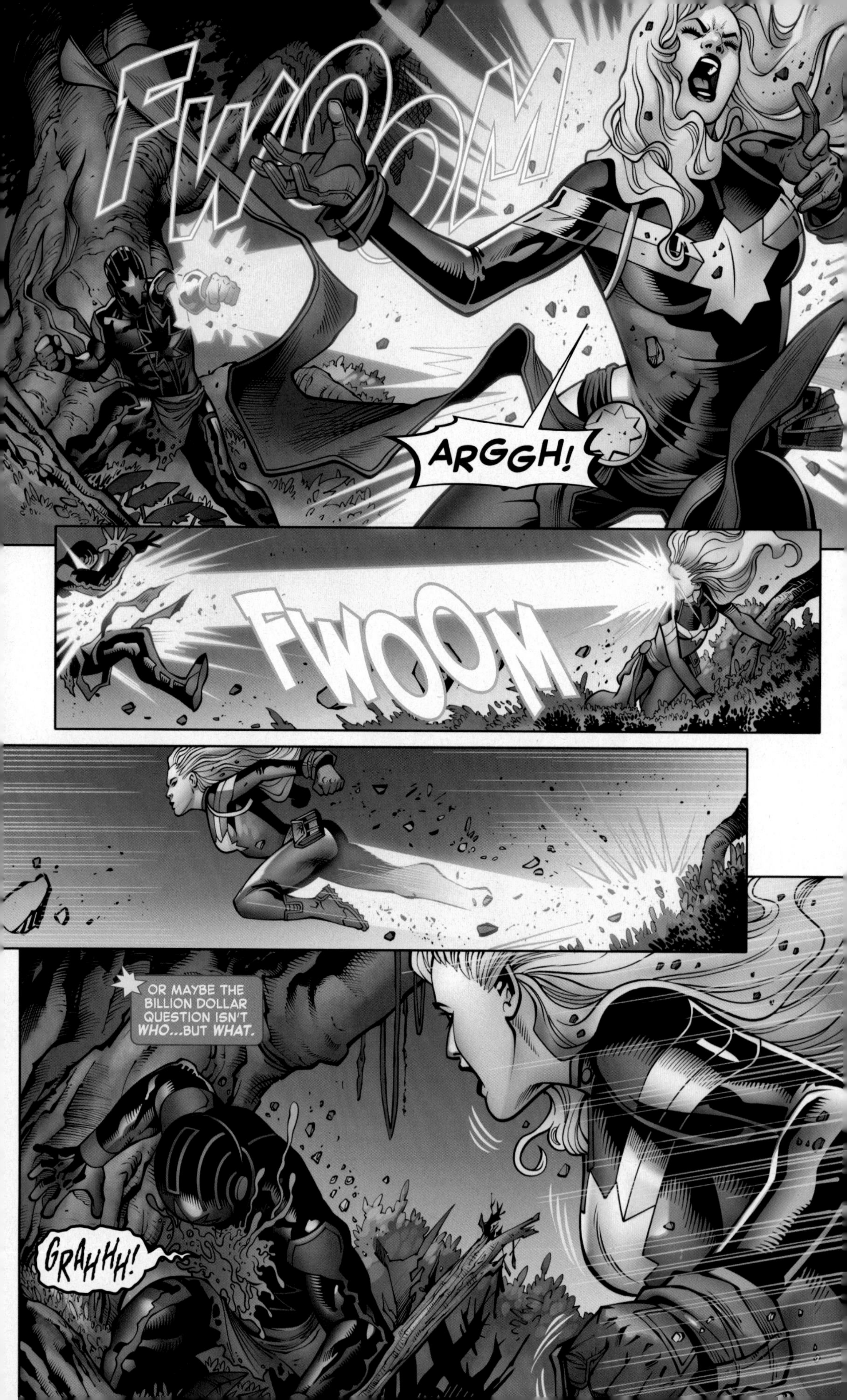
FWOOM
ARGGH!
FWOOM
OR MAYBE THE BILLION DOLLAR QUESTION ISN'T *WHO*...BUT *WHAT.*
GRAHHH!

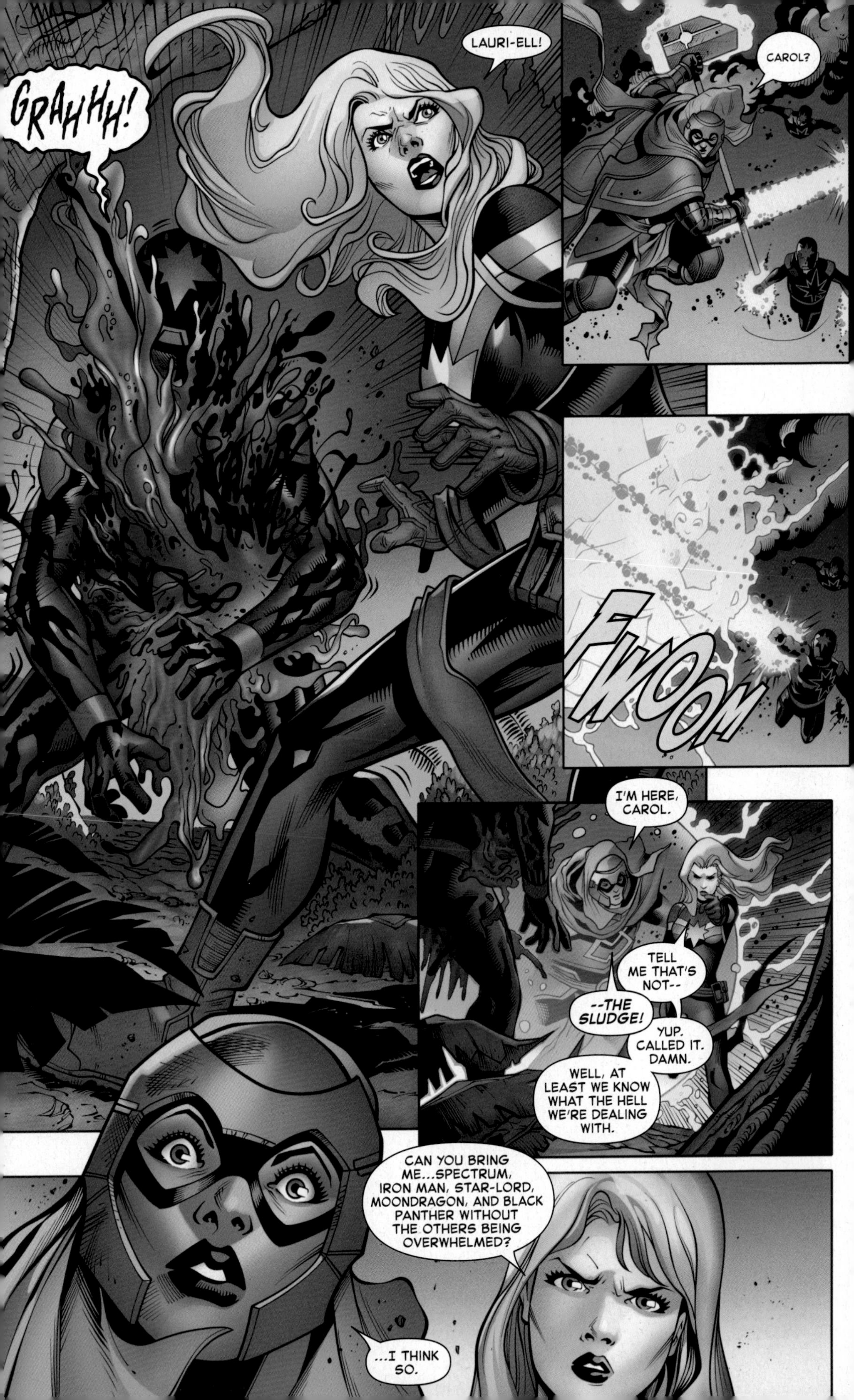
GRAHHH!
LAURI-ELL!
CAROL?
FWOOM
I'M HERE, CAROL.
TELL ME THAT'S NOT--
--THE SLUDGE!
YUP. CALLED IT. DAMN.
WELL, AT LEAST WE KNOW WHAT THE HELL WE'RE DEALING WITH.
CAN YOU BRING ME...SPECTRUM, IRON MAN, STAR-LORD, MOONDRAGON, AND BLACK PANTHER WITHOUT THE OTHERS BEING OVERWHELMED?
...I THINK SO.

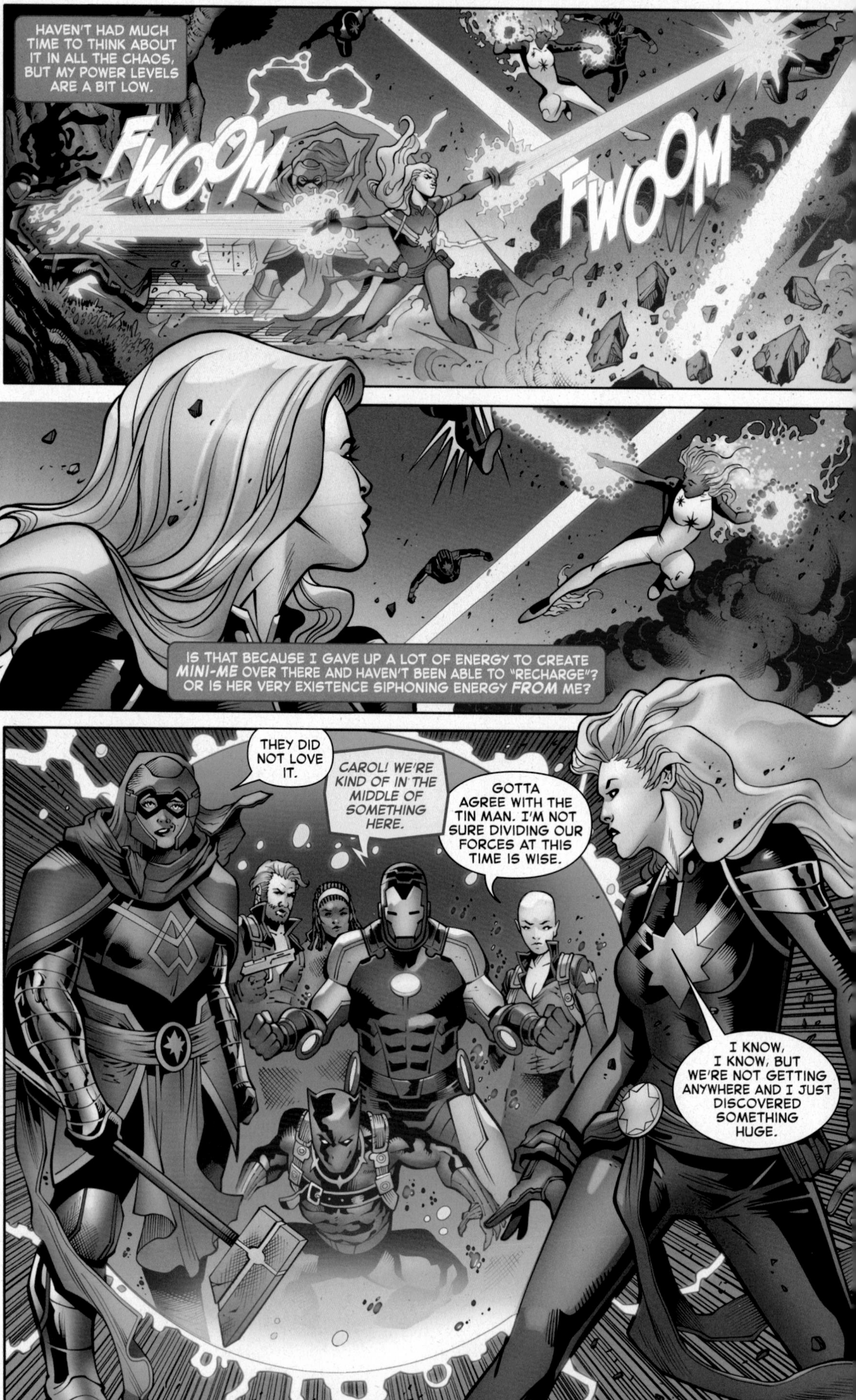

HAVEN'T HAD MUCH TIME TO THINK ABOUT IT IN ALL THE CHAOS, BUT MY POWER LEVELS ARE A BIT LOW.
FWOOM
FWOOM
IS THAT BECAUSE I GAVE UP A LOT OF ENERGY TO CREATE MINI-ME OVER THERE AND HAVEN'T BEEN ABLE TO "RECHARGE"? OR IS HER VERY EXISTENCE SIPHONING ENERGY FROM ME?
THEY DID NOT LOVE IT.
CAROL! WE'RE KIND OF IN THE MIDDLE OF SOMETHING HERE.
GOTTA AGREE WITH THE TIN MAN. I'M NOT SURE DIVIDING OUR FORCES AT THIS TIME IS WISE.
I KNOW, I KNOW, BUT WE'RE NOT GETTING ANYWHERE AND I JUST DISCOVERED SOMETHING HUGE.

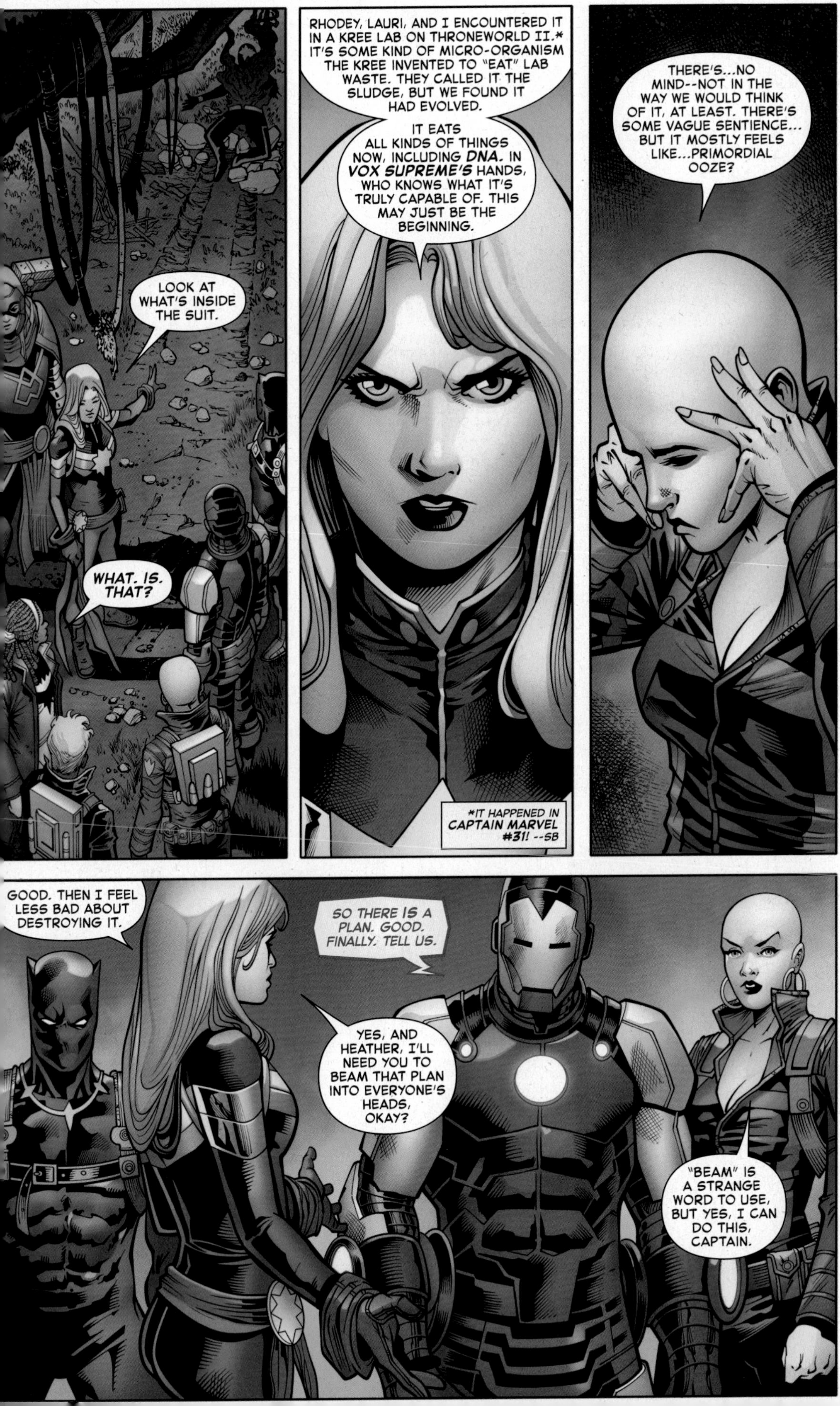

LOOK AT WHAT'S INSIDE THE SUIT.
WHAT. IS. THAT?
RHODEY, LAURI, AND I ENCOUNTERED IT IN A KREE LAB ON THRONEWORLD II.* IT'S SOME KIND OF MICRO-ORGANISM THE KREE INVENTED TO "EAT" LAB WASTE. THEY CALLED IT THE SLUDGE, BUT WE FOUND IT HAD EVOLVED.
IT EATS ALL KINDS OF THINGS NOW, INCLUDING DNA. IN VOX SUPREME'S HANDS, WHO KNOWS WHAT IT'S TRULY CAPABLE OF. THIS MAY JUST BE THE BEGINNING.
*IT HAPPENED IN CAPTAIN MARVEL #31! --SB
THERE'S...NO MIND--NOT IN THE WAY WE WOULD THINK OF IT, AT LEAST. THERE'S SOME VAGUE SENTIENCE... BUT IT MOSTLY FEELS LIKE...PRIMORDIAL OOZE?
GOOD. THEN I FEEL LESS BAD ABOUT DESTROYING IT.
SO THERE IS A PLAN. GOOD. FINALLY. TELL US.
YES, AND HEATHER, I'LL NEED YOU TO BEAM THAT PLAN INTO EVERYONE'S HEADS, OKAY?
"BEAM" IS A STRANGE WORD TO USE, BUT YES, I CAN DO THIS, CAPTAIN.

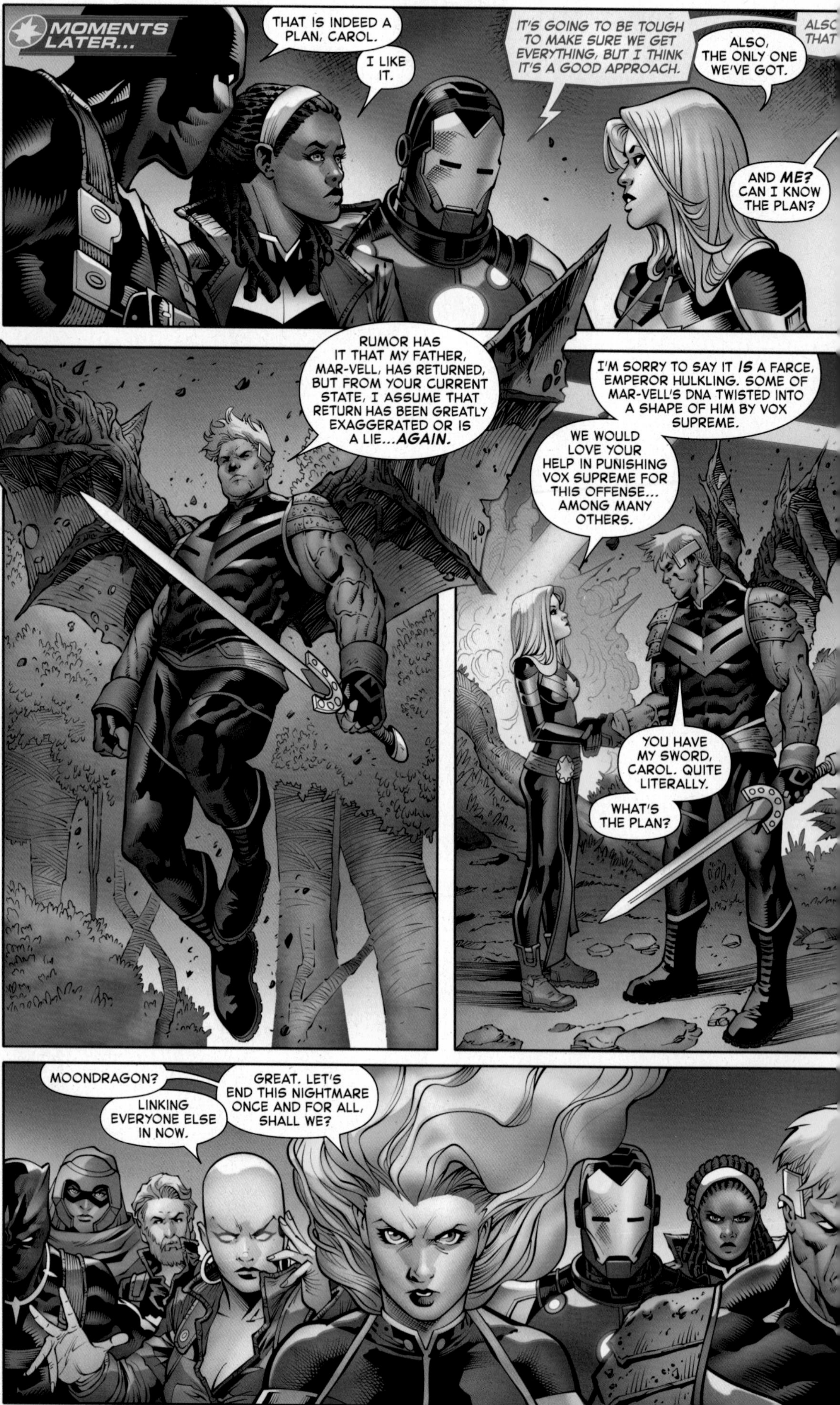

MOMENTS LATER...
THAT IS INDEED A PLAN, CAROL.
I LIKE IT.
IT'S GOING TO BE TOUGH TO MAKE SURE WE GET EVERYTHING, BUT I THINK IT'S A GOOD APPROACH.
ALSO, THE ONLY ONE WE'VE GOT.
AND ME? CAN I KNOW THE PLAN?
RUMOR HAS IT THAT MY FATHER, MAR-VELL, HAS RETURNED, BUT FROM YOUR CURRENT STATE, I ASSUME THAT RETURN HAS BEEN GREATLY EXAGGERATED OR IS A LIE...AGAIN.
I'M SORRY TO SAY IT IS A FARCE, EMPEROR HULKLING. SOME OF MAR-VELL'S DNA TWISTED INTO A SHAPE OF HIM BY VOX SUPREME.
WE WOULD LOVE YOUR HELP IN PUNISHING VOX SUPREME FOR THIS OFFENSE... AMONG MANY OTHERS.
YOU HAVE MY SWORD, CAROL. QUITE LITERALLY.
WHAT'S THE PLAN?
MOONDRAGON?
LINKING EVERYONE ELSE IN NOW.
GREAT. LET'S END THIS NIGHTMARE ONCE AND FOR ALL, SHALL WE?

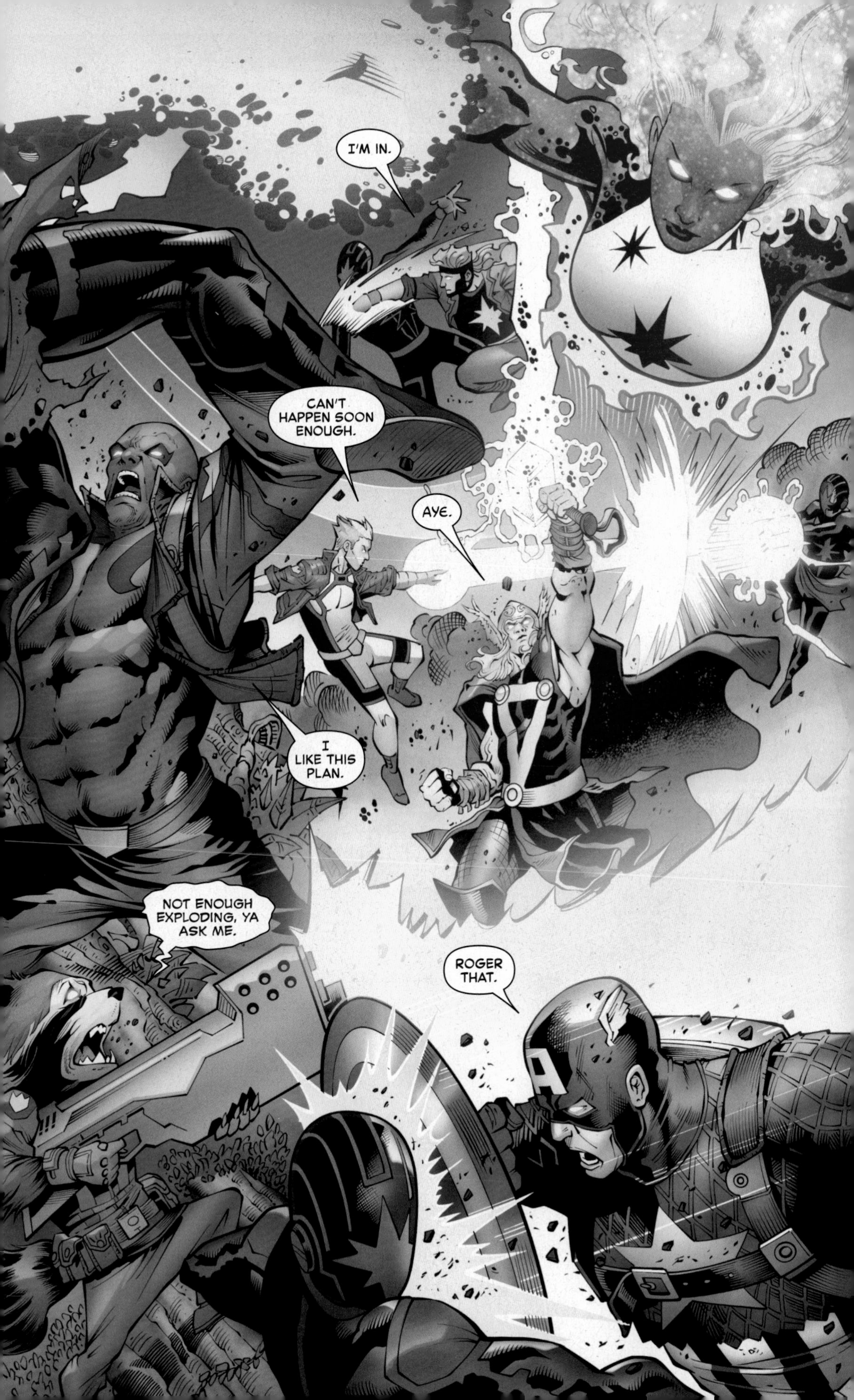
I'M IN.
CAN'T HAPPEN SOON ENOUGH.
AYE.
I LIKE THIS PLAN.
NOT ENOUGH EXPLODING, YA ASK ME.
ROGER THAT.

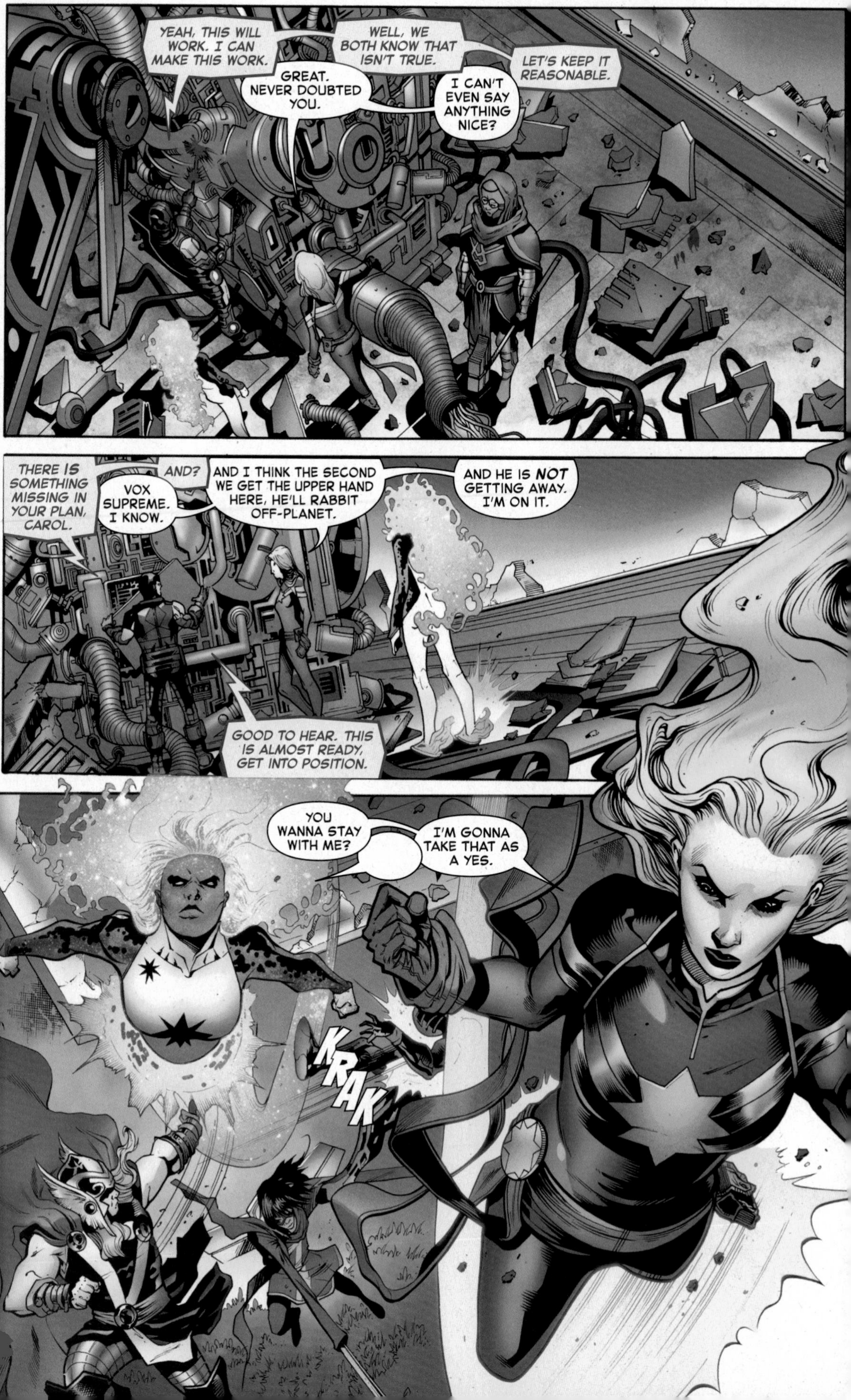

YEAH, THIS WILL WORK. I CAN MAKE THIS WORK.
GREAT. NEVER DOUBTED YOU.
WELL, WE BOTH KNOW THAT ISN'T TRUE.
I CAN'T EVEN SAY ANYTHING NICE?
LET'S KEEP IT REASONABLE.
THERE IS SOMETHING MISSING IN YOUR PLAN, CAROL.
VOX SUPREME. I KNOW.
AND?
AND I THINK THE SECOND WE GET THE UPPER HAND HERE, HE'LL RABBIT OFF-PLANET.
AND HE IS NOT GETTING AWAY. I'M ON IT.
GOOD TO HEAR. THIS IS ALMOST READY, GET INTO POSITION.
YOU WANNA STAY WITH ME?
I'M GONNA TAKE THAT AS A YES.
KRAK

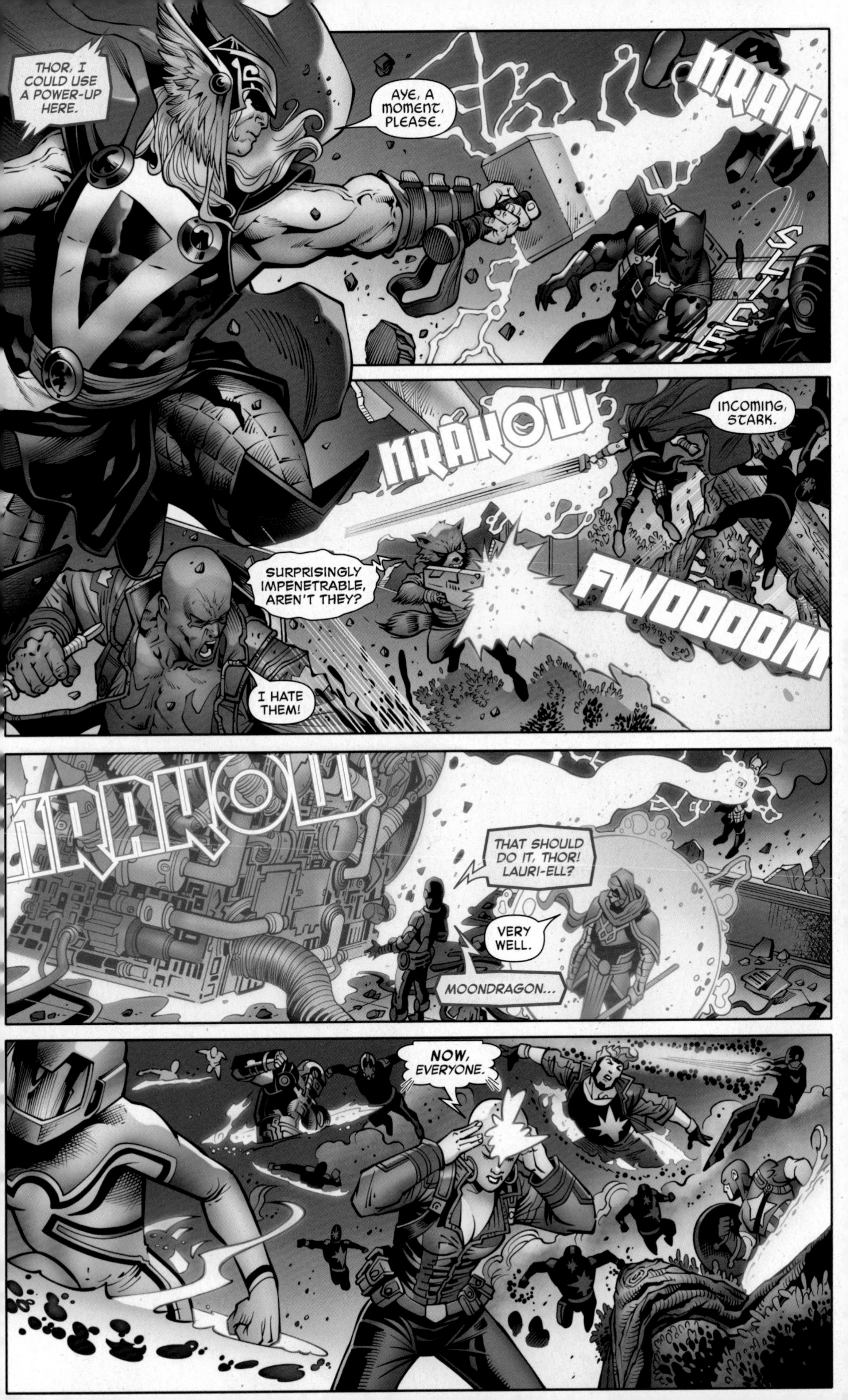
THOR, I COULD USE A POWER-UP HERE.
AYE, A MOMENT, PLEASE.
KRAK
SLICE
KRAKOW
INCOMING, STARK.
SURPRISINGLY IMPENETRABLE, AREN'T THEY?
FWOOOOM
I HATE THEM!
KRAKOW
THAT SHOULD DO IT, THOR! LAURI-ELL?
VERY WELL.
MOONDRAGON...
NOW, EVERYONE.

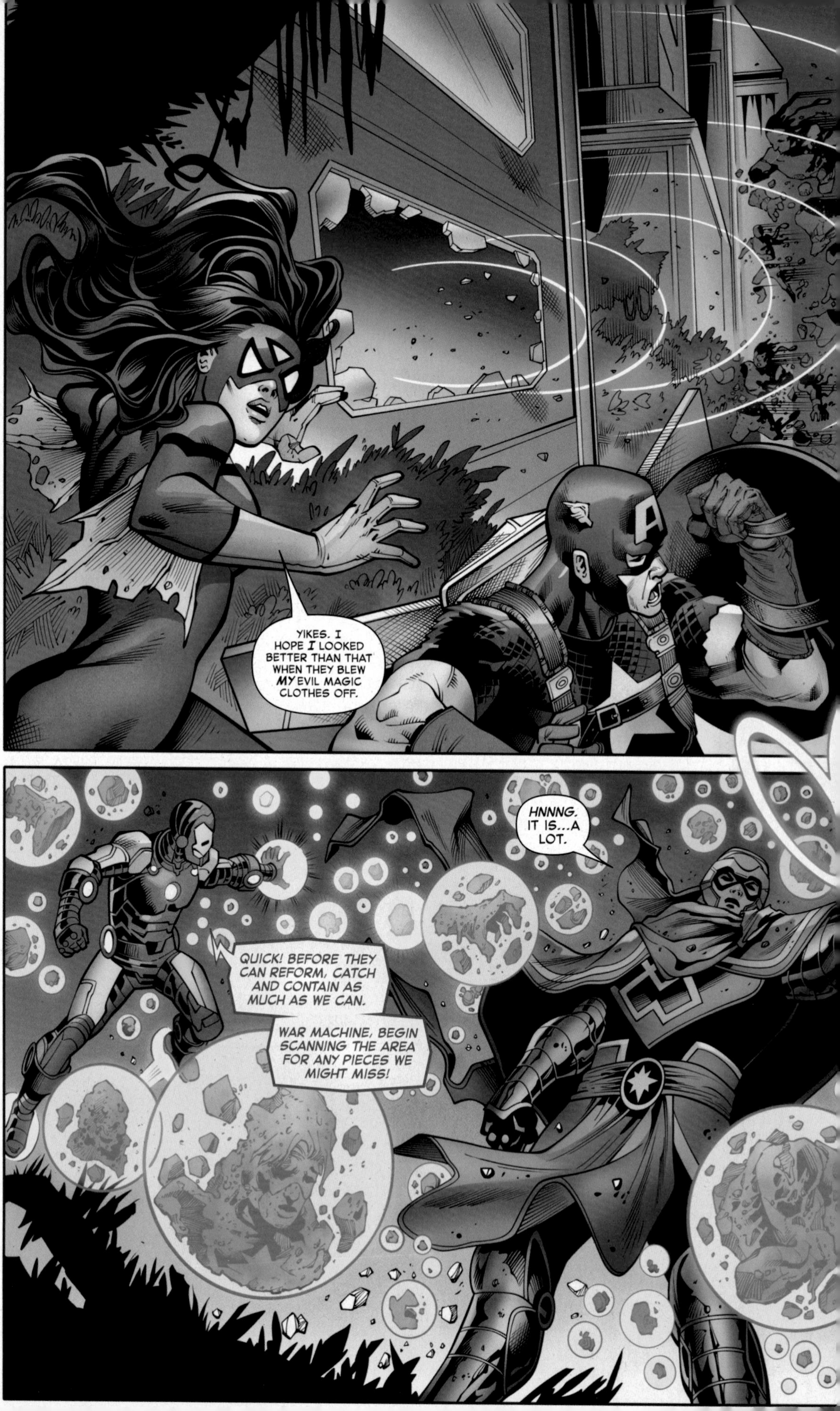
YIKES. I HOPE I LOOKED BETTER THAN THAT WHEN THEY BLEW MY EVIL MAGIC CLOTHES OFF.
HNNNG. IT IS...A LOT.
QUICK! BEFORE THEY CAN REFORM, CATCH AND CONTAIN AS MUCH AS WE CAN.
WAR MACHINE, BEGIN SCANNING THE AREA FOR ANY PIECES WE MIGHT MISS!

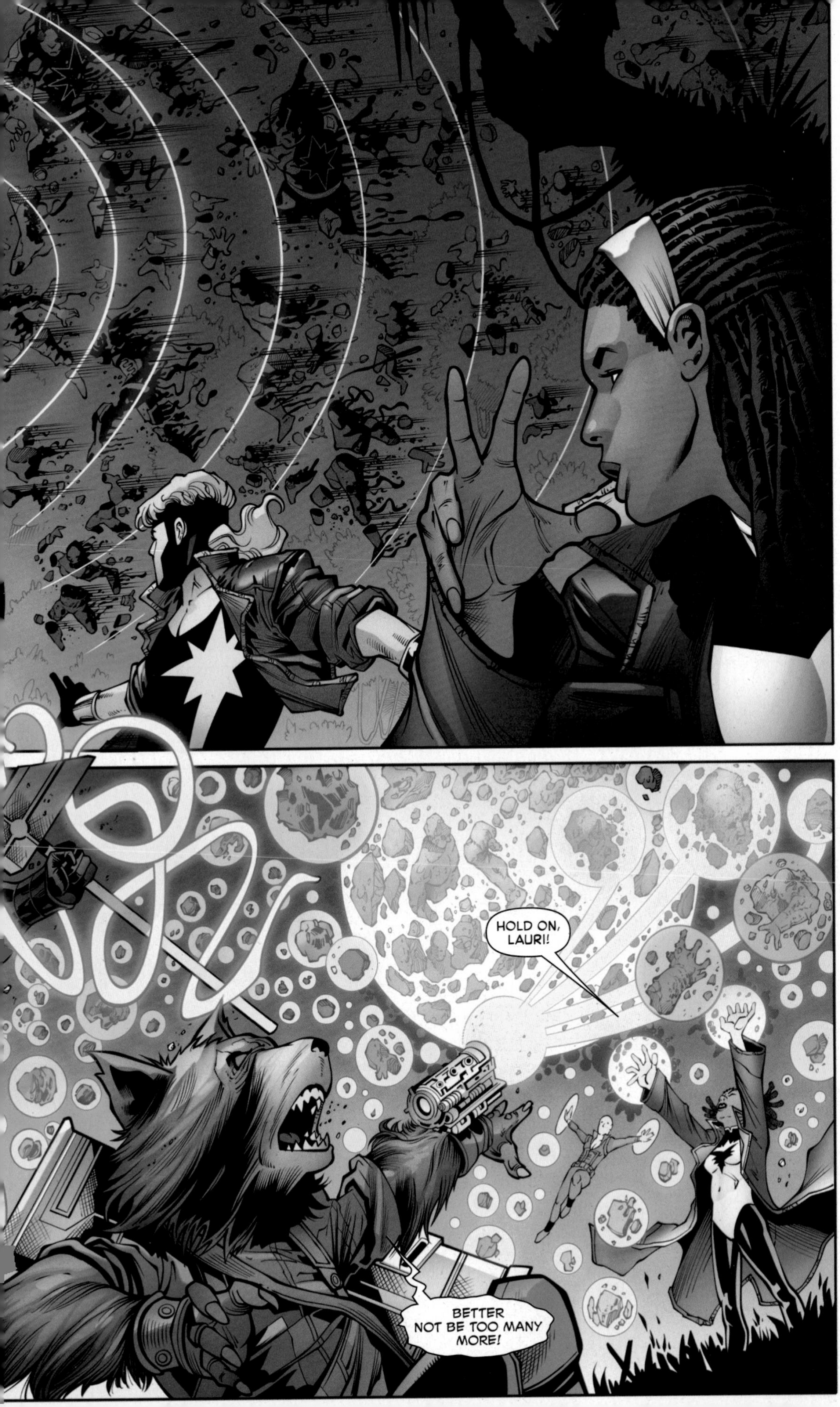
HOLD ON, LAURI!
BETTER NOT BE TOO MANY MORE!

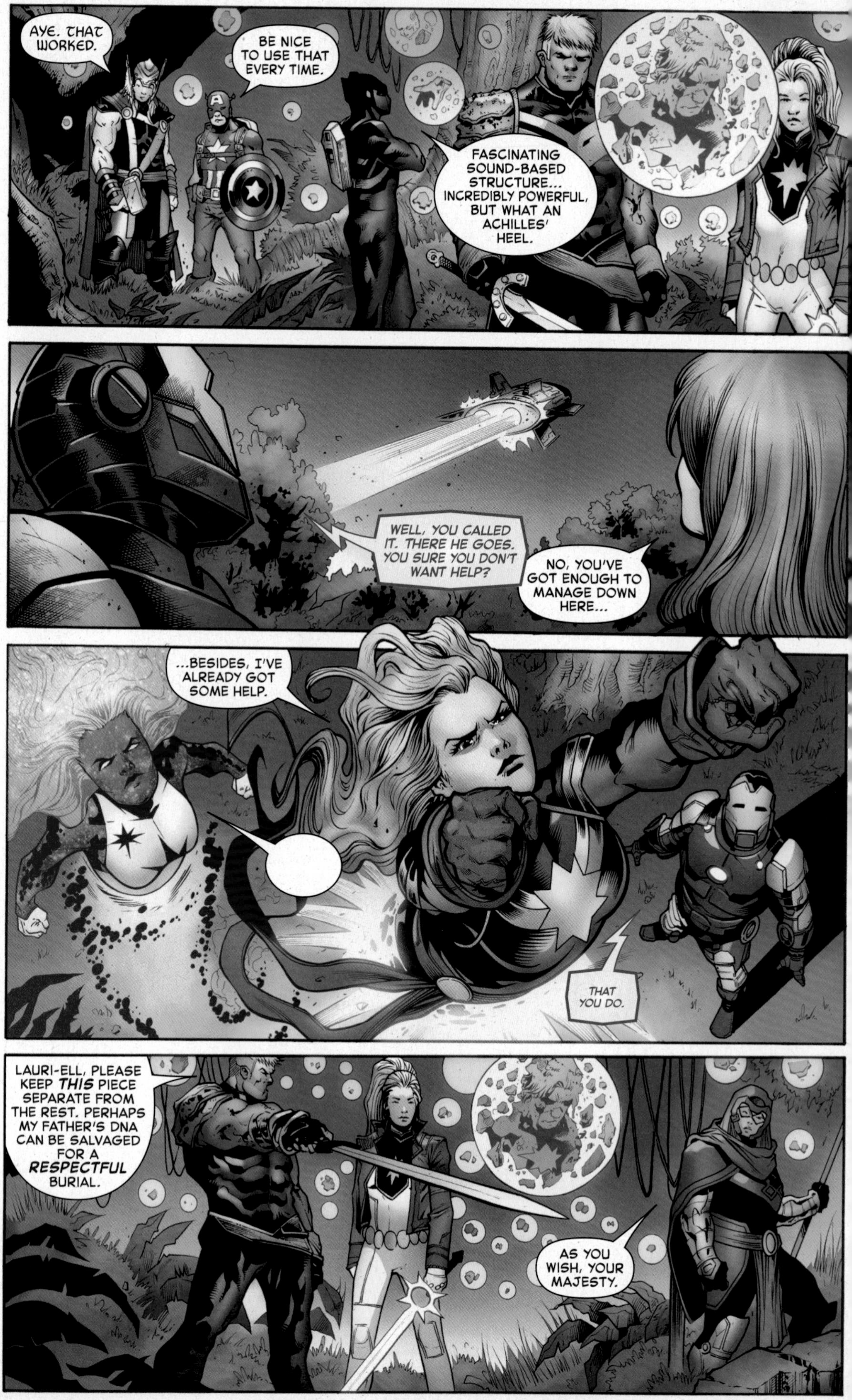

AYE. THAT WORKED.
BE NICE TO USE THAT EVERY TIME.
FASCINATING SOUND-BASED STRUCTURE... INCREDIBLY POWERFUL, BUT WHAT AN ACHILLES' HEEL.
WELL, YOU CALLED IT. THERE HE GOES. YOU SURE YOU DON'T WANT HELP?
NO, YOU'VE GOT ENOUGH TO MANAGE DOWN HERE...
...BESIDES, I'VE ALREADY GOT SOME HELP.
THAT YOU DO.
LAURI-ELL, PLEASE KEEP THIS PIECE SEPARATE FROM THE REST. PERHAPS MY FATHER'S DNA CAN BE SALVAGED FOR A RESPECTFUL BURIAL.
AS YOU WISH, YOUR MAJESTY.

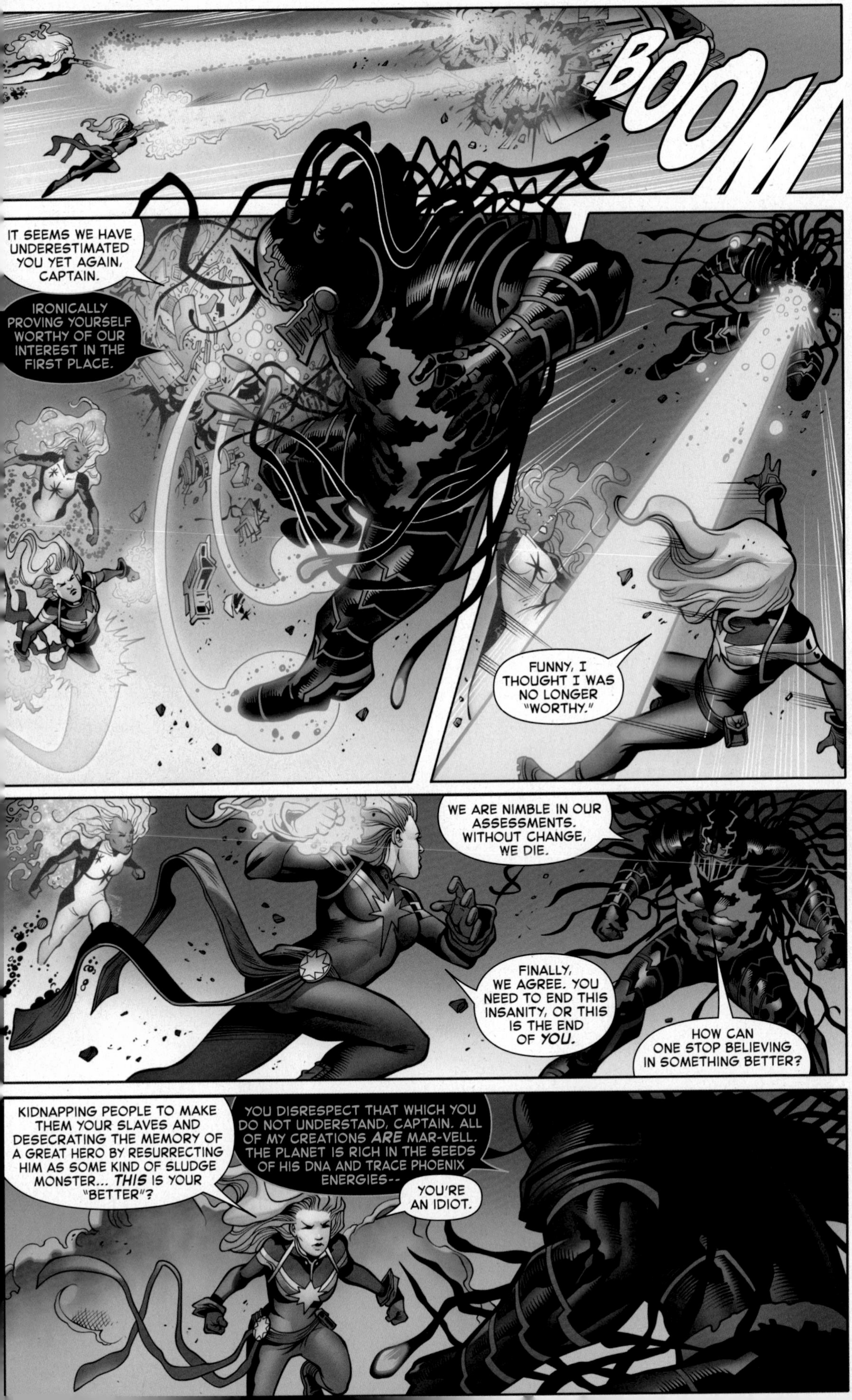
BOOM
IT SEEMS WE HAVE UNDERESTIMATED YOU YET AGAIN, CAPTAIN.
IRONICALLY PROVING YOURSELF WORTHY OF OUR INTEREST IN THE FIRST PLACE.
FUNNY, I THOUGHT I WAS NO LONGER "WORTHY."
WE ARE NIMBLE IN OUR ASSESSMENTS. WITHOUT CHANGE, WE DIE.
FINALLY, WE AGREE. YOU NEED TO END THIS INSANITY, OR THIS IS THE END OF *YOU.*
HOW CAN ONE STOP BELIEVING IN SOMETHING BETTER?
KIDNAPPING PEOPLE TO MAKE THEM YOUR SLAVES AND DESECRATING THE MEMORY OF A GREAT HERO BY RESURRECTING HIM AS SOME KIND OF SLUDGE MONSTER... *THIS* IS YOUR "BETTER"?
YOU DISRESPECT THAT WHICH YOU DO NOT UNDERSTAND, CAPTAIN. ALL OF MY CREATIONS *ARE* MAR-VELL. THE PLANET IS RICH IN THE SEEDS OF HIS DNA AND TRACE PHOENIX ENERGIES--
YOU'RE AN IDIOT.

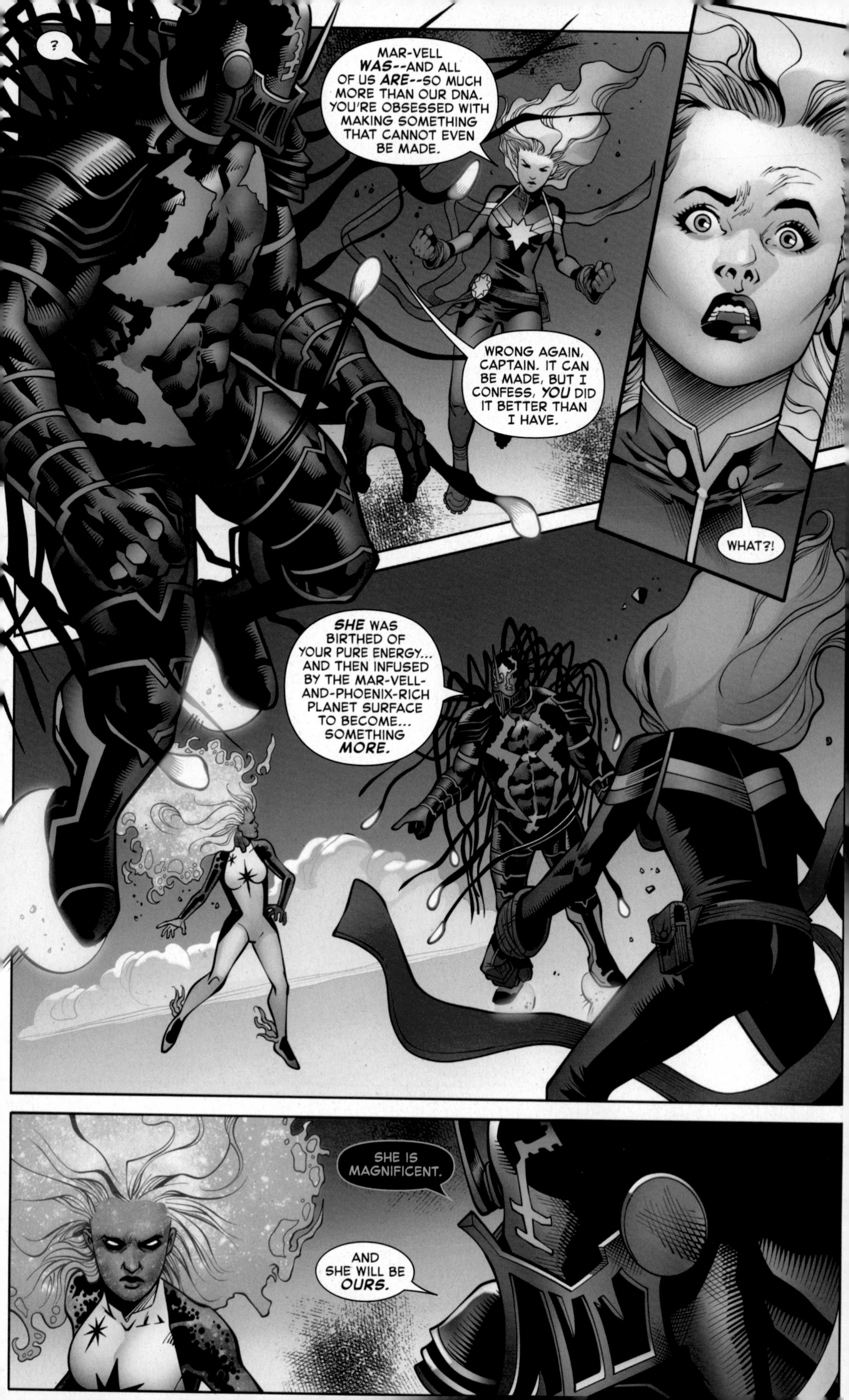
?
MAR-VELL WAS--AND ALL OF US ARE--SO MUCH MORE THAN OUR DNA. YOU'RE OBSESSED WITH MAKING SOMETHING THAT CANNOT EVEN BE MADE.
WRONG AGAIN, CAPTAIN. IT CAN BE MADE, BUT I CONFESS, YOU DID IT BETTER THAN I HAVE.
WHAT?!
SHE WAS BIRTHED OF YOUR PURE ENERGY... AND THEN INFUSED BY THE MAR-VELL-AND-PHOENIX-RICH PLANET SURFACE TO BECOME... SOMETHING MORE.
SHE IS MAGNIFICENT.
AND SHE WILL BE OURS.

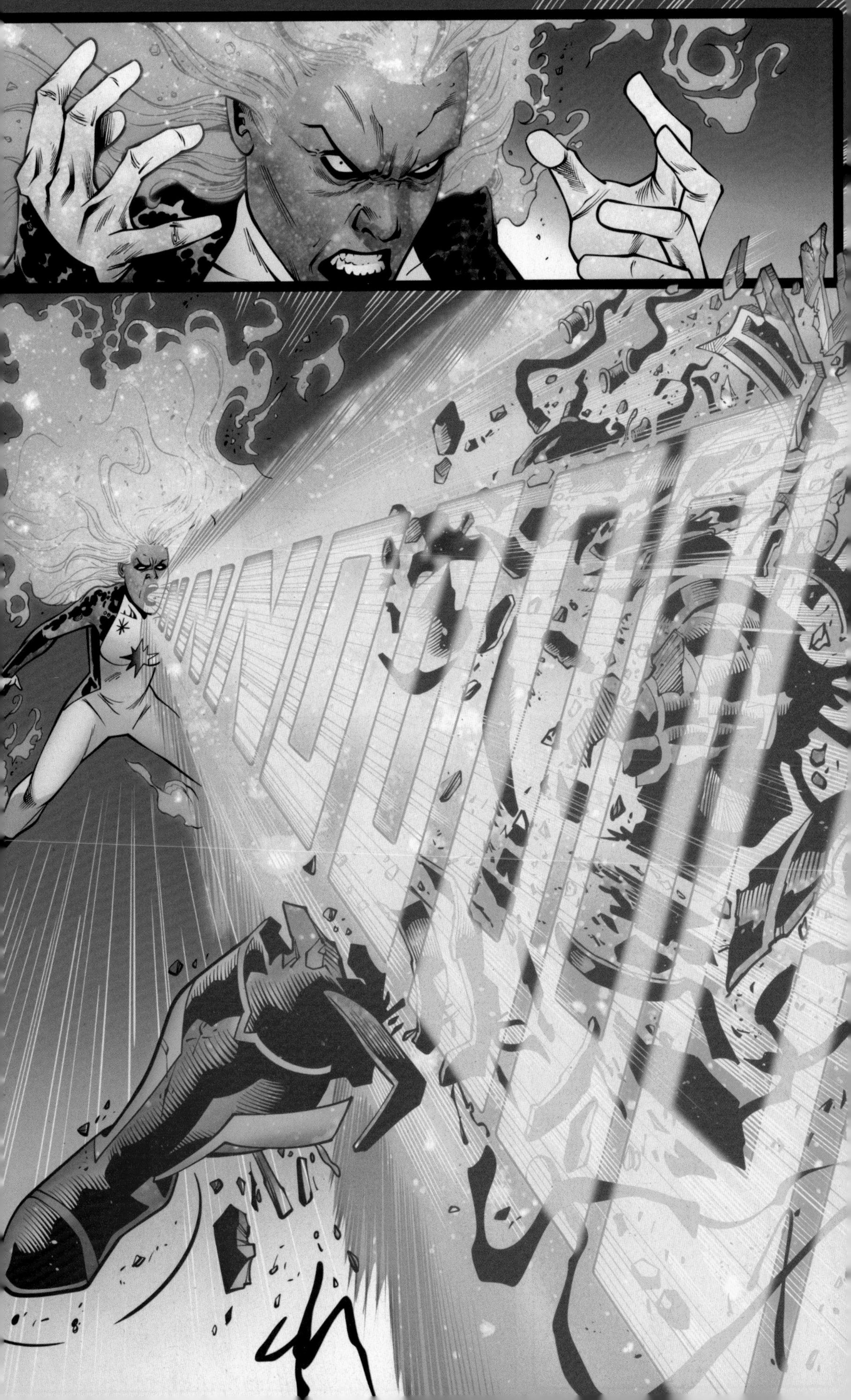

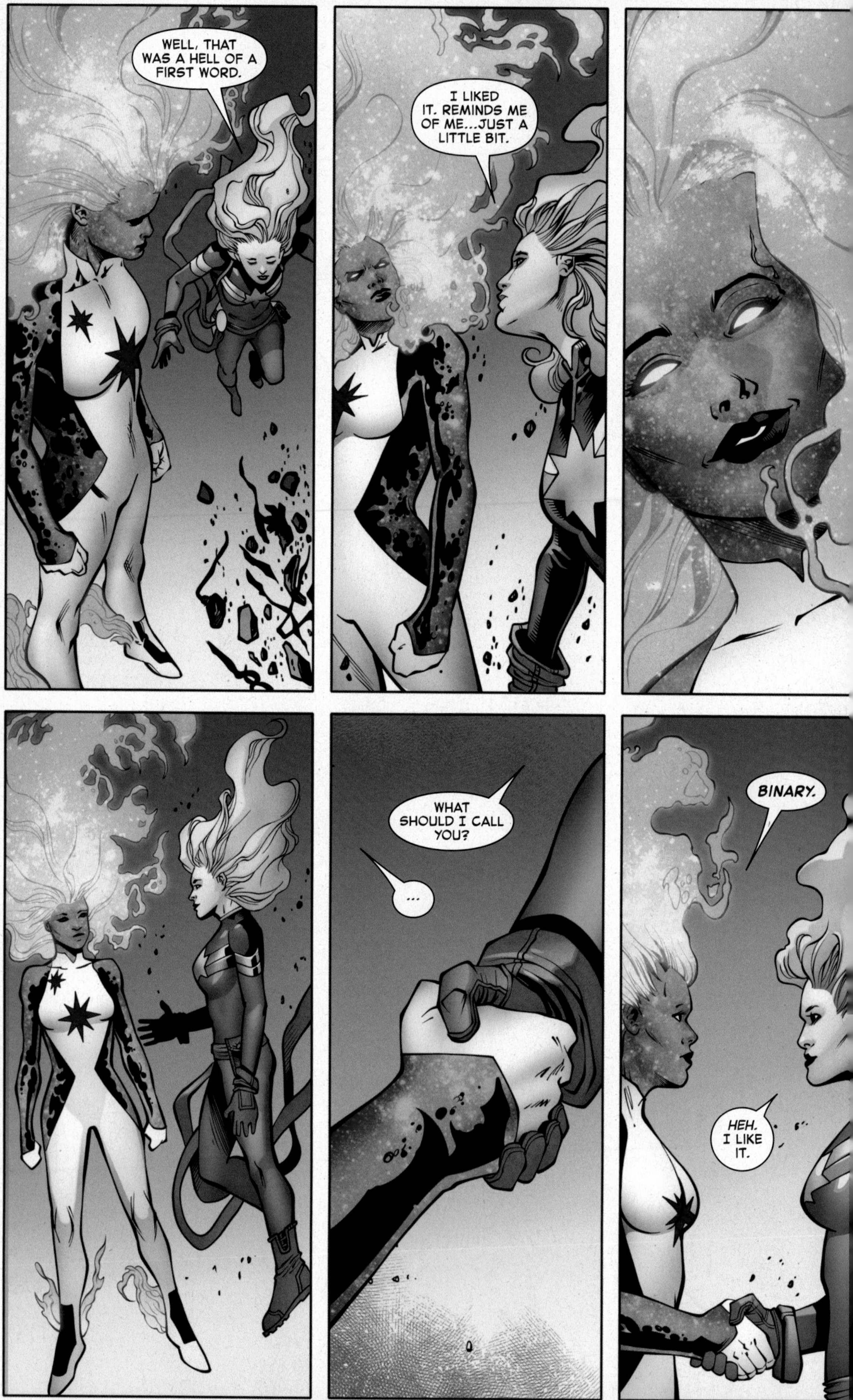
WELL, THAT WAS A HELL OF A FIRST WORD.
I LIKED IT. REMINDS ME OF ME...JUST A LITTLE BIT.
WHAT SHOULD I CALL YOU?
...
BINARY.
HEH. I LIKE IT.

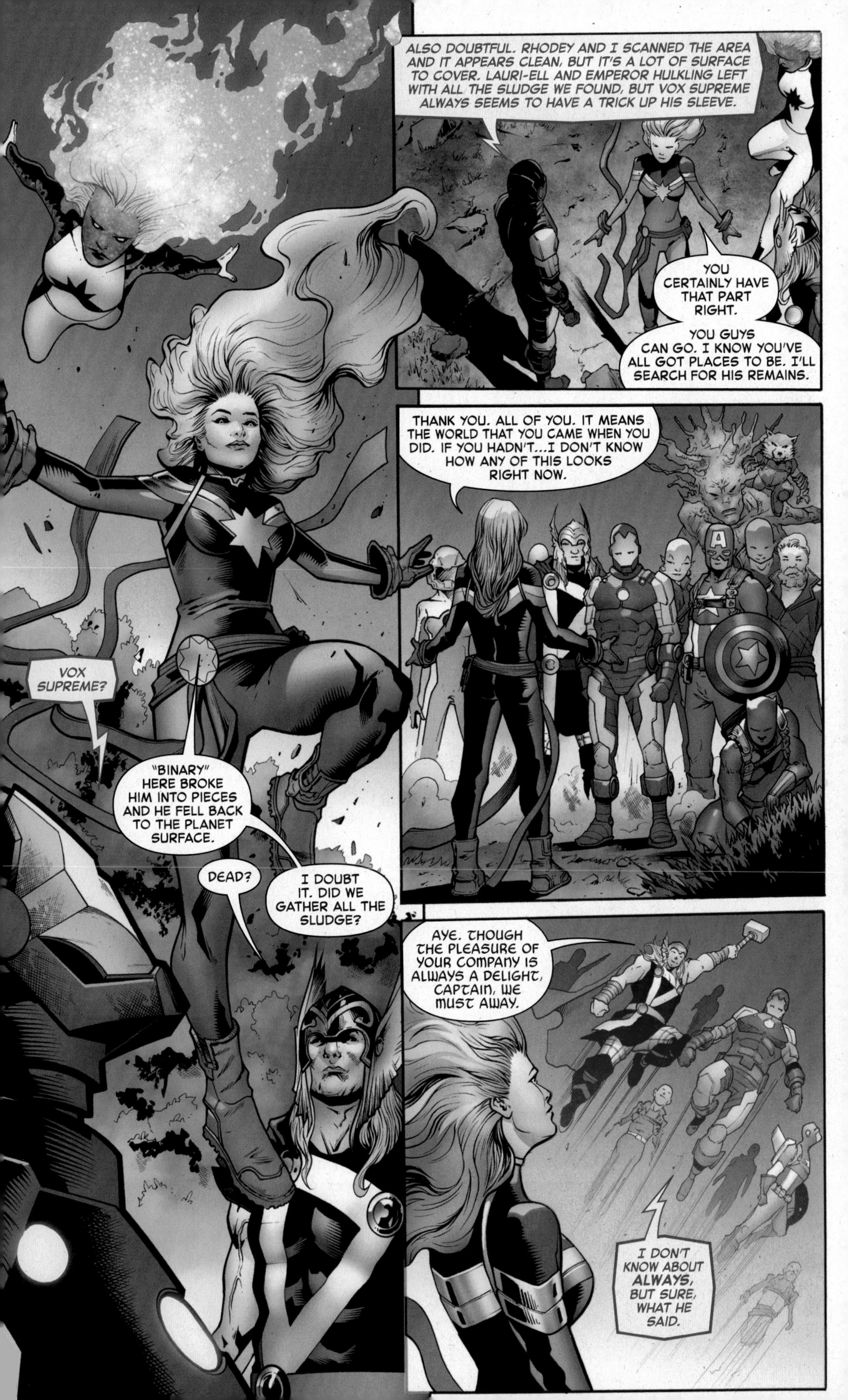
VOX SUPREME?
"BINARY" HERE BROKE HIM INTO PIECES AND HE FELL BACK TO THE PLANET SURFACE.
DEAD?
I DOUBT IT. DID WE GATHER ALL THE SLUDGE?
ALSO DOUBTFUL. RHODEY AND I SCANNED THE AREA AND IT APPEARS CLEAN, BUT IT'S A LOT OF SURFACE TO COVER. LAURI-ELL AND EMPEROR HULKLING LEFT WITH ALL THE SLUDGE WE FOUND, BUT VOX SUPREME ALWAYS SEEMS TO HAVE A TRICK UP HIS SLEEVE.
YOU CERTAINLY HAVE THAT PART RIGHT.
YOU GUYS CAN GO. I KNOW YOU'VE ALL GOT PLACES TO BE. I'LL SEARCH FOR HIS REMAINS.
THANK YOU. ALL OF YOU. IT MEANS THE WORLD THAT YOU CAME WHEN YOU DID. IF YOU HADN'T...I DON'T KNOW HOW ANY OF THIS LOOKS RIGHT NOW.
AYE. THOUGH THE PLEASURE OF YOUR COMPANY IS ALWAYS A DELIGHT, CAPTAIN, WE MUST AWAY.
I DON'T KNOW ABOUT ALWAYS, BUT SURE, WHAT HE SAID.

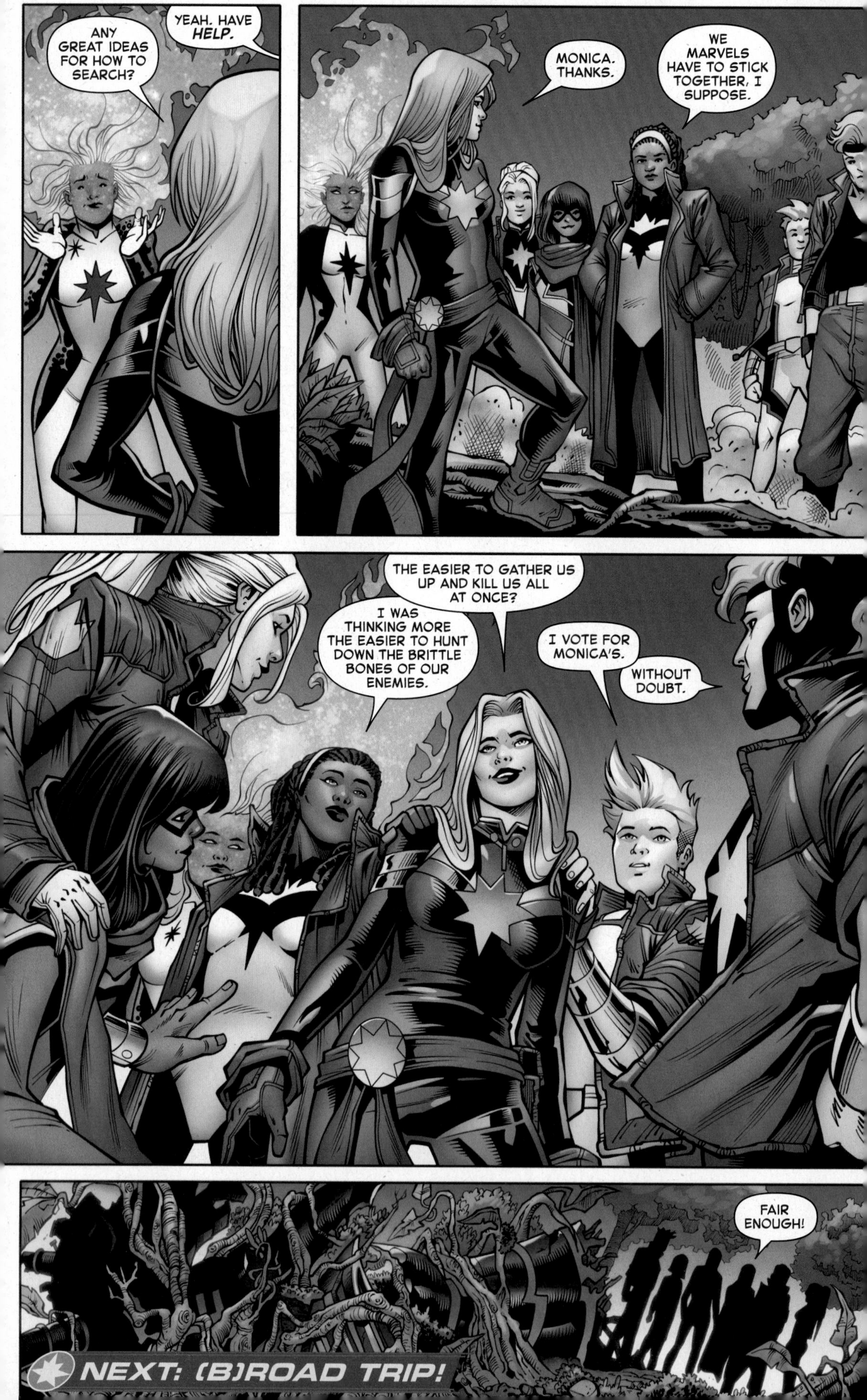
ANY GREAT IDEAS FOR HOW TO SEARCH?
YEAH. HAVE HELP.
MONICA. THANKS.
WE MARVELS HAVE TO STICK TOGETHER, I SUPPOSE.
THE EASIER TO GATHER US UP AND KILL US ALL AT ONCE?
I WAS THINKING MORE THE EASIER TO HUNT DOWN THE BRITTLE BONES OF OUR ENEMIES.
I VOTE FOR MONICA'S.
WITHOUT DOUBT.
FAIR ENOUGH!
NEXT: (B)ROAD TRIP!

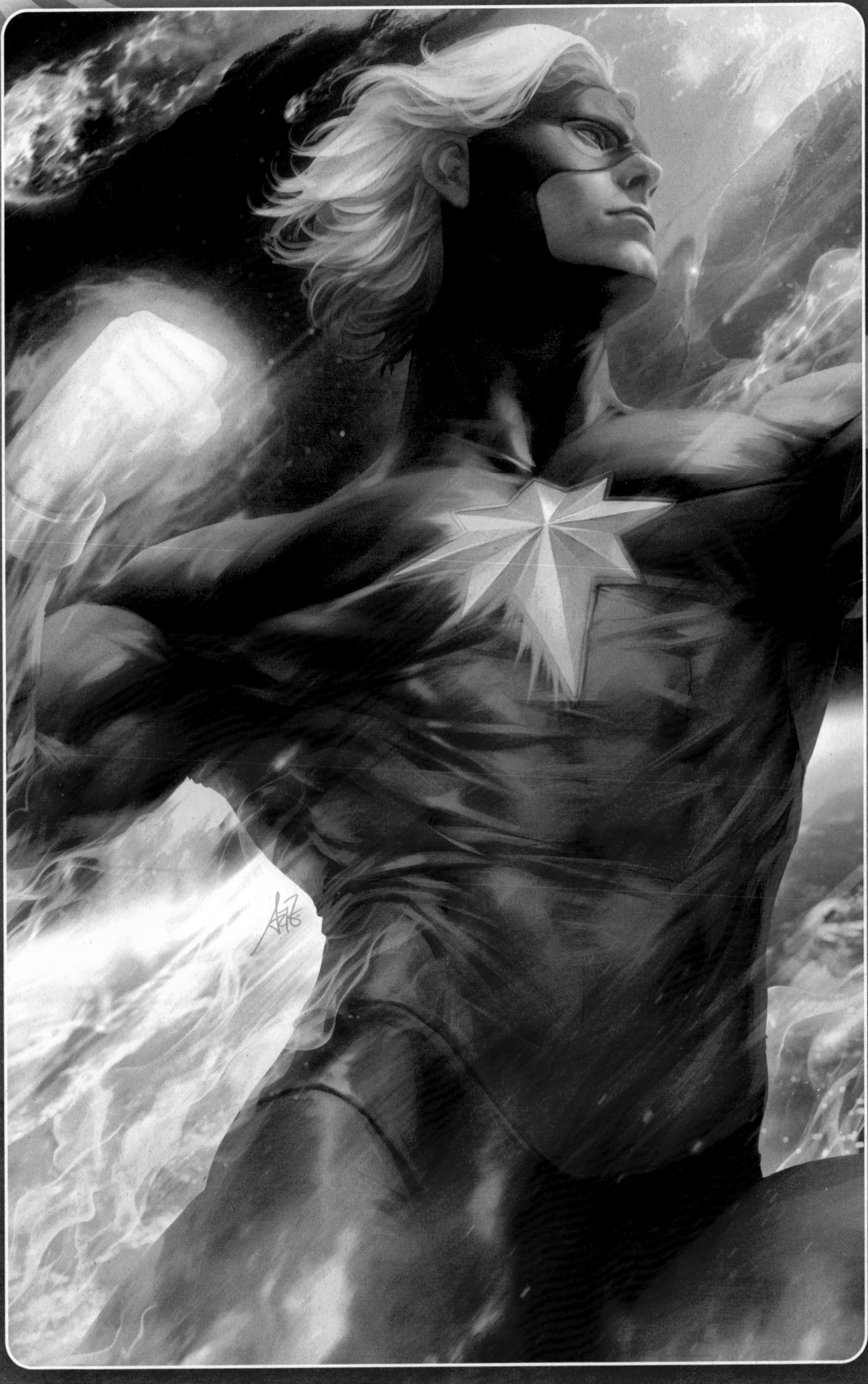

STANLEY "ARTGERM" LAU
#34 VARIANT

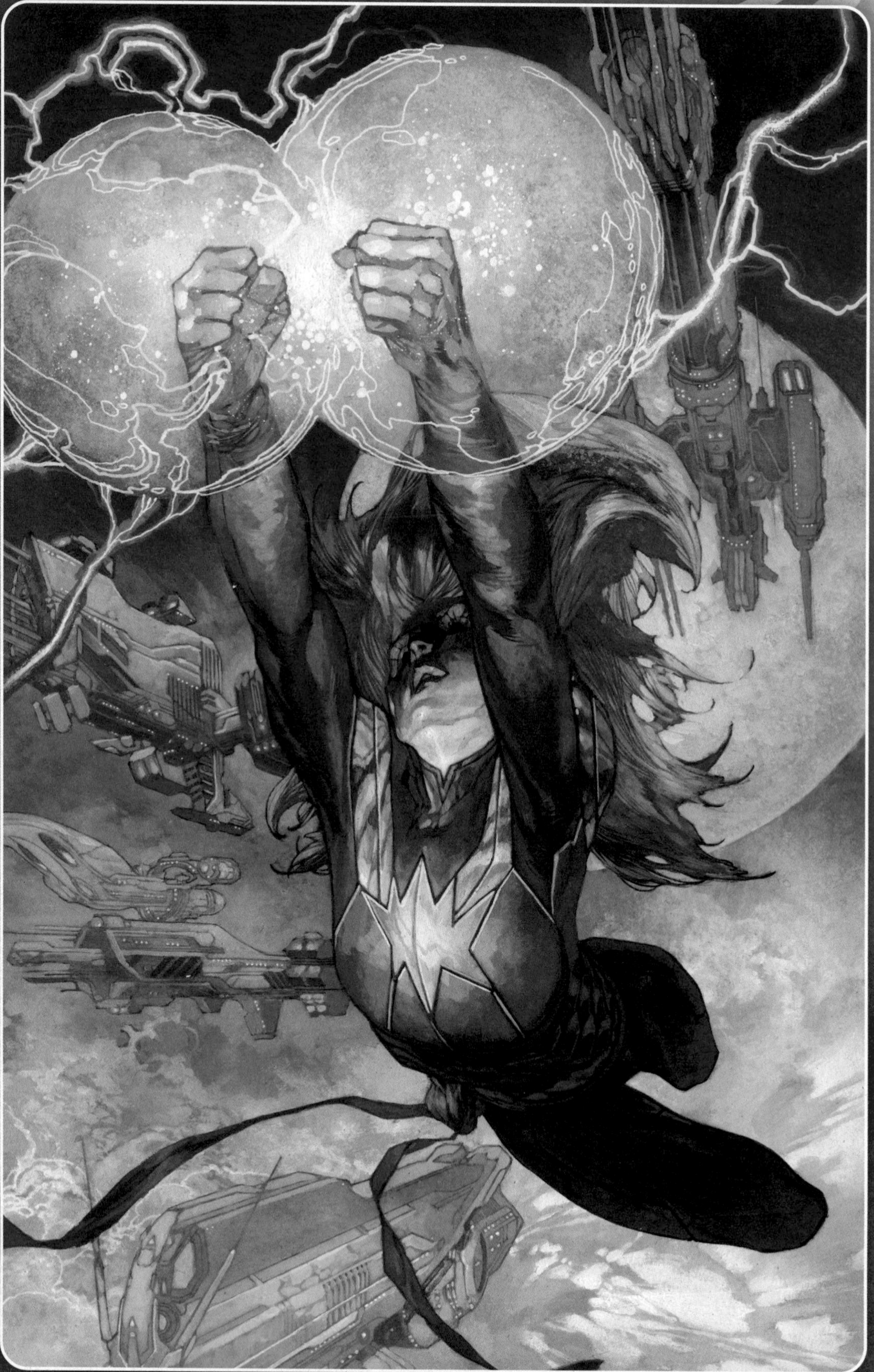

SIMONE BIANCHI
#34 VARIANT

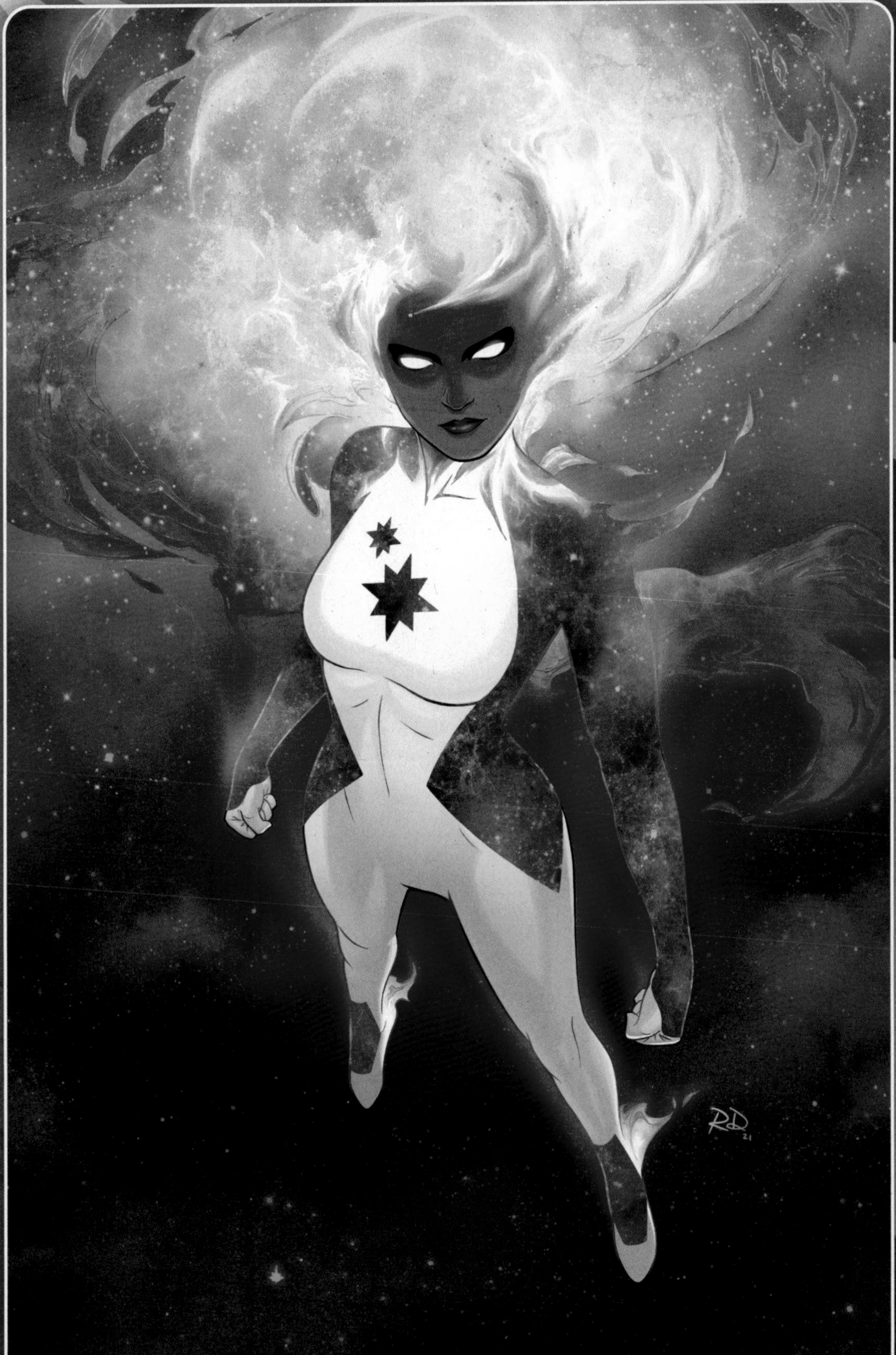
RD 21

RUSSELL DAUTERMAN
#35 SPOILER VARIANT

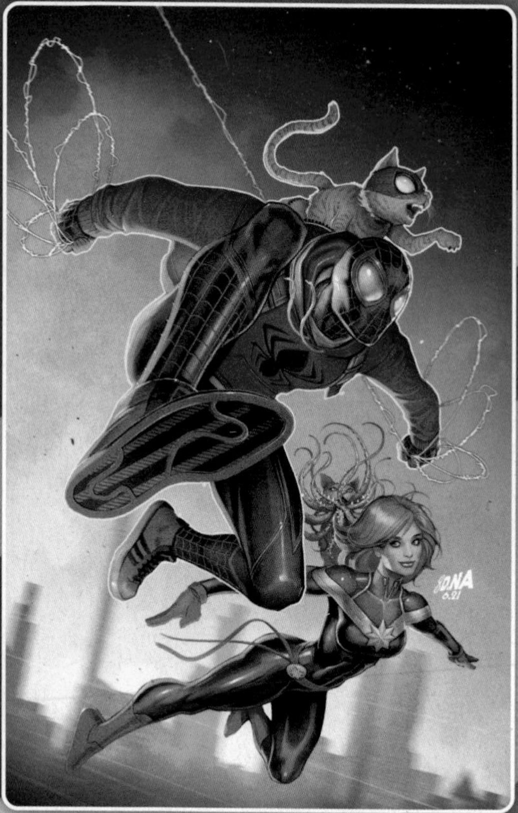

DAVID NAKAYAMA
#32 MILES MORALES: SPIDER-MAN 10TH ANNIVERSARY VARIANT

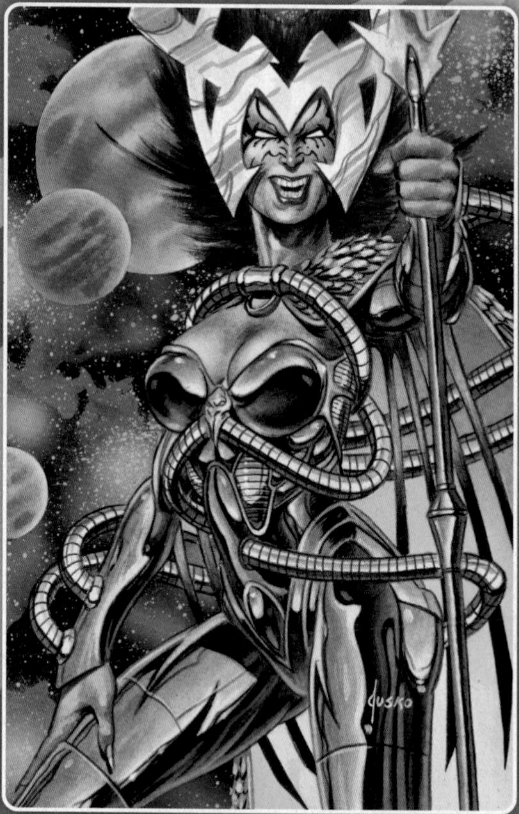

JOE JUSKO
#33 MARVEL MASTERPIECES VARIANT

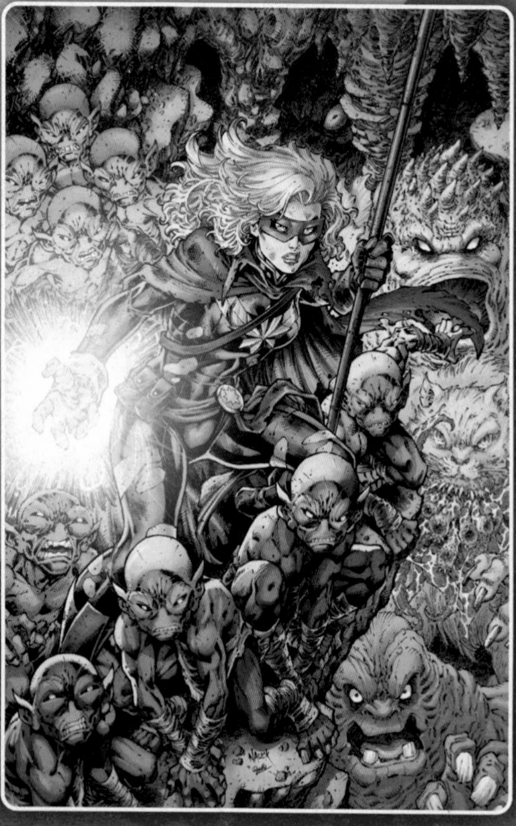

TODD NAUCK & RACHELLE ROSENBERG
#35 DEVIL'S REIGN VARIANT

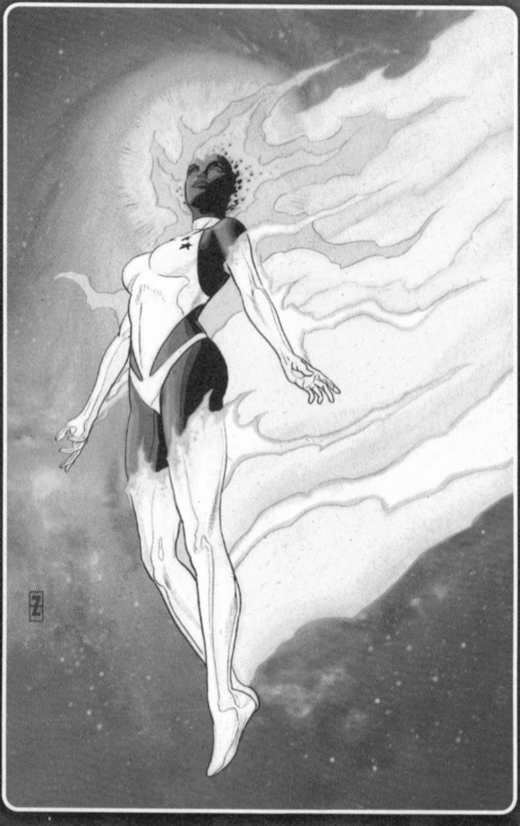

PATCH ZIRCHER
#36 SPOILER VARIANT